THE ULTIMATE GUIDE TO RAISING MONEY FOR GROWING COMPANIES

THE ULTIMATE GUIDE TO RAISING MONEY FOR GROWING COMPANIES

Michael C. Thomsett

Dow Jones-Irwin
Homewood, IL 60430

658.159
T 481

Sponsoring editor: Jim Childs
Project editor: Jane Lightell
Production manager: Ann Cassady
Jacket design: Michael Finkelman
Compositor: Spectrum Publisher Services, Inc.
Typeface: 11/13 Times Roman
Printer: Arcata Graphics/Kingsport

Library of Congress Cataloging-in-Publication Data

Thomsett, Michael C.
    The ultimate guide to raising money for growing companies /
Michael C. Thomsett.
      p. cm.
    ISBN 1-55623-240-3
    1. Small business—United States—Finance. 2. Small business—
United States—Growth. I. Title.
HG4027.7.T48 1990
658.15'92—dc20

                                89-25745
                                   CIP

Printed in the United States of America
1 2 3 4 5 6 7 8 9 0 K 7 6 5 4 3 2 1 0

PREFACE

Why and when should you allow your business to expand? And should you expand with equity or with debt capital?

These are critical questions for every business owner. The decision may lead to unimagined success or to utter disaster. Great emphasis is placed on business and market planning and year-to-year budgeting, forecasting, and other internal controls. But all too often, little attention is paid to the process of defining and redefining long-term priorities and direction.

Successful business owners are able to step back and review their progress, not only from one year to the next, but in terms of their own goals, both personal and business. Part of that process includes an analysis of growth and an understanding of how growth will change the nature of your operation—for better or for worse.

This book is designed to help you tackle these important but complex questions. We start by examining the many reasons for raising money, problems that every start-up company faces, and methods for putting together a preliminary business plan. We then analyze the characteristics of entrepreneurs versus managers, and show how to overcome the problems you encounter as you undergo the transition that comes after the start-up phase. The first five chapters define the challenge every business owner faces; and suggest a way to solve the problems you will face as your business grows from small to medium.

The second section of the book explores debt capitalization from several angles, concluding with an outline of what to include in a business plan bankers and other lenders will want to see.

The third section explains how equity capitalization plans should be put together. Because equity and debt are vastly different, and because lenders and venture capital sources view your business with different risk factors in mind, your plan should be designed to emphasize the issues that are important to each group. Detailed business plans for debt and for equity capital are included at the back of the book.

In each chapter, you are challenged to ask yourself the salient questions that will define a logical approach to your capital requirements. We introduce concepts like "profitable debt," the idea that it only makes sense to borrow money when your future profits will increase above and beyond the cost of borrowing. We examine the question of whether or not you should give up part of your equity, and the ramifications that taking on a partner might have for you.

This book also shows you how to improve your chances for getting the money you need, by looking at risk from the other side. When you are able to demonstrate to a lender or potential partner how their risks are reduced through your plan, you're taking the extra step that small business owners most often overlook.

None of these ideas are revolutionary or complex. They are really nothing more than good, common sense. Many small business owners are able to achieve growth rapidly for the first few years, only to run into a transitional hurdle. Current volume and profits are inadequate to continue supporting your growth plans; but any further growth will demand additional capital.

At this point in your operation's life, you face the greatest opportunity and the greatest peril. Profitable growth can be achieved if it's well planned, and if the rate of expansion is controlled rather than allowed to just happen on its own. Trying to achieve expansion without adequate capital can result in deterioration in quality, employee relations, reputation, and your own morale—even in failure of the operation itself.

To an extent, a young business can survive just on the will power of a motivated and entrepreneurial owner. But the ability to maintain a shoestring approach is finite. Permanent, long-term growth demands planning, careful time management, and constant reevaluation of your goals and direction. As your business grows, planning and control should become ever-growing priorities for you.

If you're able to steer your business in the direction you want it to go, your chances of succeeding will be vastly improved. Successful growth rarely occurs by chance. In virtually every success story, it's the founder's dedication and hard work that leads to well-deserved financial and personal success. With that in mind, this book is dedicated to you and to the success of your business.

Michael C. Thomsett
January, 1990

CONTENTS

CHAPTER 1

DEFINING YOUR ISSUES

> Live within your income,
> even if you have to borrow
> money to do so.
> —*Henry Wheeler Shaw*

Whether you are about to start your business or you have reached the point of expansion and need capital to expand, you now confront one of the most critical decisions for a small-business owner: whether or not to raise money from the outside.

This chapter examines the issue of debt and equity capital, including the advantages of pursuing both, the rules for borrowing and the way in which lenders evaluate your application, when equity capital should be brought into your business, and how your financing needs must be constructed within the business planning process. These points are presented as a general overview and set the premise for more detailed discussions and explanations that will come in later chapters

What is your purpose for wanting to raise money? Every loan officer in every bank knows that a large segment of the population lives with misconceptions about how loan decisions are made; and everyone in the position to invest in a business must contend with the business owner who does not appreciate their concerns. If there is any secret to successfully raising money for your business, it must be this:

> In order to convince others to take risks on your business, you must first understand those risks; and you must have a specific plan for the profitable use of money.

Notice the use of the word *profitable* in describing the use of money. As a basic idea, you must conceive a plan in which raising capital produces future profits that exceed the cost (in terms of interest payments or equity) to finance your business. Without that single attribute, there simply is no good reason to raise money.

For the start-up business, the problems of capitalization can prevent the doors from opening or make the difference between operating on a shoestring or becoming the next major growth company. For the going concern, the need for more capital may present the greatest threat to your business, or it may be the moment of opportunity. Example: One small company meets with success from the moment it opens. Sales volume is higher than the owner expected, and a net profit is earned in the first two years. The owner wants to expand, but needs a larger office and warehouse space, a bigger staff, more expertise, and fixed assets—machinery, equipment, and furniture. One year later, the business is reporting a net loss, bills are going unpaid, and the owner is working longer hours than before. Eventually, the doors close.

Why does this occur in so many small businesses? Why do some enterprises continue to grow and expand, finally going public and bringing wealth and success to the founder? The answer is not luck, financing, or the capital the owner is able to raise. Simply stated, businesses fail because owners do not plan realistically and because they do not manage their money well.

Once you know how capital must be managed and when you are able to put together a sound business plan, you will be equipped with the tools needed to reduce the risks of growth or even the risks of going into business in the first place. The critical point to remember is

> You will raise money through diligent planning and not as the result of luck or connections.

As a small business owner, you must already realize this point. However, when it comes to raising capital, a lot of people overlook this fundamental but unavoidable fact.

DEBT AND EQUITY

To raise money, you have two choices: either borrow money from a lender or raise equity by giving away part ownership. In either case, you give up something to gain the benefits that come with additional capital. If you overlook this reality, you will regret the decision.

A well-planned capitalization program takes place as part of a comprehensive business plan. However, the plan itself is not what determines whether or not you will succeed in raising capital. Lenders and investors look to other points in their decision, such as your experience, the business you are in, the level of competition, and your prospects for future growth and profits.

Lenders are accustomed to receiving loan applications from small-business owners who apply for the wrong reasons. For example, if you need a loan because your cash flow is poor, the commitment to a debt will only make your situation worse. If you have not planned ahead for the use of the money or for the method you will employ to repay your loan, a lender will naturally shy away from taking a risk on you.

Someone considering investing in your company will take the same attitude. Before someone gives you money and takes an equity share in your venture, they will want to know that your business is healthy, that you have a realistic growth plan, and that you are in control.

Some business owners create a capitalization problem. They do not seek outside financing until they are in trouble, believing that loans and investments will come to them as a solution to their problems. In fact, the successful business owner realizes that when a business is under stress, chances of raising money are slim—and the greater the problems, the lower the opportunities to raise any form of capital.

Debt capital must be managed as carefully as your own money. This might seem obvious; but many would-be borrowers fail to demonstrate to a lender that they hold this perception. Lending money is a risk to the lender, as well as to you. If borrowed funds are not well-managed (meaning that the availability of cash creates profits in excess of the interest costs), then taking out a loan will harm your business.

A poorly conceived borrowing plan is a negative. Interest expenses will affect both profits and cash flow, meaning your net worth will be lowered. Thus, no real growth can occur in the future; the loan itself lowers the value of your business.

Recognizing this problem, some business owners decide to take on a partner. They seek capital and are willing to give up part ownership to overcome the capitalization problem. However, is it easy to overlook the fact that sharing equity is a business marriage. You must enter into a joint ownership plan for the right reasons, and you must be able to live with the conflicts you and your equity partner might encounter.

Debt and equity financing must be evaluated with the use of several tests—for cost, cash payments, profits, cash flow, growth, and overhead.

1. **Cost.** The cost of debt financing is the interest a lender charges. To justify borrowing money, the interest must be reasonable, in light of your plan for use of the money, your repayment schedule, and the purpose of borrowing. Equity financing also has a cost: the sharing of future profits and growth.
2. **Cash payments.** The requirement for repayment of a debt—debt service—will be an immediate and recurring commitment. An equity partner may require dividends or a draw, which could be immediate or deferred. The timing of payments to an equity partner may determine how advantageous it will be to take this route.
3. **Profit test.** Borrowing money makes sense when profits will result from borrowing and will exceed the cost of taking out a loan. For equity, the potential future growth and profits must exceed the profits you are likely to earn on your own.
4. **Cash flow test.** Cash flow must be improved as the result of raising capital. In too many cases, the opposite is true: The additional risks of expansion create a worse problem than before.
5. **Growth test.** Capital must improve or create new growth in your business. You must be prepared to demonstrate this point, or you cannot expect anyone to take the risk of giving you the capital you seek.
6. **Overhead test.** If borrowed money increases sales more than expenses, a loan makes sense, and equity will decrease or stabilize overhead levels.

The six points of comparison and tests for raising capital are summarized in Figure 1–1.

THE PLANNING ISSUE

Successful business owners are good planners. They know that time must be spent looking to the future and taking steps today to turn their goals into realities. However, you can effectively plan only for the short or intermediate term. Once your plan moves beyond the next year or two, many unknown factors will come into the picture, such as

1. Changes in your goals or in your perceptions of your own business.

FIGURE 1–1
Comparisons: Debt and Equity

BASIS	DEBT	EQUITY
cost	interest	share of future profits
cash payments	recurring payments – immediate	dividends or draw – immediate or deferred
profit test	profits must exceed the cost of raising capital	
cash flow test	cash flow must be improved with additions of capital	
growth test	capital must create or allow growth in net worth	
overhead test	increases in sales volume exceed overhead increase	capital decreases or stabilizes overhead

Example: A consultant begins his business offering accounting consultation. However, two of his largest clients need help in developing internal automated systems. Within five years, the owner becomes an expert in systems and automation and abandons the original premise of his business.

2. Restrictions coming from changes in the economic climate, both nationally and—of greater concern—in your region.

Example: A real estate professional opens her own brokerage firm during a period of high demand for housing. For the first two years, volume is high. Then the major employer in the region cuts back its staff and operations. Many people leave the depressed area, and the real estate business dries up.

3. Competitive factors, including the growth of companies in business today and the emergence of new competitors in the future.

Example: A draftsman starts his freelance operation and develops contacts with architects, contractors, and engineers. Three years later, he finds that competitors are taking business away from him. He cannot match prices offered by better-financed firms using faster computer-aided design (CAD) systems.

4. Industry changes, including new technology that affects the way you can operate in the future.

   Example: In 1905, a blacksmith found a high demand for his services, and he expected to be in business for many years to come. Imagine his disappointment when the automotive industry rendered his business obsolete.

5. Supply and demand changes, which operate on specific cycles. These are easy to identify in hindsight, but much harder to anticipate and time. This factor is not only economic; many trends turn out to be fads and will pass.

   Example: In the early 1970s, the popularity of waterbeds led many entrepreneurs to open small retail operations. Business was good. Everyone wanted their own waterbed, and the future looked promising. So the more adventurous owners invested money in equipment and facilities and went into the manufacturing business. Two years later, the fad died away and most of these operations had to close their doors.

None of these changing factors can be known well into the future, at least not for most forms of business. Thus, a realistic plan can only be dependable and operational for the next year or two. Beyond that, it is mere guesswork.

This is not to say that you should neglect long-term planning. Given a series of assumptions that are valid today, you must certainly develop a long-term plan. However, the financial specifics cannot be known or estimated with any degree of certainty. The farther ahead you plan with specifics and numbers, the less dependable your plan.

BORROWING: PRO AND CON

When does it make sense to borrow money? Most forms of business expansion require capitalization. If you expect to grow, you may be able to achieve your goals by using borrowed funds—but only if you take this step at the right time and for the right reasons.

Borrowing provides you with the following advantages.

1. **Profits will exceed interest expense.** This is the profit test mentioned before. You must be able to prove to a lender—and to yourself—that you will increase your profits beyond the cost of taking out a loan.

This test is fundamental to the planning process when the question of borrowing is involved. If you cannot establish a reasonable expectation for improving your profit picture, then you should not borrow money.

2. **You establish business credit.** Borrowing money and making timely repayments establish business credit. Even if this is not essential today, it might be in the future when you will need lines of credit or other short- and long-term financing assistance from lenders.

3. **Interest is tax-deductible.** The cost of borrowing is partially subsidized by the tax system. Your net borrowing cost is lower than the rate you pay to a lender, based on the effective tax rate for your business. However, tax benefits should not be the deciding factor in taking out a loan. This is just one of the benefits that comes from borrowing, and it must be included in the equation.

4. **Borrowing allows expansion.** Making your business grow means investing in facilities, staff, and assets. None of these necessities produce a direct and immediate profit, but all are essential for growth. Every expanding business comes to a point where immediate growth opportunities are present, but capital is not available.

Borrowing might hold potential for your business, but with that potential, you must also face risks. Whenever you use other people's money, you accept a commitment. If your plans do not work out, financial problems will result. You can avoid and reduce risks through complete planning, responsible management and control, and concentration on directed business goals. Every business owner must also realize that risk is a permanent factor of their lives. For most entrepreneurs, risk is an acceptable price to pay for independence.

Some of the disadvantages of borrowing are the following.

1. **Cash flow is strained.** Cash flow—the money available from operations—is the critical test of business health for every company, large or small. When you borrow, the debt service (repayments of principal and interest) create greater demands on your cash flow. That is why your plan is essential. You *must* be able to prove that borrowing money will add to cash flow and not impede it.

2. **Borrowing is a business risk.** A short- or intermediate-term plan

is fairly dependable in comparison to a long-term plan. However, even in the immediate future, the conditions and priorities of your business can change, often due to circumstances beyond your control. Thus, you must recognize that borrowing money is always a form of risk.

3. **Expansion might be temporary.** In some cases, opportunities to expand might not be permanent. However, borrowed funds are used to increase facilities, staff, and the investment in assets. If higher volume is not permanent, but overhead is expanded and capital is invested, then you will face a problem of business survival. Recognizing a permanent growth opportunity requires in-depth planning.

RULES FOR BORROWING

Anyone who starts their own business already knows about risks. They have also learned how to apply creative thought to the creation of a new idea. Chances are, you have taken an innovative approach in the way you market your product or service, in setting standards for quality, and in your point of view of independence and opportunity.

These positive attributes are typical of the successful entrepreneur. However, one of the pitfalls you must overcome is forgetting to apply that same attitude to the management issues you face every day. You might begin with very bold, creative ideas, only to lose that point of view in the day-to-day routine of operations.

Insight is the attribute that sets you apart from the thousands of others who remain working for someone else, wanting to be independent but never taking that initial step. Insight is your most valuable asset, and it can be applied to every situation; indeed, it must be applied if you want to stay in business. Consider how this applies to the question of borrowing money:

> The only way to gain the advantage is to thoroughly understand the risks from a lender's point of view.

You have already established your talent for recognizing an advantage by identifying your own business opportunity. That same approach must be taken in the way you apply for a loan. Follow these rules for beginning the process of borrowing money.

1. **Work from a complete plan.** Lenders will want to know how you intend to use the money you borrow. You must be prepared with a complete plan, designed to prove that the risk of lending money to you is low and that you have a timetable and a method for producing profits with the borrowed funds.
2. **Develop a repayment schedule.** You must also prove your ability to repay the loan. Most borrowers overlook this fundamental requirement. The lender cannot be expected to know all about your cash flow or future profits; chances are, the lender knows very little about your business. So it is your task to show how operations will free up the money you will need to make timely payments.
3. **Prove your plan's validity.** Your plan must be completely accurate and valid. Anyone can develop the numbers to show their *future* success; realizing it is not always possible. Test your plan, challenge your own assumptions, and develop a "worst-case" example of the future. Show the lender how you plan to deal with risks and how you will ensure your own success.
4. **Eliminate the lender's risks.** The best way to get approval of your loan application is to identify and then eliminate the lender's risks, the greatest of which is that you will not repay your loan. Show that this will not occur, because your plan is conservative, farsighted, and realistic.
5. **Understand the lender's criteria.** Before submitting your application, meet with the loan officer. Find out how they evaluate loan requests, what information they look for, and the preferred organization of a business plan. Identify the criteria for making a decision, and then address those criteria in your proposal.

A checklist for the steps in preparing to borrow money is summarized in Figure 1–2.

THE LENDER'S CRITERIA

Every lender has its own specific areas of interest and will structure its lending policies to emphasize those applicants who fit the model. For example, one bank opens branches in areas where a number of medical offices are located. That bank seeks customers of a specific nature. The

FIGURE 1–2
Checklist: Rules for Borrowing Money

1. Work from a complete plan

2. Develop a repayment schedule

3. Prove your plan's validity

4. Eliminate the lender's risks

5. Understand the lender's criteria

law may require the bank to accept business from a broader cross section of the business and personal community, but the emphasis should be kept in mind when you select a bank as a potential lender.

Banks create distinct operational objectives. Many small community banks concentrate on short-term personal loans, whereas others will seek out small-business customers. A bank may take a highly conservative approach in its lending policies and apply strict review and approval guidelines. Others may be able to give you an answer in less than 24 hours.

Your first step in finding a likely lender must be to first identify the candidates who want to grant the type of loan you seek in the same way that you identified a market when you opened your own business. As a rule, every lender will apply the same basic tests to every loan application. There are six generally understood criteria, known as the "six C's for lenders".

1. **Capacity.** Do you possess the experience, talent, and responsibility to handle money well, repay the loan, and appreciate the lender's risks?

2. **Capital.** What have you invested in your own business? No lender will carry all of your financing; they want you to have a vested interest in succeeding.

3. **Collateral.** Most business loans will be granted on a secured basis. The lender will want to be able to assume ownership of some asset in the event you are unable to repay your loan. An unsecured loan will be granted only in those cases when credit is well-established and you can demonstrate your solvency.
4. **Circumstances.** What type of business are you in? Is volume and cash flow seasonal? How much money is owed to you, and what portion is current? What is your competitive posture?
5. **Character.** How do you view borrowing? Have you developed a business plan that demonstrates your ability to plan ahead, arrange for repayment of your debt, and take your responsibilities seriously?
6. **Coverage.** The lender is aware of the risks they face, not only in the event of a reversal in your business, but as the consequence of an unexpected loss. These risks include your own death, disability, or poor health; casualty or theft of business property; and liability you face in dealing with customers. A lender may require you to assign a life insurance policy, arrange for credit life insurance, or inquire into other forms of coverage you hold.

The six C's for lenders are summarized in Figure 1–3.

TIMING STRATEGIES

Be aware of the timing of your loan request. Of course, the circumstances that dictate outside financing might arise when you least expect it and when conditions are not in your favor. However, when you are aware of the conditions favoring loan approval, you will better know how to prepare for your meeting with a loan officer.

The timing of borrowing money is most favorable under the following conditions.

1. The bank has recently formed and is looking for new business. In order to put future profits on the books, the bank will actively seek loan business today. Under this condition, the bank will be more receptive to you and will not be likely to impose restrictions a more established, conservative institution will demand.
2. Interest rates are low. The supply-and-demand cycle for money favors your application at this time, because capital is relatively

FIGURE 1–3
The Six C's for Lenders

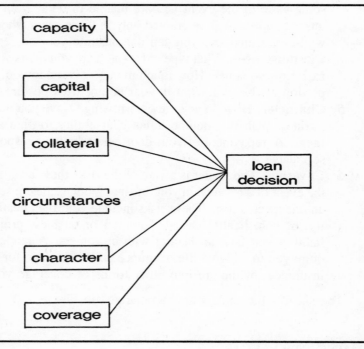

available. This also benefits you, because your interest expense
will be lower than during times of low money supply.

3. Banks in your area are competing for business. They will lower
   their requirements and even ensure fast approval.

4. The economy is healthy. When inflation is low and real growth is
   occurring, bankers become more optimistic, and getting a loan
   will be easier.

When conditions are not best for applying for a loan, but you need
financing now, you will still benefit by knowing the situation. This
information will help you prepare for your meeting with a lender. Conditions are less favorable under the following conditions.

1. Interest rates are high. Bankers have less capital to lend, and they
   raise rates accordingly. You will have to accept a higher interest
   expense to get the same amount of money.

2. The bank is at or near it's regulatory limit for reserves (measured by a ratio between loans and deposits). As money moves out of an institution or the rate of deposit growth declines, the bank must become more selective in the loans it grants.
3. Competition is low in your area. Some banks simply do not want to deal with small-business loans and will not seek your business. In that case, your task is a difficult one: to convince a loan officer that the risks to the institution are low.
4. The economy is in a recession. When interest rates rise, inflation moves upward, and business activity slows, lenders shy away from aggressively increasing their loan balances. In this condition, you must convince the lender that in spite of the overall economic conditions the timing is right for vou.

BORROWING STRATEGIES

Loan officers and borrowers review lending from entirely different points of view. You will be a more successful applicant if you employ a few basic strategies with this point in mind—and if you make an effort to review your application with the lender's risks in mind.

It's simply not realistic to believe you deserve a loan because you need the money. In many cases, the greater your need, the greater the lender's risks. Your objective must be to demonstrate how you will use the money in such a way that the lender is assured of repayment and that the risk of default or late payment is slim.

In order to appreciate the lender's perspective, set rules for yourself. The first rule is

> Always meet the loan officer in person before you ask for the money.

Even when a bank has automated its review process, the face-to-face meeting does make a difference, not only when you want money, but in every business relationship. Introduce yourself, establish a banking relationship that includes checking and savings accounts, and discuss your plans. Ask the loan officer for advice. Once you have established a relationship, your loan application will come in not from a stranger, but from a local business owner known to the bank.

The second rule is

> Ask to see a properly completed loan application, and request a list of information required.

Be sure you know how to fill out the paperwork, and get copies of everything the lender needs. This will probably include business and personal financial statements, copies of two to three years of tax returns, and a listing of other credit sources, business and personal.

The third rule for developing your loan strategy is

> Take your application into the lender in person.

Even when the mail is more efficient, take the time to deliver your loan application in person. Make an appointment to see the loan officer, and hand your paperwork to him or her directly. Ask at that point whether any additional information will be required.

The fourth rule is

> Do not ask for more than you need, as dictated by your plan.

Your loan application should be accompanied by your business plan, designed to demonstrate how the money will be used and how you plan to repay it. This plan must demonstrate that the expense of borrowing money will be justified in increased profits and that cash flow will be adequate to reduce the bank's risks. However, do not make the mistake of asking for a cushion. Some borrowers ask for more than they need, which is unnecessary and demonstrates unclear thinking.

Rule number five:

> Never assume that you cannot qualify for a loan. Try another institution.

If your loan application is turned down, that does not have to be the end of the story. Never give up after just one attempt. If you have a personal relationship with your banker, ask for advice in submitting another application—to the same bank, to someone else, or even to the type of institution you should try. Be persistent and be willing to alter your presentation.

EQUITY CAPITAL: PRO AND CON

Most people think of taking a partner into the business as a means for raising money, without going into debt. In fact, many sources for equity look for an eventual takeover and will want to control the operation of your business. This may be achieved over a number of years as a transition of management or take place immediately.

If you are not interested in giving up control of your operation, you must be aware that few investors will be content with silent partner status.

You're more likely to be expected to give up control to the new investor.
If you are able to locate someone willing to go into business with you, a rule worth keeping in mind is

> The cash an equity partner puts up should be only part of the value brought to your operation.

Cash is the most obvious benefit of giving away part ownership. For a joint venture to work to everyone's satisfaction, however, there must be much more. If you share ownership only because you need cash to support operations, you might regret the decision later. A beneficial venture should involve a combination of benefits:

1. **Cash investment.** If you give up part of your equity, you should also ask for some amount of cash. Determining the correct amount of money someone else will invest and the percentage of ownership they should receive will come from financial analysis on both sides, accounting review, perspectives of potential future value, and negotiation.
2. **Equipment and facilities.** Mergers often are motivated by the need to combine forces. Two competitors realize that by pooling their invested assets, they will be better able to operate profitably in the future.
3. **Expert talent and resources.** Some capable entrepreneurs have a particular talent, based on training and experience; but to continue growing, they need to bring in someone with a different emphasis. You may find someone in a similar business who compliments your skills or who has employees with the talents your business requires.
4. **Efficiency in larger volume.** Every new business faces a problem of expansion. You get to the point where further growth is not possible without additional capital or without consolidation with other interests. Bringing in an equity partner or merging two companies is one solution that makes larger volume both possible and efficient.

REASONS TO SEEK EQUITY PARTNERS

Most singularly owned businesses find it impossible to grow beyond a specific size without losing some degree of quality, without placing a strain on management, and without taking considerable financial risks. A solution to this problem might be to bring in an equity partner, but only if that ensures continued quality, relieves the strain on your management responsibilities, and reduces the risks associated with business growth.

Assuming that an equity partner's resources and talents will improve profits, equity is preferable to debt, because the decision *improves* profits without adding the often troublesome element always present when you borrow: the requirement for recurring monthly repayments. In most situations where additional capital is needed, the problems to be solved will stretch over the intermediate term or the next two years.

Example: Your expansion plan as you envision it will require investment in equipment, geographic market expansion, a larger staff, and a lease commitment to more space than you have today. An equity partner can finance this two-year expansion, taking compensation in the form of a salary. The point here:

> The equity partner produces while drawing a paycheck; a lender must be paid every month without enhancing profits beyond the initial loan proceeds.

You must be willing to give up part ownership, and perhaps even a controlling interest in your company, as the price of equity capital. This is a point that many business owners overlook or ignore, because they *need* the money to stay afloat today.

If you plan to consolidate forces rather than bringing in someone new, your guideline should be to eliminate competition or to strengthen your competitive posture. Some of the best-advised mergers consist of two relatively small competitors joining forces and ending up with one much larger company. This does away with the need to share a limited market and also strengthens the market position for both concerns.

Raising equity capital can be a problem as well as an advantage, especially when it isn't necessary.

Examples:

1. You might not need to bring in other owners. If you can achieve your plans without giving up part ownership and without the resources a partner brings to the business, the equity route might not be best for you.
2. You could already possess the expertise you need for expansion. You and your employees might be able to fill in the gaps, or you might be able to recruit the talent you need, not through coownership, but with employees.

3. You might give up more than you intend. When you give away ownership, you also give up the *potential* for future growth and profits, a factor that only you understand fully in regard to your own business. This disadvantage must be evaluated in comparison with the yield you can achieve on your own, assuming you borrowed money instead of giving up equity.
4. You might be unwilling to share. Remember your reasons for wanting to break away from the corporate world and striking out on your own. You were probably driven by the desire to succeed on your own. So bringing in a partner will inhibit that freedom. You must account to your co-owner, share in decisions about operations and overall business direction, and contend with another strong personality in your business.
5. Consolidation might not improve your competitive posture. If you cannot gain a distinct business advantage to combining your business with someone else's, the merger is probably a poor idea.

THE PLAN IN CONTEXT

Your business plan will play a critical role in determining whether or not you succeed in raising capital, either through borrowing money or raising new equity. The specifics of how your plan should be put together and what purposes your plan serves will be explained in detail in later chapters. For now, in the overview of money-raising purposes and attitudes, we need only to understand the context of your business plan, both for the immediate and the far future

How far ahead should you plan? The answer depends on the purpose you have in mind when presenting your plan to someone else or in using the plan to monitor and control your own operation. There are four distinct segments in the planning process, each with its own purpose.

1. **Overall business objective.** A statement of your business objective establishes your purpose in operating your business and describes the product or service you offer, your primary market, and your belief concerning quality. The statement must be clear but brief. It defines your operation.
2. **Short-term goals.** What do you hope to achieve during the next year? Goals are designed to solve current problems or to achieve

a plateau of volume, profits, cash flow, or facilities and equipment you do not have today.

3. **Budgeting.** The budgeting process is the control mechanism by which you manage your business. Budgeting as an overall practice involves predicting and anticipating future levels of sales volume, costs and expenses, and cash flow. In the interest of clarity, we will refer to these three segments of the budgeting process throughout this book in the following way: a *forecast* is the estimate of the coming year's income; a *budget* describes estimated cost and expense levels; and a *projection* is of the next 12 months' cash flow.

   Although budgets are traditionally prepared for a full year, the realistic control period cannot be expected to exceed six months. This is why most companies revise their budgets at the half-year mark. For your own control, income forecasts, cost and expense budgets, and cash flow projections are of practical value for a maximum of six months only.

4. **Long-term growth and marketing strategies.** Given your available and estimated future resources; your competitive posture; the nature of your business; your objective, goals, and plan, you establish a long-term plan. This describes the general direction in which you will take your business. Most people who review a five-year plan know that it involves predictions that become progressively undependable as the time span grows; but the plan provides valuable indications of what you want and how you plan to achieve it.

Budgetary controls, goals, and long-term plans each have a time context that distinguishes their application in the management of your business. This time context is illustrated in Figure 1–4.

Planning is an essential management tool that every successful business owner must practice. However, it is easy to forget the distinction between the two purposes of preparing a business and marketing plan. The most immediate use and value of your plan comes from the standards you establish. You must evaluate and control your operation against the standards you set for yourself. The budget is the most obvious standard and one that is familiar to everyone in business. However, the use of the plan extends well beyond the sixth month of the full-year budget.

The second purpose of a plan is to tell your story to a lender or equity

FIGURE 1–4
Time Context of Planning

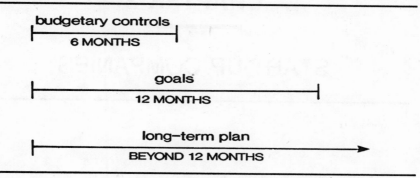

source. The document you prepare for this purpose must demonstrate how you plan to manage your company in the future and how you will produce profits and compete in your market. However, it must also contain the information that someone else will need in order to decide whether to risk their money on you.

With the overviews provided in this chapter, you are ready to begin evaluating your need to raise money, based on the current status of your business and the purpose for future borrowings or additional capital. The next chapter discusses financing for a start-up company.

CHAPTER 2

START-UP COMPANIES

> Young people, nowadays, imagine
> that money is everything, and when
> they grow older, they know it.
> —*Oscar Wilde*

To the would-be business owner, money *is* everything. Without it, a concept remains a concept and can never be put into action. With it, an idea grows into an organization, providing product or service, giving people jobs, and bringing success to the founder.

Your start-up company can only be a concept until you find a way to raise money. Not only must you finance the obvious business investment—inventory, advertising, facilities, and initial expenses—you must also provide for your own living expenses until income begins to exceed the cost of initial operations.

This chapter explains the methods for evaluating a new business concept, with the following concerns.

1. Solving the problem of raising money before you are open for business.
2. Analyzing the problems and risks of a new business, and developing your strategy for dealing with them.
3. Evaluating the competition, and identifying the market for your idea.
4. Preparing a realistic analysis.

All of these steps will be necessary if you plan to seek financing from an outside source. Lenders and equity sources will perceive every new business as a high risk to a greater extent than any going concern. So you must be able to demonstrate how and why your idea has a better than average chance of success.

DEFINING CAPITAL REQUIREMENTS

Anyone who provides you with capital for your new business will be concerned with return on the investment. For a lender, the return comes in the form of interest; and for the equity source, the return is represented by future profits. Both forms of return will be evaluated in terms of risk. This is a critical point to remember whenever you approach a source for capital: It does not really matter how much *potential* for success you have with an idea. What counts is how well you are able to show how the risk of investing in your company can be reduced.

A good starting point is to break down your capital requirements by specific categories.

Organizational Capital

You will need a sum of money to pay for the costs of preparing a location and opening the doors. The costs and expenses involved in this are easily identified by asking the right questions locally. You must determine the rent you'll have to pay, including security deposit and initial rent payments; deposits to telephone and utility companies; cost of purchasing equipment, machinery, and furniture; insurance premiums; legal and accounting fees; special permits and licenses; improvements to your leased space, including material and labor; stationery and signs; and initial inventory.

To raise organizational capital, you will need to list these costs and demonstrate that you have done your preliminary investigation. The more specifically you are able to identify the exact amounts involved, the better. For example, if you approach a lender with a vague idea of what you will need and ask for a round number, that will not be very reassuring. The lender will want to see that you take a responsible attitude toward your new business and will respond more favorably if you present a thorough summary of organizational costs.

Living Expenses

The second category of capital is the amount of money you will need to pay your own living expenses during your start-up period. Depending on the type of business, the level of costs and overhead expenses, and the market, this number will vary considerably. It will also vary based on what you need to support yourself and your family each month.

It is difficult to get financing for this form of capital, because a lender or venture capital company will not realize a return on their investment from advancing money to you for personal expenses. You have a better chance of succeeding in raising money for your business if you are able to exclude living expenses from the total amount you will need. That can be achieved in several ways.

- Reducing personal expenses (for example, paying off your home mortgage).
- Depending on other income (from your working spouse, for example).
- Borrowing living expense money from a relative.
- Using your personal savings.

Chances are your original estimate of what you will need to replace income lost from a previous job will be low; and the time required until you can support yourself from your new venture will be greater than you believe. With these points in mind, it is a smart idea to try and estimate your personal living expense requirements on the high side.

Working Capital

Once your new business is up and running, you will need capital to pay for the merchandise you need to replenish inventory (in a retail store, for example), for payroll, and for other operating costs and expenses.

This is separate from organizational capital, which covers only those costs necessary to get started. Once you begin operating, your costs and expenses will come up on a regular basis, while income will not necessarily come in as readily. For example, if you run a service organization, you will bill clients for your hours and expect payment within 30 days. You must pay your employees, rent, utilities and telephone, and other expenses promptly. However, receipts could be delayed beyond the date you expect.

Hopefully, this problem will be a temporary one. In many instances, new businesses fail because the problem of working capital presents itself on the first day and never disappears; if anything, it gets worse with time. So to raise initial working capital, you must convince a capital source of three things.

1. You are aware of the common problems that new businesses face concerning cash flow, and you have a management program in mind to control and monitor the use of cash.

2. You have identified the reasonable period of time required to get over the initial lack of working capital and have developed a plan that will bring in working capital by the end of that period.
3. You know how much money will be needed each month and can present a pro forma budget for the initial period.

Expansion Capital

Once your operation is firmly in place, with established customers and controlled cash flow and profits, you will look for ways to grow. Expansion can be achieved in terms of geographic location, number of employees, sales volume, and market lines. Regardless of *how* you measure expansion, it is only worthwhile if your profits increase at the same time. It is possible to double your sales volume, but report lower profits—an important issue to the lender or equity source that will be approached for new money.

It is a mistake to ask for expansion capital before your business is up and running. However, many people with new venture ideas do include this in their initial search for financing. Expansion should take place only after you have established yourself and proven several things:

- Your business is running profitably.
- You are able to manage money and create profits.
- There is a potential expansion market.

A smart approach to a money source is to exclude the anticipated need for expansion capital, at least when you first present your plan. However, include your expansion plan with your first application to show that you are thinking well into the future. Your plans might change later, based on what you discover after you open your doors and start operations. However, showing that you are a farsighted potential business owner makes a good impression, and a long-term growth plan demonstrates your ability to see beyond just "getting the money."

The four categories of capital are summarized on Figure 2–1.

DEALING WITH INITIAL RISK

If you are able to realistically identify risks and then demonstrate how you plan to eliminate or reduce them, you have the best possible chance for raising the capital you need. This assumes, of course, that you plan to

FIGURE 2–1
Capital Requirements

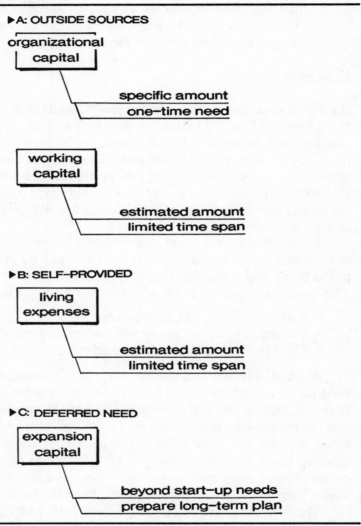

▶A: OUTSIDE SOURCES

organizational capital

specific amount
one–time need

working capital

estimated amount
limited time span

▶B: SELF–PROVIDED

living expenses

estimated amount
limited time span

▶C: DEFERRED NEED

expansion capital

beyond start–up needs
prepare long–term plan

start a business with a ready market, at the right time, and in the right place.

To better understand the nature of risk, we must first examine some of the misconceptions people have about how to borrow capital to finance a new business. Watch out for the following ideas.

1. **The more money you raise, the lower your risks.** If you are able to finance your business entirely from your own funds, then you certainly do away with the most common risk for the new business: inadequate capital. However, the same argument does not apply when you seek outside financing. The truth is, the more money you borrow or the more equity money someone else puts up, the greater your risks, and the more difficult it becomes to exceed a breakeven point.

2. **The bigger the investment, the bigger your growth potential.** Some applicants approach capital sources on the premise that their concept can become a major, big operation—if there is enough capital available. This sets too high a standard and brings too much risk into the picture for most sources. Remember that a new venture presents the greatest risk to an investor or lender. Start with what you need to *survive* and worry about a major expansion much later on.

3. **If you start small, you'll always be small.** This is another version of the belief that you must start with a lot of money. There is no flaw in starting out modestly. If you have a good idea and are willing to take the time needed to build your business from its small beginning, you can grow as much as you want. The financing will be there once you establish early successes and build financial strength. Businesses rarely start out in a big way, and most small businesses must operate with limited finances, at least until they establish themselves in the immediate market. In fact, the greatest threat to your survival is not at the onset, but later, when you begin to seriously consider expanding. That is when controls can fall apart, when you find you have no time to manage and overhead can begin to creep upward, finally killing the business as you originally planned it.

The first problem to overcome is getting your doors open with the capital you need to achieve that. Later, when you have overcome the initial difficulties that every business faces, you will be better prepared to confront the problems associated with expansion. For the first step in this process, you must deal with the important question of risk—both to you and to the source of capital.

Begin by studying the issue of risk in the various forms that every business must face and overcome. The most obvious risk you face is that you will be unable to get your business idea off the ground, due to lack of adequate capital. You also face other risks:

1. **Poor timing.** You might decide to go into business just at the time the money supply tightens up in your area. Interest rates rise, lenders become very selective in approving applications, and the general climate for financing is poor.
2. **Strong competition.** You must be able to get a market share, or your business will be unable to generate the volume needed. For example, you identify a market with little local competition. At about the same time you open, a larger, better-financed company also opens its doors.
3. **Product or service obsolescence.** With rapidly changing technology, notably in automation, some businesses can become obsolete overnight. For example, you provide a computerized service that soon becomes available to everyone on their home computers—at a cost well below what you charge.
4. **Economic events beyond your control.** Anticipating economic cycles is virtually impossible with any degree of certainty. For example, a real estate broker starts business when there is a high demand for housing. Within a year, interest rates are up, there are more sellers than buyers, and the market is at a standstill.

Each of these uncertainties can be dealt with in a number of ways at the time you approach a capital source. It makes sense to raise the potential risks you will face, if only to demonstrate that you are able to look ahead and that you have a contingency plan.

Underlying the "what-if" picture you draw is a comprehension of another form of risk: the risk that the lender or other capital sources faces when they advance money to you. If any of your specific risks become realities, they stand to lose money, too. In the next chapter, an initial business plan will be explained in more detail, including examples of addressing contingent risks. For now, begin thinking about the risk issues of concern to a capital source. Some guidelines:

1. **Identify the possible risks.** Taking a positive approach, explain the risks your business might face, and then show how you plan to deal with those risks. Although you certainly do not want to present a plan preoccupied with negatives, you must be able to show that the risk to the capital source is minimal.

2. **Summarize your market research.** Investigate the market for your product or service, including competitive forces, and summarize your findings. If you have a good idea, your research will support your contention that the risks to a capital source are low. To succeed in your new venture, you must be prepared to familiarize yourself with your market and to prove your point with thorough, relentless investigation.

3. **Explain your contingency plan.** Research alone does not do away with risk. Thus, you must address each area of contingent threat to your business' health, and then tell how you will deal with it.

4. **Support your timing.** Explain why this is the best time for you to enter your business. Support your case with facts and statistics, referring especially to the local economy and competition. If your business will be seasonal, explain why your planned start date is strategically right to take maximum advantage of a high-volume period of the year.

5. **Analyze the competition.** It is a mistake to ignore competition in your area. You will make a much stronger case for yourself by telling a capital source exactly who else is out there, how they operate, and how you will fill the gap. If your idea is sound, there must be a niche you will be able to fill. Perhaps your competitors are large companies, and you plan to emphasize personalized service. You have a particular twist that no one else has thought about. You may have a new product or service idea that is in demand, but that no one else is supplying.

6. **Anticipate market obsolescence.** Just as individuals fear being replaced by a computer or by cheaper labor sources, a capital source will be concerned that your business concept will become obsolete in the future. If you plan to enter a business that's vulnerable to this idea, you must present a contingency plan. For example, you might diversify the services you offer, so that when new technology makes your original idea obsolete, you will be prepared to take a market share of an advanced technology; or you offer services so personalized that automated systems can never replace them.

7. **Investigate economic trends.** Gather facts about your potential market. If your customer will be the consumer, you must be aware of local population trends, demographics, and employ-

ment statistics. Business customers or clients will also be affected by local economic trends. The information you collect should support your idea, showing adequate stability or growth in your demand market. A capital source must be concerned with the possibility that your market will disappear due to economic factors. The more sensitive your product or service is to interest rates, housing trends, and population, the more risk is involved in starting your business.

The guidelines for risk evaluation are summarized in the checklist in Figure 2–2.

EVALUATING THE COMPETITION

Assessing the state of the market fairly is one of the most difficult problems for the perspective business owner. Your idea might be based on an initial assumption that later proves to be misguided. Yet, because

FIGURE 2–2
Guidelines: Risk Evaluation

1. Identify the possible risks

2. Summarize your market research

3. Explain your contingency plan

4. Support your timing

5. Analyze the competition

6. Anticipate market obsolescence

7. Investigate economic trends

the desire to go into business is a strong one, you can easily make a common mistake: looking for conclusions that support your initial assumption.

This problem might be solved by hiring someone else to perform an objective appraisal. However, in many consulting arrangements, you might get what someone else *believes* you want to hear, rather than a truly impartial market study. In addition, you will probably have difficulty locating someone who understands your potential market well enough to provide meaningful insights.

You will likely end up studying the market on your own. Checking with local civic groups and business associations might be a good start; but you will discover that your Chamber of Commerce, Better Business Bureau, and other business organizations rarely represent enough of a total market to give you what you need. The nature of information you seek probably is not available from such organizations, either.

The first step in performing your own market research is to define your proposed territory. If you will operate in one locale only, you must analyze competitive factors in an isolated area. However, if you will operate over a broader range of territory, the task is more complex. If you plan to provide services through the mail or through intermediaries over a wide section of the country, a close analysis of your competition could be a formidable task.

Once you know the limits of your territory and the types of customers you will serve, the next step is to find out what existing companies already serve the market. You must determine the following.

1. Are your competitors local companies, or are they headquartered somewhere else?
2. How long have these companies been operating?
3. Do they provide the same service that you want to provide or a variation?
4. Besides the service or product you want to offer, do competitors offer more?

The purpose in getting these answers is to determine whether you will be going head-to-head with a well-established, well-financed organization—perhaps one that offers much more than you will—or whether you will be filling a need no one else does. Remember that your purpose in identifying the nature of competition is to develop a "plan of attack," that is, a method for taking advantage of the market as it exists. Don't allow yourself to plan defensively at this point. Remember:

Only the established company needs to operate defensively. The newcomer must look for opportunities and then exploit them.

A second point to remember in formulating your plan for dealing with the competition is that you cannot afford to take on a better-established company in the identical market. As a basic strategy, you must plan to work around established competitors, either offering something they cannot or will not offer (like personalized service or a better price); or you must find a gap between what the competitor provides and what the customer demands.

Your strongest asset as a new competitor is that your company is young. You have not built up a bureaucracy, and you are not restricted by several layers of authority and responsibility. Do not try to go up against a large organization on *their* terms. Set your own rules for a different market, and then make the most of it.

Identifying the competition and its weak and strong points is a good start. However, that still does not tell you how to find out what the other companies are doing. So where do you go for this information?

The fastest way to get answers and the best source for information is the competition itself. Start your research by visiting established companies, large or small, and asking questions. You might be surprised at what you will learn. If your competitors are willing to talk to you, make yourself available.

Example: Several years ago, an accountant decided to start his own public bookkeeping and tax service. With a large number of small retail establishments in the area, he believed there was enough demand. His first step was to visit the existing bookkeeping and tax companies in the area, introduce himself, and state his intentions. He asked the following.

1. Is there enough demand for another bookkeeping company in this area?
2. What services in particular do you suggest that I offer?
3. Are there ways that you and I can work together?
4. What other advice can you offer?

You might discover that some competitors are not competitors at all. They might specialize in a narrow segment of the total potential market and even welcome you as a new *resource* for themselves. In the case of the bookkeeping business, one competitor served individuals, partnerships, and small corporations, but did not become involved in estate tax returns nor in certain types of businesses.

Dispelling the Myths

The purpose in studying the competition closely, preferably at first hand, is to develop a clear and tangible perception of the market. That condition, as it exists today, will dictate whether or not a lender or equity source will be interested in taking a chance on you. So the more insights you are able to provide at the time you ask for the money, the better.

Pointing out the negative factors at work will help you obtain your financing, because you will discuss those negatives in terms of contingency plans and opportunity. Ignoring the disadvantages only makes your plan and proposal incomplete. If there is to be any assumption on the part of the company considering your application, that assumption will be that you did *not* study the market thoroughly. You must plan for this and disclose as much as possible as the result of your investigation.

In pursuing information about your competition, be aware of several myths that new business owners often believe.

Myth 1. The Competition Is the Enemy.

In the sense that you and your competitors must fight for a respectable market share, you are in an adversarial position. But in most cases, you and your competition do not need to avoid one another. Chances are there are many aspects of each business that are complimentary rather than directly opposed.

Myth 2. If Well-Established, the Competition Will Always Be Tough.

The exact opposite is often the case. You might be led to the idea of starting a new business for this very reason: poor service from a larger company. An emphasis on personalized service and quality will always be an advantage to the smaller organization.

Myth 3. There Is a Lot of Competition Out There.

Once you define exactly what you want to offer and how you will offer it, you might find that there is absolutely no serious competition at all. This is amazing, but true in many cases. Even in businesses considered to be highly competitive, you might find that your customers are hungry for service that is dependable, prompt, and worth the price.

Myth 4. All the Good Ideas and Markets Are Already Tied Up.
There is never a shortage of demand for high quality and a fair price. When the perceived competition is well-entrenched, that in itself might prove to be your greatest advantage. When a company that leads the industry is asleep on the job, that is where the young, new enterprise has its greatest chance for success.

Preparing a Realistic Analysis

The way you explore and explain the competitive factors in the report you present to a capital source will to a large extent set the tone of your application. You do not want to present a negative perspective on your proposed business, so dwelling on highly unfavorable conditions will not help your case. At the same time, you do want to disclose the facts in a *positive* way.

Make the competitive situation a plus in your report. To do this, see the examples in the next chapter. The key is to turn apparent disadvantages into obvious guidelines for the successful start-up. For example, if you discover that two other companies offer the same product you want to market, and their prices are lower than what you think you must charge, identify the ways you will overcome those facts:

1. You will concentrate on a segment of the market that the competition is ignoring.
2. You will emphasize quality, which your research indicates is not provided by your competitors.
3. You will include your product as part of an innovative product and service package that no one else has thought of before.

The possible list of methods for overcoming existing competitive factors is endless. You are limited only by your imagination, based on your insights about the market as it exists now and as you envision playing a part in its future.

A lender or venture capital company will certainly review your business plan and proposal with a thorough understanding of the risks you and they will face. If the competitive factors in your business are so extensive that your idea simply will not work, then you must accept the fact that there is little prospect for succeeding in your new business, unless you are able to develop a creative but realistic method for delivering your goods to the market.

The much-discussed "better mousetrap" can be discovered in any industry. You are never too late. No mater how well-cornered a market seems to be, the customer will always respond to a needed product or service, provided you can deliver it with quality and care.

The next chapter explains the methods for putting together the initial business plan, intended to interest capital sources. This is not a detailed plan that will include complete budgets and forecasts; that comes later. For now, you must be able to demonstrate to the money source that you have a sound idea, that you have done your research, and that *their* risks are reduced by the way that your risks will be managed.

CHAPTER 3

YOUR INITIAL BUSINESS PLAN

> The reason why everybody
> likes planning is because
> nobody has to do anything.
> —*Edmund G. Brown, Jr.*

Business planning has earned itself a negative reputation in many circles, because the process has been made overly complex. No matter what you have heard before, any plan for *your* business should be simple, brief, and easy to prepare. Planning, as it often is practiced, consists of an exercise on paper with little reality. However, planning can and should be much more—the demonstration of your ability to manage and look ahead, to anticipate future risks, and to show how you are anticipating them today.

You can hire an expensive consultant to put together a 200-page document called a "business plan," complete with endless computer-generated projections, high-level language that no one understands, and attractive comparative financial statements and forecasts. This document will cost you several hundred dollars in fees, but it will prove to be of little value where it counts—in the hands of someone who must decide whether or not to take a risk on you.

The business plan should be nothing more than a written explanation of who you are, the business you are in, and the goals you have set for yourself. Considering that no one knows these matters better than you, a key point to always have in mind is

No one is as capable of writing your business plan better than you are.

This chapter describes the first document you will present to a lender or equity capital source. The preliminary plan is a simplified description of your business as it exists today and as you envision it in the future. You must also prepare a more detailed plan, which will be described in later chapters.

THE SIMPLIFIED PLAN

The simplified plan should run only a few pages. It is prepared to show a venture capital source or a lender exactly what ideas you have for your business and what you will do with additional capital.

This plan is part financial document and part marketing tool. Your business is much more than the money issues you must face. Your initial plan must convey more than just the bottom line: It must also convey the soundness of your ideas and your personal enthusiasm for the direction in which you are headed.

If the capital source is interested in your simplified plan, you will be asked to present more details. Thus, you must have an extended, fuller plan available. The first document is nothing more than a synopsis or summary.

The first page should provide an orientation for the plan reader with a brief history of your company. What is your background? What type of product or service do you offer? Who is your customer? When was the company started? Where are you located? This section should require one to two paragraphs and should not run over one double-spaced page.

The second page should include a one-paragraph statement of your primary business objective. You must carefully write this brief statement. It must convey the sum of your purpose for being in business, specifically and simply. In one or two sentences, you must define your product or service, customer, and quality standards.

Some examples of objective statements:

1. **Professional service company.** Robert Carter and Associates provides management planning and consultation services to small- and medium-sized manufacturing companies. We ensure every client that as a result of retaining our service we will produce greater tangible cost savings than we assess in fees.
2. **Retail establishment.** Americana, Unltd. is an antique dealer with several stores, offering the highest-quality, authentic an-

tiques to the serious collector and investor. We sell and restore American furniture from the period before 1900.

3. **Construction.** Woodward Home Remodeling is a licensed contractor specializing in renovation and additions. We serve homeowners in a two-county territory and guarantee the highest quality and satisfaction to our customers.

The third page of your simplified plan should describe your requirements for additional capital—expressed in terms of specific business goals. For example, you see an opportunity to expand territory, add another outlet, or offer additional products or services; and these changes will require capital.

It helps the reader of your plan when your capital requirements are tied as closely as possible to the actual expansion plan. It's not enough to merely state that you want to add another store and that will require a loan of $30,000. You must list estimates of organizational costs, inventory purchases, licenses, employee costs, and advertising. You must also estimate the time that will be required for your changes to produce enough revenue to produce a return on your investment.

Take this approach: As the owner of your business, you want to raise capital for specific expansion ideas. That means buying inventory, building shelves and counters, hiring clerks and training them, getting an operating permit, placing deposits on a lease, and advertising your opening. Then, once open, you estimate gross sales, costs, expenses, and net profits over a specific schedule. This should show when cash flow will be adequate to (1) break even and (2) produce a profit. As part of this brief pro forma description, be sure to include estimates of time required to repay a loan (if you will be borrowing capital) or generate profits adequate to build net worth (if you are looking for a partner or venture capital).

The next section states your assumptions. This is a very revealing section from the lender's or equity source's point of view, because it shows what beliefs underlie your request for additional capital. Many business plans overlook the need for a list of assumptions, so that the reader of your plan must apply assumptions of their own. That is not advantageous to you, because you are in the best position to describe your business environment.

Assumptions may include any number of statements. For example:

- The market demand for our services is going to increase in the future.
- We have little competition today; but as we grow, we expect other companies to enter this market.
- The timing for this move is perfect, because the economic signs point to a healthy increase in demand next year.

After setting down your assumptions, define your marketing strategy. There are three segments to this.

1. **Expansion.** How do you plan to make your company grow? Describe the opportunities for the type of expansion you have in mind (territorial, service or product, or potential market).
2. **Support systems.** What will your growth require? List the capital assets, staff, facilities, and additional overhead involved with your expansion plan.
3. **Time requirements.** What deadline have you imposed on yourself to complete your expansion plan to the point that you will be able to produce a profit? This is crucial to the explanation of your goals. You must have a deadline and must be able to prove that it is realistic. Chances are the investment you must make in expanding will not produce an immediate profit or even the cash flow to support the changes you propose—that is why you need additional capital.

PROVING YOUR POINT

Every lender or equity source knows how easily a plan can be made to look profitable on paper. If every written plan came true, we could all be millionaires. This is one of the great flaws in preparing a plan. To make your ideas convincing and compelling to the reader, you must confront the risk issue and prove that your goals are sound.

Begin by introducing the elements of risk that your plan involves. Express these risks in terms of likely solutions. Show that you have thought through the risks, both as a business owner and from the point of view of the company that you are asking to forward capital.

You must raise the issue of risk as it relates to your particular business. Each venture contains specific, inherent risks of its own (for example, some businesses face unusually high exposure to lawsuits, are at the mercy of the weather, or require unusually high overhead and can remain profitable only with volume). In addition, you should address four general areas of risk:

1. **Timing.** Why is the timing of your request for capital better now than it was six months or a year ago? Why not wait a few months? Is this a seasonal question or one involving competitive or demand factors?

   Express this point in a positive tone. Any negative statement can be turned around.

   Examples:

Negative	Positive
This business suffers from very poor cash flow during the winter months.	Cash flow is seasonal, requiring careful planning and control.
In a few years, there will be so many other companies offering this product that our market share could be minimal—unless we act now.	We are faced with an opportunity to take a leading role in expanding today; the demand is there, and the competition does not yet exist.
We cannot keep up with the high volume of orders for our product and need to hire more people just to respond.	Demand is high. We must increase our fulfillment staff just to meet our existing order volume.

   Notice that, in each case, the *risk* is addressed in the positive statement, without avoiding the issue. You face specific risks—poor cash flow, emerging competition, and high volume of orders—that all could affect your ability to remain at your present size. The solution, which is a positive expression of those same risk elements, establishes the value of adding capital to your business today.

2. **Competition.** How does your business stand in terms of competitive forces at work in your territory? Are you the only company offering your services? Are you the leader, in the middle of the pack, or the struggling newcomer?

In some businesses, your "territory" is geographic. In others, it is a market. For example, a freelance writer must compete with an uncertain number of other writers, and there are a limited number of publications that will buy a limited number of articles from "the market" each year. Thus, the limitations of territory relate not to a physical boundary, but to what the market will absorb.

In this segment of your plan, define the competition in terms of territory as it relates to your business. If you have a small operation, do not claim a larger territory than you can serve, and do not make your plan so ambitious that you anticipate moving from one town to national market penetration within a year or two.

Express competitive factors as positive solutions.

Examples:

Negative	*Positive*
A number of better-financed, larger companies control this market. But they do not offer quality or personalized service.	We see an opportunity to offer personalized service and quality, features that larger competitors are not able to provide.
We will lose market share as larger companies enter the field. If we do not act now, we will eventually be forced out of business.	We intend to strengthen our market share by expanding the range of products we offer. This will place us in the best position.
Our competition is too strong for us to take more market share than we have today. We are forced to concentrate on only a small portion of the total market.	Rather than confront better-financed companies directly, we concentrate on a small segment of the total market.

Competitive forces must be addressed directly in your plan. They cannot be ignored, and your plan's reader will most surely be concerned about how you size up in the overall market. Thus, your statements must show how your limited size is an advantage, how you anticipate maximizing future competitive trends, and how you plan to grow not by confronting larger companies, but by making your specialized niche a stronger one.

3. **Obsolescence.** The third form of general risk is that your product or service will lose its market in the future, as the consequence of improved technology, changing demand, or cheaper competition. Your plan must show why your services cannot become obsolete or, if there is a risk, how you plan to position yourself to change with the new environment that might emerge in the future.

   Express these ideas as positive solutions rather than as problems. Examples:

Negative	Positive
The company's service is aimed at customers who do not have their own computers. If new technology is developed enabling customers to replace our service, we will lose our market.	New technology will eventually make our existing services more widely available. We intend to expand the range of services we offer in anticipation of this trend.
We cannot predict whether the existing demand for our product is a fad or a sign of permanent change.	Recognizing that the demand for products changes with time, we will diversify our lines to offer more than we have today.
The greatest threat we face is that with volume competitors could offer the same product at a much lower price.	Our strategy calls for expansion of sales volume, as well as diversification in our product lines.

As automation becomes more widespread, a growing number of businesses must face the question of product or service obsolescence. Anyone who will weigh risk factors in lending or investing money must proceed with caution if your business is vulnerable in this regard. The solution is to devise a plan that allows you to change with the times, to grow with new technology, and to combat the problem of obsolescence in a progressive manner.

4. **Economic factors.** Economic risk is a constant issue that few businesses can avoid. The immediate demand for your product or service will invariably be affected by negative trends in the

economy, even when those trends do not directly affect your customers. For example, if your goods are sold to other businesses, a reduced demand for new residential construction will affect you in the future. The leveling off of population growth reduces market share for local businesses (your customers), which must translate to a lowered market share for you.

Some examples of ways to express your perception of economic risks:

Negative	Positive
Interest rates are low today, but we believe they will rise in the coming 24 months. This could adversely affect our volume and profits.	Our expansion plan anticipates rising interest rates in the next two years. By diversifying, we will minimize the effects of this contingency.
The population in our region is rising; this may level off or fall in coming months, which would adversely affect our sales volume.	Our plan to expand product lines and to extend territory beyond the present, limited area will offset a decline in local population growth.
Our financial services are unavoidably tied to investment market sentiment. A falling market will create a more conservative customer base.	Our plan anticipates the effects that will be created in the event of a falling market.

Mentioning the effects that economic factors will have on your business and on the health of your plan is a necessary feature to include. However, by striving for a positive expression of those effects, you make a better impression. When explained in the context of how your plan is designed to anticipate and *reduce* risks, you demonstrate your farsightedness. The contingencies do not have to act as detriments to your getting the money you need; they can be turned around, incorporated into your plan, and used to support your expansion goals.

The last section of the preliminary plan also supports the points you want to make. Include financial statements to demonstrate that you have the capitalization to support your expansion, to afford to repay a loan or produce profits from equity capital, and to remain a strong competitor in your market.

The major sections of the initial plan are outlined in Figure 3–1.

FIGURE 3–1
The Initial Plan Outline

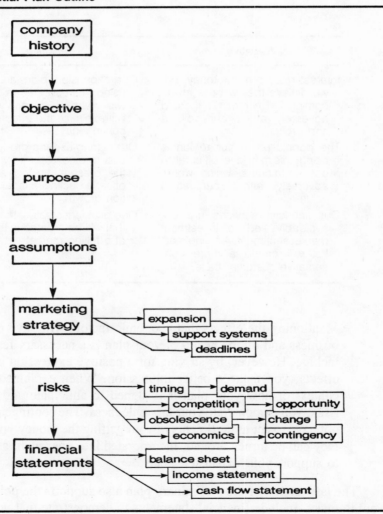

AN IDEA WITH MERIT

The initial plan presents the highlights of the larger, complete plan. At this point, you do not need to show detailed budgets and forecasts or to take up the reader's time with long explanations of your marketing strategy and competitive position. This document should interest a lender or equity source. If they want to see more, you can provide it with the complete plan.

The point to get across is that you have the ability to think through the process of raising capital—not just to the point of getting the money, as the majority of business plans do, but all the way to producing a return on someone else's investment. The properly constructed initial plan will show the reader that you are aware of risks and that your expansion goals were built with those risks in mind.

Your plan must not dwell on negatives or express risks in highly negative terms. At the same time, you do not want to hard sell the reader by ignoring the risks that you face. Remember that your risks will be shared by the company that advances money to you.

Try to convey your belief in your own plan. A sense of enthusiasm should be perceived by anyone who reads about your company, your product or service, and your goals. If you are confident that you can maximize the competitive opportunities you have isolated and that you can continue to earn a profit in the future, then you will fit the profile of a business every money source looks for. The problem, from the lender's or equity source's point of view, is identifying the business that really does meet their criteria.

The solution is to disclose—in a positive way—how your plan mitigates *their* risks. You must prove one essential point with your plan:

> Additional capital will enable you to increase profits and net worth in the future—to a greater degree than is possible without an infusion of capital.

This is the essential information that every capital source wants to know, the proof they seek, and the point on which a decision will be made. You must show that, given the risks you face, there's a good chance that you will earn more money than it will cost to raise capital. A lender will get back its principal and interest, or an equity partner will profit from growth in future net worth. Everyone must win, or you will not be able to attract new money.

You might have an excellent plan for growth, and this might be the best time to start your expansion plan. If you cannot express that idea and prove it, then you will probably look like so many other businesses competing for the same loan or equity who might need the money just to cover ever-increasing cash flow problems or to support a business that does not produce enough profit to survive.

An oversimplification of this important idea is to say that "you can only raise money when you do not need it." There is some truth in this belief, in the sense that no one will advance money to you if you are on a sinking ship. However, lenders and equity sources also know that growth demands capital. They will be willing to take risks when they are convinced that you have the strength and management skills needed to make that growth happen, when you are in a strong competitive position (or will be with capital), and when you understand your risks and have positioned yourself to overcome them.

A SAMPLE PLAN

The following is an example of how an initial business plan can be written and presented. For our example, we have used a small sole proprietorship with a limited service line, one employee, and a single location. This selection was made in the interest of simplicity. However, the principles shown in this sample plan can be applied to any business, regardless of its nature, size, or scope.

The plan includes the brief sections we have described above. Excluded are pro forma income statements that will be included in a more comprehensive business and marketing plan; forecasts, budgets, and projections for future periods; and narrative sections concerning your markets and how you plan to approach them. These specifics will be described and shown in the chapters dealing with the full plan.

AUTOMATED BOOKKEEPING SERVICE
Business Plan Summary

1. History

Automated Bookkeeping Service (ABS) is a sole proprietorship operated by Andrew Harrison and one full-time employee. The company was founded seven years ago and is located in the Commercial Building at 114 Main Street, Suite 15, Scottsdale, Arizona.

ABS provides batch-processing services and offers consultation services to clients during acquisition of automated systems. We assist with conversions and training, support partially automated systems, and create operator documentation. Our market is the small-business owner with monthly volume exceeding manual capacity, but inadequate to justify the investment in fully integrated computer systems.

2. Objective

Automated Bookkeeping Service fills a gap in an ever-growing automated business environment. We help our small-business clients to overcome the fear of automation and work directly with company owners and staff to achieve the desired level of efficent, working automated systems.

3. Purpose

This plan is presented as a brief description of how ABS plans to expand its current range of services, not only to existing client markets, but to larger companies in the immediate area. In order to achieve our three-year expansion goals, we will need to raise $30,800 in additional capital, to pay for

- Larger office space.
- Office furniture and equipment.
- New computer hardware.

We have identified specific expansion goals:

1. Upgrade our hardware with faster, more efficient technology that will enable us to remain competitive. The list price of the hardware we need is $13,500.
2. Expand our current staff over the coming year to take advantage of increasing customer demands. This will require larger facilities than our present office. The employee and facility costs will add to existing overhead. We estimate adding gross receipts to cover overhead within three months. The 90-day cost of overhead is $7,700.
3. Add fascimile transcription and photocopying equipment in our offices to better compete with other firms in the same business. The purchase cost of these machines is $9,600.

4. Expand our consultation services, where recent demand has been growing. No additional capital cost is anticipated.

4. Assumptions

This plan is based on the following assumptions:

1. The recent increase in demand for automated bookkeeping and related services will continue in the coming five years.
2. As automated systems become more common in business use, the demand for training and consultation will also grow.
3. The current conditions in our area make expansion a practical move. We expect the number of small-business owners requiring automation to increase.
4. We will increase profits through expansion to a degree that is more than adequate to repay a loan in three years (based on 12% interest and monthly payments of $1,023).

5. Marketing Strategy

Our expansion plan takes advantage of current market conditions. A growing number of small businesses in this area require automation; yet, the majority of owners have little or no experience in buying and operating their own computers.

Most of our customers face three alternatives:

1. Take the chance of investing in hardware and software.
2. Continue processing by hand.
3. Use a remote time-sharing service, which offers little in the way of affordable and ongoing support.

ABS is the fourth alternative. By working closely with clients and their employees, we ensure successful completion of an automated program designed especially for the business owner's needs.

Demand is growing. Based on population trends, we expect the rate of new business starts and existing business growth to continue. Our expansion will require investment in computer equipment and office furniture for a larger staff; the cost of adding staff and relocating to larger facilities; and temporary coverage for our higher level of overhead (which we expect to offset with newly generated volume within three months).

The expansion we plan will be completed within two years. The initial thrust will involve adding one employee, moving to larger quarters, and purchasing the new equipment needed to expand services. These steps will produce immediate new volume, both in existing service lines and new consultation. Within 12 months, we expect to add one additional employee. Over the following year, we expect volume to produce profits and cash flow that is more than adequate to repay a loan to finance this expansion plan.

6. Risk Factors

As with all expansion plans, this proposed change contains elements of risk. However, we believe that the indicators and trends mitigate those risks:

1. Timing. Market and demand factors all favor expansion now. ABS is working now at full capacity, and several large clients have asked for more hours and services in the near future. Ours is a low-overhead business that has yielded a profit in each of its seven years in operation. We contend that with existing clients and the expected growth in businesses in the area demand will continue to grow at an accelerated rate.

2. Competition. Our competitors are batch-processing service companies that offer a limited range of services (primarily in automated general ledger and accounts receivable billing). These services offer no consultation and will not work with clients on a one-to-one basis. We see a trend in increasing demand for the direct involvement of a flexible consultation firm in helping the business client to overcome conversion problems and the needed training and support associated with automation.

3. Obsolescence. Systems now in use are efficient, but more efficient hardware is available. Our plan calls for replacement with faster, more compatible equipment and a larger data base.

    We do not anticipate computer literacy and comfort level to become realities within the next generation to the extent that small-business owners will be able to operate without our services. On the contrary, with advances in technology, we expect demand to increase.

4. Economic factors. Existing clients are well-established in the local economy, and economic trends in this area have been strong over the last two years (to a greater extent than in the national economy). With population on the upswing, we

expect increasing demand for service from the types of businesses we serve. The economy in this area is diversified. Thus, economic health is not dependent on one industry or industry group. In the event of even a severe recession, we believe that demand for our services will continue.

7. Financial Statements

(Here, the latest balance sheet, income statement, and cash flow statement, with footnotes, are included. If audited, reviewed, or compiled, the appropriate accountant's notation and statement should be included. If not, they should be marked "unaudited.")

Double-spaced, an initial plan like this one will take up less than 10 pages. For a lender's or equity capital company's review, this will provide enough of a summary of your plans to make an initial decision, without having to read a time-consuming volume of details and—at this point—information not yet required. It lays the groundwork for more investigation. If interested, the reader can then request your more expanded business plan.

The initial plan should be accompanied with a cover letter, explaining that you have a more detailed business plan and will submit it once you hear back. This will be appreciated by the busy loan officer, for example, who must review several applications per week. If you are able to show your planning abilities, your initial plan will certainly draw attention to itself. If your assumptions are reasonable and your plan is realistic, then you will be well on the way to raising the money you need.

CHAPTER 4

ENTREPRENEURS
AND MANAGERS

While a general sense of optimism
is essential, a manager's sense of
harsh reality is his trump card.
—*Lester R. Bittel*

Notable differences exist between the entrepreneur and the manager. These differences will affect the way that a money source perceives an applicant, and that perception can be detrimental if not planned for. But regardless of whether you consider yourself more of an entrepreneur or a manager, you can certainly function in both roles.

Perception on the part of a lender or venture capital company becomes significant in review of a proposal and plan and will not be limited to the impression made by the market opportunities. Attitude, demeanor, and emphasis will add to the equation; but, in fact, the attributes that separate entrepreneur and manager are not necessarily in conflict.

In this chapter, you will see how the differing priorities and interests of entrepreneurs and managers can be reconciled, how the transfer from process to practice must be made to give comfort to a capital source, and what to do when you cannot successfully make the transition from entrepreneur to business manager.

IDEA PEOPLE AND DESK PEOPLE

Can a creative, fast-moving, risk-taking entrepreneur find happiness sitting behind a desk each day? Can this person, who might even be addicted to the process of achieving goals, become a manager of risk rather than a risk taker?

That is the question that everyone must answer when they start a business. Invariably, the entrepreneurial spirit that generates the start-up proves intoxicating, even for the operations person. A transition will occur for everyone who manages a young business, which is often a difficult transition.

This transition frequently occurs just at the time that the new business owner begins seeking financial help. It might even be that the motive for attempting to locate money is to move away from the operation. The owner might use funds to hire a manager and delegate day-to-day operational responsibilities, to sell the business to someone else, or to expand into new territory to get away from the office routine.

From a lender's point of view, when an entrepreneur seems restless in the role of manager, a new element of risk surfaces. Obviously, the lender hopes that the young business is directly and personally managed and nurtured by its founder. The lender realizes that responsibility for a recently launched business can seldom be completely delegated.

From the venture capital point of view, the entrepreneur is better understood. However, the package deal might include provisions for the founder to remain at the helm for a period of time and continue running the operation. As a broad assumption, your money source will want to believe that *you* and your style and perception make the business the opportunity what it is and that your individual efforts are a great part of the value involved.

These issues do not change the planning and motivation behind the search for outside money. However, they are issues that the lender or equity source care about and are aware of—both from the point of view of risk and long-term business health. The differences between entrepreneurs and managers are significant.

The traditional conflict between the two comes from the attributes and motives that drive the individual. Although these attributes are generalizations and do not apply to everyone, the characteristics will certainly affect how you originate your business, what types of risks you take, and what kinds of long-term prospects you have for producing profits.

The generalization assumes that entrepreneurs are driven by the process of making new ideas happen. The entrepreneur is creative, enjoys taking risks, and is motivated to achieve something when the odds do not favor it. On the other hand, the manager is analytical, prefers to avoid or manage risks, and works best with well-defined goals that are realistic and predictable.

The general traits of entrepreneurs and managers are compared in Figure 4–1.

1. **Risk.** The entrepreneur seeks calculated risks and might appear to be reckless when, in fact, the actual degree of risk is minimal. In comparison, the manager's job more often involves planning to avoid or reduce risk.
2. **Approach.** Entrepreneurs tend to approach problems with a creative attitude. They are impatient and want to resolve things as quickly as possible. They cannot tolerate details. A manager, though, is methodical and was trained to operate "by the book." Problems are solved analytically. Details are an everyday reality.
3. **Future potential.** Another important distinction has to do with the way that an opportunity is perceived. Entrepreneurs are more

FIGURE 4–1
Attribute Comparisons

ENTREPRENEUR	MANAGER
seeks calculated risks	seeks risk reduction
creative; impatient; not detail oriented	methodical; analytical; detail oriented
recognizes investment potential	recognizes profit potential
understands the formation process	understands the operational process
point of view: marketing	point of view: financial
prefers to delegate recurring tasks	accumulates a range of responsibilities
seeks recurring change and discovery	seeks stability and a predictable environment
responds to ideas	responds to problems

likely to recognize investment potential, often to the point that they do not even care about whether or not a business earns a profit over the intervening years. A manager tends to think in fiscal blocks. How much profit will be earned next year? Is it acceptable? Is it an improvement? What is the *profit* potential for the future? The ultimate investment value of a business or even of a business decision is a secondary concern.

4. **Processes.** The entrepreneur understands and enjoys the start-up process. The opportunity to beat the odds and the statistics is enticing to the entrepreneur. However, the manager understands how to operate a business and does not function as well during the uncertain period of testing and market contact.

5. **Point of view.** Entrepreneurs tend to come from marketing backgrounds where the customer or client is well-understood and serves as the focal point for directing energy and effort. The manager is probably more financially oriented and knows how to use the numbers to predict trends, hold down costs and expenses, and prepare budgets and business plans.

6. **Tasking.** Entrepreneurs will invariably want to delegate recurring tasks, preferring to spend their time negotiating the next deal. Managers, though, define their role in an organization by accumulating a series of related tasks and responsibilities. Even when delegating to others, managers are inclined to keep a hand in, at least at the supervisory level.

7. **Change.** Entrepreneurs can remain happy only when their environment is constantly changing. They live for discovery and challenge and cannot easily settle for a quieter, more predictable life. Managers, though, work to create and maintain a stable, predictable, and controlled work environment.

8. **Response.** Entrepreneurs respond to ideas and consider development of the promising idea the ultimate accomplishment. By the time operational problems arise, the entrepreneur may well be out creating the next idea. Managers respond to discovered problems and gain satisfaction by solving them. Ideas are of less value to the manager, because they are not tangible until they are transformed into working, real situations, complete with problems waiting to be solved.

These comparisons are, of course, very general. However, as traits, they are certainly distinguishable, and they do point out the strong and weak attributes of each individual. There must be a resolution of the dissimilar characteristics. Before a business owner can claim to be aware of all of the marketing and administrative problems to be faced during expansion, the two disciplines must be merged.

The entrepreneur cannot expect to make a career out of starting businesses that are abandoned on opening day. The founder must be willing to make a commitment of several months—as a minimum—to create a profitable new enterprise. The entrepreneur, however, does tend to lose interest once the origination phase is complete. In comparison, the "pure" management personality cannot be expected to launch the new business in the same way as the entrepreneur. The manager's background, experience, and tendency moves toward predictability and risk reduction.

Many successful businesses have been launched by people with strong management backgrounds and have succeeded. A good many entrepreneurs have discovered and developed their management skills on the job. The two disciplines can be reconciled and combined in many respects. For example:

1. A manager who is able to combine risk taking and risk management has a broadened point of view for making decisions and evaluating risks.
2. A manager who has experienced the satisfaction of starting a new business can learn to apply that entrepreneurial spirit to internal expansion programs.
3. The entrepreneur who learns how to manage a business as it develops might be better trained than someone whose training takes place in the classroom. Practical experience may be expensive, but it is also more valuable.
4. By recruiting talented specialists with different backgrounds and delegating responsibilities or by using outside services, the entrepreneurial founder can avoid being forced into an uncomfortable role.

From an outsider's point of view, the differences between entrepreneurs and managers might be troublesome. Can a lender afford to take the risk that the founder will be able to run the business for the next three years? Can a venture capital source depend on continuing individual management to protect their investment?

Be aware of the potential problem based on attributes you will be assumed to have. Also be prepared to raise that issue when you approach a money source. Explain how you are solving the problem of becoming a manager, how you are already coping with the gaps in your own experience and training, and how changes in your business are being planned in conjunction with executive staffing demands.

HOW EACH FARES

The two extreme ends of the entrepreneur/manager scale are the salesperson and the bureaucrat. The salesperson sees everyone as a customer and refuses to understand the importance of recordkeeping, planning and budgeting, and long-term money management. Today's quota is the issue. When a person with this mentality proposes a new business (or expansion of an existing one), the emphasis is on gross volume, expansion, and an unlimited market. One observant lender identified this individual by saying, "Just remove three zeros from all the projections he shows you, and you'll be closer to what might happen in the future."

The bureaucrat has one product: files. He or she is not concerned with customer contact and does not appreciate or even acknowledge the market. The only thing of any importance is the audit trail and paperflow. The more, the better. Just as the salesperson believes in expansion of customers and volume, the bureaucrat is motivated to create a larger, more complicated filing system.

Virtually everyone falls somewhere in between these extremes. However, outside capital sources will tend to label everyone as a "marketing" person or an "accounting" person. Convincing someone that you can carry off both disciplines will require a good deal of demonstration—both on paper and with your own track record.

A marketing person will approach a capital source with a "sure thing." It will be impossible to lose money on the idea, and today's small-business operation will be tomorrow's largest publicly listed corporation. However, the plan—if one even exists—will consist of the concept only, with no dependable financial forecasts or marketing plan.

A bureaucrat believes that analysis tells the entire story. The business plan will be so long and complex that it, too, is of no value to an outsider. Chances are the entire plan was formulated on historical information and statistics, but the would-be business owner has never seen a customer.

When either of these extreme personalities does open a business, the inevitable failure of that enterprise is predictable, for obvious reasons. Both extremes represent different aspects of business management and operation, but without the required balance.

Once a business has been started, the tendency of the owner toward the sales or the bureaucratic side will determine how growth is planned, the degree of risk involved, how effectively it can be achieved, and whether or not outside capital will be found when needed.

OFFSETTING WEAK POINTS

If your background is strong on the marketing side, plan to pay special attention to the planning aspects of expansion. Too much emphasis on potential sales volume can hurt your case rather than help it from the capital source's point of view. If you come from an administrative background, develop a very detailed marketing plan. Be able to show that you have a realistic sense of who the customer is and how large a market is available to you. You might need outside help to add the balance in emphasis to your application and plan.

Example: A highly entrepreneurial marketing executive left his job and formed a financial services company. His talent was in recruiting independent sales companies to work with him on a representative and brokerage basis. Within two years, he had 11 offices in two states fully operational, and profits were high. He constantly sought to expand more, preferably as quickly as possible. However, to do so meant having to borrow money. His first trip to the bank resulted in a rejection, because he had no detailed plan and could only describe the potential of the market to the lender. After that, he hired an accounting consultant to write a plan. The owner handled the marketing side of the plan, and the accountant filled in the pro forma financial information, developed a tentative forecast and budget, and established a timetable for completion. The plan included a precise identification of how the money would be spent and the profits and cash flow it would produce.

Example: A secretary used the proceeds from selling her home to start an answering service. She used local contacts to gain her first few clients, but wanted to open a second and third location in larger communities in the next county. This required outside financing. She did not know how to structure a marketing plan, so she asked a friend who worked as a marketing manager to give her a hand. Her business plan now included a study of the market, the competition, projections of volume and profits from expanded operations, and a strategy for advertising and customer contact.

Inevitably, the business owner who wants to present a balanced plan—one that explains both the marketing and the financial side—must plan to use outside help. This will certainly add value to your plan for a loan application or proposal to a venture capitalist; it will also help you to fine-tune your plan for your own use and implementation. Write your own plan, but strengthen it with outside help where needed.

THE ENTREPRENEUR'S DILEMMA

The perception that some lenders *might* have of the entrepreneur must certainly be addressed in an initial plan. This is especially the case in trying to finance a business not yet up and running. Even after the operation is established and earning a profit, the emphasis the owner places on marketing and sales potential can affect how a lender perceives their risks.

Beyond this initial risk, however, the entrepreneur faces a more complicated dilemma. Most new businesses do not succeed. In fact, the U.S. Small Business Administration has estimated that as many as 80 percent of all new ventures do not make it. This is not a precise statistic, however; it does not include the large number of part-time business enterprises that start up each year. The owners of those businesses are not entirely dependent on profits to earn a livelihood, so the chances of surviving through the first three to five years are much better than the odds for the full-time venture.

The boom in small-business starts means the small business has more competition today than ever before. More than half a million new tax returns were filed between 1980 and 1987, according to the Internal Revenue Service (IRS). Of the more than 18 million businesses active in the United States, the IRS reports that 80 percent are sole proprietorships and that three-fourths of all small businesses hire no employees.

The significance of these numbers must be remembered when you seek outside capital. From the point of view of someone who will be taking a risk advancing money to the "average" small business, the risks are varied and high.

1. Most small businesses do not succeed.
2. Most are one-person operations or are run by husband and wife. Thus, illness or death means income ceases, and the lender or venture capitalist loses out.
3. Sole proprietorships have less flexibility than corporations, because stock cannot be traded or sold. In order to change the capital structure of the operation, it must be disbanded, and a partnership or corporation formed in its place.
4. With more small businesses being formed today than ever before, the competition in the market is more intense—even with a more active economy.
5. The small-business market is cyclical or will be hit especially hard by adverse economic conditions.

The small business is more mobile and flexible and can operate without the expensive support systems required of the large corporation. Thus, a great demand exists in the marketplace for the very small company. However, when you are no longer the only small business on the block, your potential market share must be smaller. This factor limits your growth and profit potential.

The industries dominated by small businesses often are affected by conditions beyond their control—such as the national and regional economy; the competition from larger, better-financed firms; and even the weather. Forty-three percent of all small businesses are retail and construction firms. Retail establishment volume depends largely on buying trends, which are affected by the health of the economy, interest rates, and inflation. The construction industry is especially sensitive to interest rates, new building trends, and the money supply:

Small Business Industries

Retail trade	29.33%
Services	22.44
Construction	13.99
Wholesale trade	10.82
All other	23.42
Total	100.0%

Source: U.S. Small Business Administration.

The sensitive nature of the retail and construction industries are risk factors you must address in your plan. The market conditions and historical high risks associated with new business enterprises do not apply only to those who need money just to get started. Even after you have established a track record of profits over a number of years, many lenders and venture capital companies will shy away from the smallest concerns. The definition of *small* encompasses operations that many one-person companies would consider large. For example, a small business, as a general rule, refers to a sole proprietorship with fewer than 20 employees and annual gross income of less than $1 million.

When an established small business—one with three years or more of profitable operation—applies for new capital, showing profits might not be enough. You might also have to be able to demonstrate talent as a business manager. This is an intangible ability, but it must be made tangible by your *management* and *marketing* track record. The best vehicle for this is the well-conceived business plan, which demonstrates your ability to accurately predict and forecast the future, to anticipate and plan for problems, and to plan profits as part of the plan for obtaining outside capital.

PLANNING FOR DELEGATION

The ability to locate the right people to get a job done is increasingly becoming the necessary attribute for success. This is as true in big business as it is in the small-business community. Yet, many small-business owners have trouble recruiting employees for key management positions.

A top-notch executive may be hesitant to invest a career with a small business. The reasons are similar to those that a capital source will have in mind. Many small businesses fail, notably as they begin to expand beyond a comfortable, localized operation. So the risks of changing careers to go to work for a small organization are everpresent.

A second factor the career executive or manager will have in mind is limitation. In a small operation, the key employee will be able to gain power and influence in a relatively short time; but what is lacking is the large number of divisions or departments to which one might want to transfer later on.

Smaller companies cannot afford the cafeteria plans, headquarters facilities, and retirement benefits that bigger companies offer as a matter of course. Those perks might be worth more than half the annual salary offered by a large company and are hard to resist for an executive considering more than one option.

For hiring an employee directly, the market is limited. An executive search agency *might* be helpful. There, too, the emphasis and time is spent with a few large clients who recruit a number of executives each year. The smaller operation must take second place.

The skill to delegate is itself not an easy one for all owners. Even when it is essential just to complete the demanding requirements of the workday, some owners have trouble letting go. When they do, they might give the job to the wrong person.

Example: A real estate marketing firm grew rapidly when second mortgages gained popularity among investors. The president wanted to hire an executive vice president to run the headquarters' office, where 35 people worked. The president spent a good deal of time on the road and had little patience for the routines of office work. However, over a series of four years, the company went through five executives. None of them worked out and either left on their own or were asked to resign.

The problem, which was painfully obvious to the employees, was that the executives hired were not able to do the job. They were either incompetent or dishonest (one of the four embezzled a large sum of money right after his signature was added to the company's checking account). Some employees concluded that the president would never hire anyone *more* talented or capable than he was.

The problem of ego, when it involves hiring people to take over your responsibilities, can prevent you from realizing your expansion objectives. No matter what market opportunities you want to exploit, your office staff must be in working order to support your efforts. What is the point of flying around the country to make deals, if your staff lacks the leadership to back you up?

Ultimately, the real estate marketing company was dissolved. The demand for second mortgages diminished, but the more immediate cause was the problem of finding a capable, competent leader. You do not need to experience a similar difficulty when the time comes to hire someone to run your office. Chances are you can not afford the cost. The salary paid to the wrong person is only the obvious cost; you also lose time and marketing advantage by not putting the right executive in charge.

Example: When the owner of a big-city delivery service opened his doors six years ago, he acted as president *and* the only employee. He ran the business with a telephone, an answering machine, and a bicycle. Now he has 16 employees and rents a shop. His staff includes a part-time repairperson and bookkeeper and a full-time receptionist. The owner wants to set up a similar operation in another part of town, but needs to hire someone to run the first shop for him. He interviews several people for the job, making use of the contacts he established over the last six years, and narrows the field down to two people. The one he hired was given the added incentive of a graduating 25 percent equity in the business.

This approach was practical. The owner screened applicants carefully and found the best person for the job. He also let his employees know that he was looking for someone, a wise move for any owner in a small business. Now, with the first operation running smoothly, the owner felt more confident in asking for a loan to set up a second shop.

GETTING THINGS IN ORDER

If you have read brochures or other books about how to prepare to visit a lender or venture capital company, you have already heard the advice to "get things in order" before filling out the application. This usually means paying off older debts, improving the working capital ratio, and timing your request so that it follows an exceptionally profitable year.

What is often overlooked, though, is the need to get your staffing and management team in order, too. It is very reassuring to an outsider to see that you have all the bases covered.

Example: A very successful entrepreneur was prepared to expand his small two-store retail flower business into several new locations. He had the marketing expertise to achieve this, and he had identified a market demand, especially for weddings and other gatherings. However, his weakness was in the financial area. So before visiting his banker to ask for a loan, the owner hired an accountant. The mission: To establish internal systems to manage a multioutlet retail establishment. This was to include preplanning for hiring store personnel and, later, administrative support staff; putting cash controls into effect; devising a simple but effective inventory control system; creating and tracking a budget; and developing a workable business plan. When the owner went to his bank, the loan officer was impressed with his plans, and a line of credit was approved within one week.

USING OUTSIDE SERVICES

One of the best ways for the entrepreneurial business owner to fill in the missing administrative gap is by using outside professional services. This solves the problem that a young business faces: being unable to support full-time help, but needing that help on a semiregular basis.

The outside service alternative can hold down overhead while rounding off your management team—all the way from secretarial help up to top executive positions. Some possibilities:

1. **Temporary help agencies.** As big-corporation "downsizing" takes its toll, many career executives are retired well before their productive career years are ended. Many displaced executives seek part-time work and are available through temporary help agencies specializing in executive-level placement. This offers an ideal solution for both sides. The executive can remain semi-retired and enjoy greater leisure time and still use years of experience and knowledge in a productive manner. The owner of a small business benefits from that expertise, without having to make a commitment to a full-time career executive.

2. **Consultants.** In place of full-time or temporary employees, consider hiring a consultant to act as the financial arm of your small business. This helps your budget, but provides credentials that lenders and venture capital companies will expect to see.

   Be careful in your selection of a consultant. You should maintain control over the total hours and cost involved. The project duties should be specified in writing. You should list the procedures, analysis, plans, budgets, and other results you expect to gain from the relationship, including deadlines for completion.

3. **Executive suite services.** For the business too small to run from a home, but not profitable enough to justify an office, the executive suite might be the best answer. Convenience is the key. Rent usually is charged on a month-to-month basis, and office facilities (photocopy machine, phone answering service, secretarial help, conference room, etc.) are charged for on an as-used basis. The executive suite might provide much more, too. Some companies not only rent out space, personnel, and facilities, they also offer a range of consultation services, which might include executive and financial help.

Filling in the "talent gaps" you will face when you are on your own requires a thorough and complete search. Even with choices among consultants and other outside services you might use, you will eventually need full-time executive staff. Growth invariably also means having to add permanent overhead, and, for most businesses, payroll costs are the most substantial portion of that change. Once you begin hiring people, you increase your administrative and recordkeeping burden, extend potential liabilities, and take on the responsibility of an employer and not just an independent business owner.

The complications do not end there. Expansion itself increases the risks of management and even could threaten your solvency. Every growing business reaches a plateau, which temporarily limits development. At that point, existing resources (staff, facilities, equipment, etc.) barely support the volume of business; yet, in order to grow beyond that level, you will have to make a major capital commitment or find outside money. This is the subject of the next chapter.

CHAPTER 5

THE THREE-YEAR GROWTH PROBLEM

> Success has ruined many
> a man.
> —*Benjamin Franklin*

Bigger is always better. At least, that is what we tend to think about business. This year's sales must be higher than last year's, and the profit level must grow as well. Expansion, though, can become the greatest threat to profits and even to your ability to keep your doors open.

Every business owner eventually faces the problem and the opportunity for growth. The first big break often occurs at about the time the business has been operating for three years. At that point, a market niche has been established, the start-up problems have been ironed out, and personnel are in place. The next logical step is to grow.

If you attempt to force expansion, you may find yourself stretched far beyond your capital resources. The quality of product or service you offer to your customers will deteriorate and, as a direct result, profits will fall. For many, the question should not be how to achieve greater volume, but when to stop growing.

Growth itself is a misunderstood process. Many of us believe that growth occurs as a matter of luck—being in the right place at the right time. We might even fool ourselves into thinking that when a company becomes a big success, the owner is just along for the ride.

The truth is far different. Successful companies are led. Growth is planned and controlled by management, not allowed to just happen. It cannot be forced and it cannot be allowed to run free. It must be allowed to happen when you are ready for it. Your task as the owner of a business is to make the determination about the best time to allow growth—based on the two primary resources at your disposal: people and money.

The human resource may be more difficult to find than the financial resource. Having capital, by itself, will be of little permanent good if you do not surround yourself with the right talent. As your business expands, you must be prepared to delegate large segments of authority and responsibility. Although we are primarily concerned with a discussion of raising and using capital, you must not overlook the critical importance of having talent in place as an intrinsic requirement for a successful and ongoing business operation.

THE NEED FOR CAPITAL

The three-year growth plateau is frustrating for most business owners. Your operation has demonstrated a respectable degree of success to date; but the market has been a limited one, and you now want to expand, take a bigger market share, and move into a higher mode of operation. If it worked on a small scale, can the same approach also work on a large scale?

At this point, we must acknowledge that a larger-scale operation is vastly different than a smaller-scale one. You must face several realities that come with expansion:

1. You will have to increase your permanent staff, accepting the idea that you need executive-level management to take some of the control burden from you.
2. Support staff must be increased as well.
3. Internal systems will have to be made more sophisticated. That probably means automated processes for the high-volume transactions and records you have probably kept by hand up to this point.
4. You will have to invest in fixed assets, meaning a commitment of money that is not directly used for operations. In a sense, buying fixed assets takes away a part of your working capital and ties it up.
5. All of these changes also mean leasing larger facilities, both for the administrative and marketing of your product or services. This represents permanent overhead (at least to the extent of your lease).

Fixed overhead. All of the requirements of growth are permanent. Keep this key point in mind:

During the process of expanding your costs and expenses and adding inventory and fixed assets, you must also be able to create a permanently higher level of sales volume.

If you build in permanent overhead and invest money in inventory and fixed assets, accept a higher level of outstanding accounts receivable, and commit yourself to a three-year lease, you *must* be able to support these expensive changes. The mistake many small-business owners have made is to attempt to finance these changes with borrowed money or new investment capital rather than with a permanent increase in new volume.

Remember that a one-time inflow of capital, either borrowed or invested, is finite and that the changes you make in fixed overhead are permanent. This is a problem that every business owner confronts when attempting to expand: How do you achieve that expansion while contending with the risks of higher-level permanent commitments? It cannot be done without taking the risk, and it will not work without adequate capital.

You will need both a permanent increase in volume and the capital to survive the transition period. Unless you have a good sum of money sitting idly in a savings account, you will have to seek financing elsewhere. It is the rare operation that is able to finance expansion from its working capital.

Recognizing the need to raise capital, you must also acknowledge that the greatest threat you face is growth itself. At the three-year plateau, you are enjoying the benefits of success. You have beaten the odds and stayed in business. You have made money. You have also proven to yourself that you are a capable executive and manager. So why should you stay where you are?

Another key point to keep in mind—and to think about before you borrow money or take in new investors—is

When you go to the outside to raise capital, you give up a part of the control you now have over your business.

The owner of a securities brokerage firm faced these questions and decided he would take his company national. He wanted to expand from his 17 branch offices in five states to over 100 offices in 43 states. This required an investment in licensing, registration, and legal fees. He would have to find qualified professional salespeople to join the firm— meaning recruiting them away from other brokerage firms. Like any marketing situation, the competition in that business is in the recruitment of salespeople. So in order to make branch offices successful, it would be necessary to put together a commission scale that was more attractive than that offered by larger firms. This translates to lower profit margins for the owner, so higher volume would be essential in order to make a profit.

Initial estimates were that the expansion plan would cost more than $250,000. The owner wanted to complete his expansion plan within one year. Several problems came up, however, that inhibited both the schedule and the affordability of the plan:

1. The firm was not earning enough to finance the ambitious marketing plan.
2. The plan included hiring no less than 25 home office employees and installing an automated commission accounting system. Neither the facilities nor expertise was in-house to achieve these objectives.
3. The current office space was far from adequate to house the planned number of employees.

Even with these problems, the owner was convinced that additional profits from expansion would more than cover the higher overhead and initial capital requirements. The firm proceeded with his plan.

A year later, the company was operating in 28 states and 60 offices. Original estimates of cost proved to be too low, and expansion was slowed by a drain on working capital. Other problems were discovered as well.

First, profits from operations in remote states were not as high as they had been in the original five states. This was due largely to the smaller margins the owner offered to attract and recruit professional salespeople.

Second, the salespeople in the original 17 offices heard of the new commission rates and demanded that their scales be increased to match them. So the margins on the existing offices had to be reduced.

Third, the cost of operating remote branch offices was higher than expected. Travel, telephone, and other expenses ran far beyond budget. The owner spent a great deal of time on the road, recruiting and meeting with new office personnel.

Fourth, it proved very difficult to recruit the best salespeople, even with a competitive commission scale. In the original five states, the owner used his connections in the business. Now, he was on new ground. He discovered that even among the salespeople he did recruit, attrition was quite high. Some of the most promising recruits left the firm within the first six months.

Cash flow problems developed early in the expansion plan. Even when remote offices did produce high volumes of sales, it took several months between execution and the date that the income hit the books. Original estimates of volume were based on point of sale and did not allow for the delay time.

To deal with these problems, the owner sought outside financing. He approached his banker and asked for a loan. A $100,000 line of credit was approved at a rate of interest far above prime. The reason: It was an unsecured loan, based on existing volume of business and the promising potential of the aggressive business plan. The mistake made in this entire process was the failure to assess the expansion process realistically. If the owner had factored in all of the variables that could occur, he would have realized that financing should have been arranged up front. In addition, the schedule of expansion should have been stretched out over a longer period of time, so that it could be controlled within the limited equity and debt capital available.

The company did eventually become licensed in nearly 40 states. However, profits were far below original expectations. The distance factor was significant. It seemed there was a correlation between distance from the home office to the branch office and the level of profit. Increased fixed overhead, coupled with lower overall margins, meant lower profits for the company. Interest paid on borrowed funds further eroded profits.

When the expansion was complete, the nature of the operation had changed dramatically and not for the better. For example:

1. The company was far less profitable after expansion than before.
2. The staff totaled about 50 people, and morale was low. Before expansion, a small staff was in control, and morale was high.
3. The owner was no longer in control. There was simply too much going on, and he no longer had time to sit in on staff meetings or to be involved directly in the management of the operation.

EXPANSION AS A NEGATIVE

In a case like the one above, a forced expansion resulted in lower yields. At the same time, exposure to risk was increased and profits fell. The business was exposed to higher liability levels, fixed overhead, loan commitments, facilities leases, and salaries.

Many businesses have failed in their attempts to expand, because they either project unrealistically or fail to project at all. It is a mistake to assume that profits will be identical after expansion. In fact, if you are able to match profit margins, your expansion will be judged a huge success. In many cases, however, the rate of return will be lower, but justified by higher *permanent* volume.

A realistic appraisal of profits after expansion might reveal lower profit margins. If this is the case, is expansion worth the risk? Yes, if future profits will be greater and you believe that the risks you accept during expansion justify making your move. No, if you will be taking risks you cannot afford, and if you will be in far over your head.

Considering all of the skills you must exercise as the owner of your own business, patience might be the most important one of all. A lot of emphasis is placed on marketing ability, talent in motivating employees, the knack for identifying expansion opportunities, and other leadership skills. In fact, you are under considerable pressure to grow, whether it is good for you or not. Businesses are judged by growth, regardless of the more important factors of control, quality, and profit. If your sales do not rise and if your staff is not constantly growing, the common belief is that you have become stagnant.

What good is an expansion of commitment if you end up losing control of your business and if your profits evaporate in the process? This is not to say that growth is always bad. A young business should grow and at a healthy rate. Yes, we measure success in terms of volume and profits, and those are appropriate standards. Less tangible, though, is the measurement of your own perception of financial risk and timing.

Another point about expansion: You started your own business so that you could be in control. If you allow expansion to occur beyond your control, then you will end up just as you were before starting your business—doing work you don't really want to do, working longer hours, and making less money than you want.

Expansion is a negative when the *quality* of growth is lower than it was in the past. You must face the fact that if you don't give your customers the service they expect, then someone else will. All too often, a business loses its customer base following expansion because they sought growth for its own sake. They forgot the most important element along the way: building permanent volume through customer loyalty, meaning service after the sale, prompt response, and delivery of quality. Compare these two examples of growth:

Example 1. You double your gross volume from one year to the next, but earn only half as much in net profits.

Example 2. Your volume declines one year, but net profits are higher.

In the first example, growth resulted in lower net profits. So at first glance, it appears that the second example is a successful one. The *amount* of profit is greater, even though sales volume declines. Ironically, though, when we apply the cultural standards of business "success," the business in the second example is not doing well—but only because sales volume declined. There is a negative connotation to allowing your business volume to fall off, even when it means you make more money.

In contrast, the first example involves half the net profit as a prior year, but volume doubles. The change in profits may be justified in several ways. The owner might argue, "I'm willing to accept lower profits now, because my investment in expansion will pay off later. Also because my volume is higher, the business has a higher market value."

These justifications may be true for some businesses, however, it is not enough to merely state that a current loss is an investment in the future. What if the drain on capital and cash flow makes it impossible for you to survive financially? Many failed businesses held great promise for the future. They failed because the owner's vision did not include short-term survival.

You might be willing to accept lower profits during an expansion year in the belief that your investment will pay off in the future. In every success story, this has proven to be the case. It is completely valid to welcome acceptable losses now for greater profits later assuming two very important facts: first, that you can afford the losses and, second, that you planned for the growth curve and knew the profits would occur. This is critical because if you planned the acceptable loss and knew it would occur, then you will also know how and when the profit picture will turn around. A problem will always arise when you attempt to expand in this way beyond the means of your capital.

Putting it another way, behind every great expansion plan is a business failure, waiting for the chance to take place. Looking back after the failure occurs, one can wisely see—too late—that behind every failure was a success that was never given a chance.

You should not borrow money to expand your business unless you first understand the risks and have planned for them. Judging growth in terms of profitable and unprofitable volume is one of the best ways to assess how well you succeed in the expansion attempt.

You may equate "profitable" volume to the idea of quality. Whether you deliver a product or a service, you are certainly aware of quality as the way to build a permanent and loyal customer base. You must also be aware that many large companies are unable to compete with a smaller operation, because their size prevents them from providing the personal touch. Remember:

> As your business grows, quality will suffer—unless you make the conscious effort to grow in terms of quality first and volume second.

What this means is that the rate of growth must be limited to the speed at which you can build in a continuing dedication to customer service and to providing quality before, during, and after the sale. If you want only volume, you must certainly abandon this idea. If you want *permanent* growth, volume and quality are inseparable attributes.

SEEKING PROFITABLE VOLUME

A plan for growth must include provision for the inevitable acceleration of fixed overhead. Thus, higher levels of rent, salaries, and other expenses must be matched to the gradual plateaus of volume. Your plan cannot ignore the need for investment in certain assets associated with expansion: higher levels of accounts receivable, inventory, and fixed assets. In order to match or exceed previous levels of net profit, you must plan to constantly monitor cash flow and the use of capital. If you borrow money to expand, you must make payments on your note and for the added interest expense.

A small business might have cash flow problems by borrowing for even a modest expansion plan. For example, you borrow to pay for the purchase of fixed assets. As you spend that money, cash flow is adversely affected in two ways: First, the flow from operations must be adequate for repayment of the debt. Second, borrowed money is invested in fixed assets, which are not always directly related to the production of income.

If you buy a new desk and typewriter for the new executive you just hired, how will that investment contribute to profits and cash flow? Although these assets must be acquired, they do not directly produce income in the same way that a piece of machinery does in a plant. Your investment might be unavoidable, but the consequences of poor timing can harm your cash flow.

Evaluate expansion in terms of cash flow, and these problems will be recognized and dealt with as they arise. Do not expect higher volume to provide the working capital you need to fund your expansion, unless you can prove that outcome with an evaluation of growth.

Table 5–1 shows how volume can be increased over a four-year period in such a way that profits increase year by year—not only in the amount, but also in the percentage of yield. There are several control factors that allow this to occur.

1. The percentage of direct costs to sales is kept at the same level each year. When analyzing the nature of direct costs, you discover that they can—and should—maintain their relationship to sales. This relationship changes only when your cost factors are altered or when you relax the controls needed to maintain the proper relationship.
2. Selling expenses increase in line with the volume of sales however they are controlled. Thus, the rate of increase is not identical, rather, it slows with time. Travel, entertainment, and other selling expenses must be allowed to grow, but should do so at a rate less than the volume growth level.
3. Fixed overhead is "fixed" only in the sense that the commitment is there regardless of volume levels. Once you make this com-

TABLE 5–1
Profitable Volume

	Year 1	Year 2	Year 3	Year 4
Sales	50,000	75,000	100,000	125,000
Direct costs	28,000	42,000	56,000	70,000
Gross profit	22,000	33,000	44,000	55,000
Selling expenses	13,000	18,000	21,000	26,000
Fixed expenses	6,000	8,000	10,000	10,000
Total expenses	19,000	26,000	31,000	36,000
Net profit	3,000	7,000	13,000	19,000
Yield (%)	6.00	9.33	13.00	15.20

mitment, you are required to continue making payments even if volume drops off. For example, you sign a three-year lease for a fixed amount, and that is payable on the first of each month. As you can see from Table 5–1, "fixed" overhead does not remain at the identical level. It must be allowed to increase to new permanent levels as certain volume plateaus are attained.

You might expect to achieve a higher percentage of profit if your sales double. Without proper planning and management of the income statement relationships, this will not be possible. Remember this key point:

> Higher sales volume is not the key to greater profits. The real secret to building profits in the immediate future is constant monitoring and control of costs, expenses, and cash flow.

Next, consider the outcome of a four-year profit plan when yield drops off. This may occur even when the *amount* of profit grows each year. It may be argued that this is an acceptable outcome, as long as there is more money going to the bottom line. In the long run, this might be true. Ultimately, very slim margins are indeed acceptable, given higher levels of fixed overhead and the need to cut gross profit margins in order to compete. For the immediate future, the next two to four years, you should be able to maintain a steady net profit yield or even to create a higher yield of net profits. This can be achieved and, at the same time, the amount of net profit can be increased.

Table 5–2 shows what commonly occurs during periods of expansion without internal controls. The sale gross volume is used as the previous example, and the amount of net profits increases with each year. Is this a positive trend as long as profits are moving upward? No. For increased volume, you also take on higher levels of business risk in many forms.

- You have a higher level of liabilities when you sell more goods.
- You commit to higher levels of rent, salaries, and other permanent fixed overhead expenses.
- You must increase inventory levels and the amount of average outstanding accounts receivable, affecting the amount of cash available today.
- You must invest money in fixed assets.

TABLE 5–2
Unprofitable Volume

	Year 1	Year 2	Year 3	Year 4
Sales	50,000	75,000	100,000	125,000
Direct costs	28,000	43,000	59,000	77,000
Gross profit	22,000	32,000	41,000	48,000
Selling expenses	13,000	19,000	25,000	30,000
Fixed expenses	6,000	9,000	11,000	13,000
Total expenses	19,000	28,000	36,000	43,000
Net profit	3,000	4,000	5,000	5,000
Yield (%)	6.00	5.33	5.00	4.00

- If you have borrowed money for your expansion plan, the loan must be repaid.
- If you have taken in new investors, they will be interested in the yield trend, which represents a return not only on sales, but also on their investment.

Several problems are revealed in the analysis of unprofitable volume, including

1. Direct costs increase as a percentage of sales as the volume grows. This indicates lack of control over inventory, material purchasing, and scheduling and control of direct labor.
2. Selling expenses are growing at a rate higher than that shown in the illustration of profitable volume. With greater volume hitting the books, the tendency is to relax controls, notably over entertainment, travel, and similar selling expenses.
3. Fixed overhead outpaces the gains made in volume levels. The percentage comparison shows loss of control in these expense categories. If growth occurs too rapidly, the results might bear out the usual problems revealed by close analysis: the addition of employees before they are really needed, the addition to leased space beyond current and foreseeable needs, and relaxation of the usual control routines.

FIGURE 5–1
Profitable and Unprofitable Volume

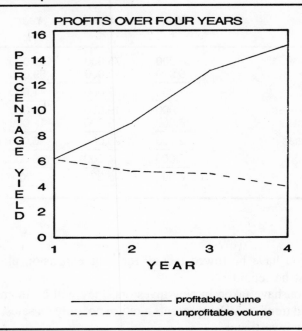

A comparison between profitable and unprofitable volume, as shown in Figure 5-1, summarizes the important differences. They are substantial. For a few thousand dollars swing in costs and expenses, volume can be highly successful or it can harm your ability to remain in operation. If you multiply our limited examples by volume on a much larger scale, the slight variances are translated into big dollars. If the trend in deteriorating controls continues as expansion proceeds into the future, the operation is headed for serious cash flow and profit difficulties.

INTANGIBLE PROBLEMS OF GROWTH

Besides these purely financial questions, expansion also creates less tangible problems you might not anticipate at the time you plan it.

We have already equated profitable expansion with the idea of quality. There is a reasonable and finite limit to the pace of growth you can achieve, given the assumption that you are concerned with quality and reputation. A great deal may be said for the small company's advantage over its larger competitors in this regard.

Most expansion plans succeed in gradual, methodical, and controlled phases. This is so because the quality issue is just as important to survival as are immediate profits. Smart management recognizes that proceeding with control today translates to existence in the long term. Many of the most successful organizations in operation today have gotten to their positions of competitive power because they recognize an important factor in the expansion equation: Customer service and product or service excellence is of greater importance than sales volume for its own sake.

A large, well-capitalized organization can afford the luxury of concentrating on quality and service. A smaller company may have to concentrate more on profits in the immediate future, or so the belief states. How do large companies get to where they are? The answer goes back to the original philosophy of management, which invariably stated that customer loyalty was the only way to create permanent growth.

The reality that successful management accepts is that the competition always inherits their dissatisfied customers, probably forever. Temporary success in sales, yields, and profit amounts do not really add to growth if customers turn over faster than inventory.

Another problem common to expanding companies is the failure to anticipate ongoing and short-term capital requirements. You can plan completely for cash flow needs with higher volume; you can control direct costs, selling expenses, and fixed overhead; and you may still run into problems.

Most businesses today allow customers to pay on time. Both service and product companies give customers lattitude in the time required to make payment, especially when profits begin to grow. With expanded volume, the tendency to relax collection procedures is a likely pitfall. Many small businesses realize this and concentrate on timely payments by customers. Then, as they grow, they overlook the need for continuing this function. Many growing businesses have been forced to close their doors with a decent record of profits on the books.

Some business owners have made the mistake of assuming that additional borrowing is the solution to cash flow difficulties during expansion. As growth occurs, volume doubles and then triples, but there's never enough cash on hand. So the owner applies for a loan or solicits outside investors.

This is the worst time to try and raise money. From the point of view of the borrower, the greatest risk is lending money to a business that is having trouble coming up with cash. The big question is: Where will they get the cash to repay the loan?

If the problem is one of lacking controls (and it usually is), borrowing money will not solve the problem, it will only make it worse. Investors would rather risk their money on well-managed companies than take a chance on bailing out an organization that has fallen into the most common pitfall of all: forgetting to exercise the most basic financial controls when growth occurs.

Lack of control cannot be disguised. An intelligent loan officer or potential investor will quickly recognize the symptoms of cash flow mismanagement. To succeed in raising needed capital, you must first do away with the problems by correcting the difficulty and installing the controls that should have been in place all along.

Yet another problem with expansion is whether or not you, as an owner, really want to expand. You might assume that you want to grow when, in truth, you would be happier identifying a comfortable, controlled level of sales and profits and then stopping. Seek no more growth and prevent it even if the opportunity comes along.

This might seem an unnatural strategy, given that our business successes or failures often are measured in terms of the most obvious forms of growth. However, your reasons for leaving someone else's employ and taking the risk to start your own business should be examined in the context of the expansion question.

You probably struck out on your own so that you could earn more money and determine your own career path. All too often, business owners lose sight of their own original motives and end up in the same situation they have been trying to avoid: working longer hours for less money than they would like to earn. They are no longer in control, but find themselves a passive rider on the full-throttled train of "success"— with no engineer up front. The result: The owner is just as unhappy and unfulfilled as he was as an employee. Anyone who allows this to occur might as well not take the risks in the first place and remain in an employment situation, working for someone else. Then, at least, they will enjoy the benefits of group insurance and a company-paid retirement plan. Why take the risks of starting your own business, only to give up its benefits?

THE MARGIN OF PROFIT

Before applying for outside financing be willing to demonstrate your ability to create profits from expanding volume—not just volume itself. You can achieve this by showing a track record of growing margins of profit or, at least, of maintaining an acceptable margin even when volume doubles or triples over previous levels. If you manage costs and expenses well, your growth will be profitable. If you are having problems with ever-declining yields, it will show up in your numbers. It is time to apply your management skills or to hire someone who can do it for you.

You might be completely justified in seeking outside financing to take advantage of growth opportunities. At times, cash flow will be poor, even when you manage well. However, as long as your margin of profit is stable or improving—a sign of effective management leading to the ability to create profitable growth—your chances of finding financing are excellent.

A healthy and improving margin of profit depends on the consistency of gross profits (sales minus direct costs) and selling expenses in relation to sales and on the control over levels of fixed overhead. These relationships are summarized in Figure 5-2. Note that gross profit and sales move on the same approximate line. This is an ideal result, while your actual curve may vary. If costs increase but you must keep prices at the same level to compete in the market, then gross margins will decline over time. In this situation, you must depend on volume to offset the narrowing margins.

Selling expenses tend to grow in plateaus related to gross volume rather than on a straight line. The level of spending directly related to sales (for telephone, travel, entertainment, and advertising, for example) will vary with higher volume, but not to the same degree as will direct costs.

The margin of profit is ultimately determined by these relationships combined with the absolute and unfailing control of fixed overhead. If the fixed portion of expenses is allowed to grow too quickly or beyond the level required by current volume, whether in response to current sales activity or in anticipation of future volume, your margin of profit will begin to erode.

Spending must be controlled and, to a degree, anticipated. However, it must also be reactive. Do not commit your company to fixed overhead before it is mandated by circumstances and becomes inevitable. For example, if your plan points to the need for hiring a larger support staff in

FIGURE 5–2
Margin of Profit

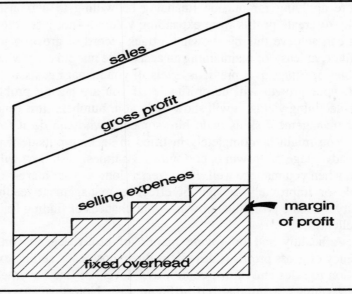

the near future, also meaning a larger office, you do not need to make a commitment until the anticipated levels of volume begin to occur.

Once you determine that the time is right to seek outside financing, you will be ready to proceed to a lender or investor and present your plan. As long as you are in control, you will be able to prove your case. If circumstances control you, raising capital will prove to be a problem.

Before approaching a lender, you should think about that process from the lender's point of view. By understanding the evaluation of risk, you improve your chances of approval. That is the subject of the next chapter.

CHAPTER 6

LOANS: THE LENDER'S PERSPECTIVE

A financier is a pawnbroker
with imagination.
—*Arthur Wing Pinero*

To achieve a worthwhile objective, you will have an advantage when you can see the issue from the other point of view. This is especially the case when you seek financing from a lender.

In this chapter, you will gain the perspective needed to understand risk from the lender's side. Several important points will be discussed, including

- Proving that you are a good risk.
- Convincing the lender that your planned use of money is sound.
- Using your plan to make your best case.
- Expressing your goals in positive terms the lender wants and needs to hear.
- Ideas that will make the lender's job easy.

Our purpose is to provide insights into the process that lenders use to evaluate loan applications and the business owners who present them. Once you know how a lender perceives you and your business, you will have overcome one of the major obstacles to successfully locating the debt capital you need.

THE LENDER'S EVALUATION

Every business owner knows quite a lot about risk. Just being in business is risky for a number of reasons—economic conditions beyond your control can change the demand for your product or service, sometimes overnight. The competition is a constant threat. You also face the risk of liability not completely covered by insurance.

There is another side to risk. The lender evaluates you and your business from a completely different perspective than you do. A lender might appreciate the risk elements with which you contend on a continuous basis and might even admire the steps you have taken to reduce those risks. However, these points relate only to *your* business risks and not the lender's.

Whenever you approach a lender to ask for a loan, remember that "risk" has a different meaning. The savings and loan, bank, or other money source wants to ensure that the money it loans out has the best chance of being repaid—on time and in full. If, for any reason, a loan officer concludes that the risks to the institution are too high, your loan will not be approved.

The lender must evaluate risk in several ways. First, there is the risk that money will be committed at a rate of return lower than the rate that could be earned elsewhere. Second, lenders are restricted in how much they can loan out and must maintain adequate reserves. Given that there is a limit on the amount of money that can be committed to loans at any time, the lender will select the strongest, most secure companies for loan approval. Third, the lender must depend on the presentation you make through your business plan, budget, and financial statements.

Some institutions actively seek small-business customers and want to make loans. Others are more conservative and will restrict their loans to secured mortgages and other outlets they consider to be safer. Your first step in successfully getting a loan is to identify the right lender to approach. The bank that wants to grant small-business loans is going to be more receptive to your application than one that simply doesn't want the business, and the approval standards will be more favorable.

Before trying to figure out your strategy in placing your application with a bank, first take these steps:

1. Ask other business owners which banks in your area are receptive to small-business loans.
2. Visit a branch office and speak with a loan officer. Explain your intentions and ask whether that institution wants the business.
3. Ask how long it takes to review an application and reach a decision. If some institutions quote an unusually long approval process, chances are the loan officer does not have the authority

to approve applications on his or her own, even for loans of minimum amounts. Seek an institution that has granted some approval rights to a branch loan officer.

4. Ask about loans as well as lines of credit. Compare interest rates. Compare policies for both short-term and long-term lending. Compare these points between institutions, looking for one that offers a range of lending products and maximum flexibility.

THE "GOOD RISK" PROFILE

Your goal must be to prove to lenders that you are a "good risk" in their eyes. This simply means that you will make payments on time and that the entire loan balance will be repaid.

Your forecast and budget must support the good risk profile by demonstrating how cash will be used to fund operations costs and expenses, as well as repayments. The broader picture, including what you intend to do with the money, must be spelled out in your business plan.

Every lender would prefer to loan money only to those businesses and individuals who are certain to repay the entire debt. Their evaluation seeks to minimize the risk that someone will default on a loan. This risk can never be entirely eliminated, and all the lender can do is make the best possible selection. Your task is to understand the review and approval process and to position yourself with the strongest possible profile.

The first method for establishing your stability and financial responsibility is through your track record. If you have always paid bills on time, this should be highlighted in your presentation. If you've had a previous loan that was repaid in full, that should be included as well. Emphasize the positive points in your track record, remembering that this is a major basis for deciding whether or not you are likely to fit the profile of a good risk.

What if your record is not that positive? If you have been late on repayments of other loans or if you have gone past due on vendor accounts, that is a definite negative. With today's automated credit system, the lender will discover these negatives early in the review process. So while you should not dwell on past problems, you must mention them—but in a very positive way.

Example: The owner of a local restaurant had problems in the past. Several food wholesalers cancelled charge arrangements and put the business on cash on delivery. One even demanded a cashier's check in payment upon delivery of goods. A loan taken out two years ago was finally paid, but nearly six months late. When the owner applied for a new loan, he knew the lender would discover these problems in the credit report. So in the cover letter to his application, the owner explained that in the past, there were cash flow problems. However, with new controls in place and with a revised, more realistic business plan, the cash position of the business had been improved and was current on all accounts.

By raising the negatives and explaining how today's situation is different and improved, the owner has a better chance of being approved. The alternative—not mentioning past problems—leaves it to the lender to assume, and that assumption will not be likely to go in your favor. Not only are there negatives in your track record, failing to mention them makes you look as if you were trying to hide them.

You also demonstrate that you are a good risk by showing how your cash flow is likely to support loan payments. Once you understand the lender's perspective on risk, you will also see the most important point of all: If you will not be able to afford loan repayments, the loan will not be granted.

A cash flow analysis—at the initial presentation—can be fairly brief. In the cash flow projections within the business plan, the cash flow summary should be provided in greater detail. Figure 6–1 shows a summarized version of a cash flow evaluation for three months.

Each month's ending balance is carried forward and becomes the subsequent month's beginning balance. The cash flow evaluation shows the lender that there will be adequate funds to take care of regular, periodic loan payments. Of course, the projection (like the forecast and budget) is only an estimate. However, as long as you can support your assumptions well, the projection will be believed. This is discussed in greater detail in the chapters dealing with the business plan.

The lender will also size you up as a risk based on the stability of business. This can be measured in a number of ways, including

- The length of time your operation has been open.
- The consistency of gross sales and profits.
- Seasonal variations, if applicable.

In a relatively small city or town, your local reputation might also play a part in the lender's assessment of you and your operation. Although the approval process might be less formal, it is also more difficult for a newcomer to find financing.

FIGURE 6–1
Summarized Cash Analysis Form

cash flow evaluation

	MONTH		
	JAN	FEB	MAR
beginning balance			
gross sales			
equity capital			
debt capital			
total			
direct costs			
expenses			
dividends			
loan payments			
total			
ending balance			

THE USE OF MONEY

The problem lenders encounter most often with small-business applications is the failure to think through the use of funds. What will you do with the money, if the loan is approved?

Although this question seems basic and obvious, a large number of applicants are taken by surprise and do not have a specific idea of how they will use the funds. From the lender's point of view, this is unsettling. Why should the lender assume a risk—on the premise that there is a sound business reason to borrow—only to discover that the owner does not know *why* those funds are needed? More to the point, why take a risk on someone who has not even answered the first question everyone should ask when applying for a loan?

You must have a solid, specific plan for the use of money you want to borrow. Give specifics. Do not settle for a vague description of purpose, such as "to consolidate other debts" or "to provide working capital." These are not reasons to borrow, and they do not describe how you plan to spend the money.

The specific reason must prove to the lender that with debt capitalization, you will be able to generate higher profits in the future than in the past. Your use of funds must be *profitable* in the sense that the cost is justified by the changes that money will enable you to create.

Example: The owner of a one-location bakery provides sales figures to a banker, broken down over a period of six months. Volume has been rising steadily. At the present, however, further expansion is not possible. A second analysis shows why: Volume in the typical day is broken down by hour. Most of the business takes place within a 90-minute period. In one shop, with limited floor space and baking equipment, the bakery is operating at full capacity. The owner also provides the lender with a breakdown of the competition. He convinces the loan officer that a second shop will be as profitable as the first.

Example: A mail-order business produces a catalog once per quarter. The owner can no longer process the increasing volume of orders without additional employees, more storage space and inventory, and an automated customer mailing and file system. The expansion will require additional capital of $45,000. The owner shows the lender how that money will enable the operation to increase its volume and profits, and the business plan includes two additional features: a summary of cash flow over the next 12 quarters and an estimate of the time required to break even after expansion.

Example: The owner of a real estate brokerage company spoke with a loan officer about borrowing $25,000 to expand. The money would be spent on recruiting more agents, advertising in the local multiple-listing service and other publications, and creating a strong local image and presense through newspaper ads. The owner included summaries of local housing and employment trends and convinced the lender that the near future promised to be a high-volume period.

Demonstrate the profitable use of funds by emphasizing potential and opportunity. Make you statements positive rather than negative. Be prepared to prove your point with thorough research, a realistic business plan, pro forma income and cash flow statements, and income forecasts. Base your assumptions on the past as well as on trends in your market area. Comparisons between statements emphasizing profits are summa-

FIGURE 6–2
Profitable Use of Funds

PROFITABLE BORROWING	UNPROFITABLE BORROWING
increases net profits	increases interest expense
coordinated with spending controls	no control measures
strengthens cash flow position	drains limited cash reserves
reduces borrower and lender risks	increases risks on both sides
facilitates permanent growth	makes growth risky and short-term

rized in Figure 6–2. Note the five areas this comparison mentions: profits, spending controls, cash flow position, risk, and growth. If you can demonstrate to the lender that you are aware of all of these points and have covered them in your assumptions and plan, your chances of approval will be vastly improved.

THE REALISTIC PLAN

Many small businesses prepare business plans, although few of them are the simple, realistic documents they should be. A plan is nothing more than a description of where you want to go, what you hope to achieve, and how long it will take to get there. The demands spelled out in the plan will dictate the need for borrowing money by proving that the plan will work.

That is the entire premise of the plan, and that is all it should be. The more complicated your plan becomes, the less realistic it will seem to a lender. It is very easy to "prove" that an idea is foolproof, as long as it is limited to the two-dimensional plan. The real challenge is to present a three-dimensional idea in black and white to the extent that the lender will comprehend and believe your assumptions.

To achieve that goal, your plan must be realistic, not only in your eyes, but also in the lender's eyes. If the lender can see the big picture you describe in your plan, you have accomplished your purpose. If the picture is so big that the assumptions are called into doubt, then you instantly become a greater risk to the lender.

Example: The owner of a new business approached a lender with a plan. It set the goal of increasing sales by 500 percent and tripling net profits—all within one year. In order to achieve this, the plan explained, it would be necessary to get a $75,000 line of credit. The application was rejected for a number of reasons—no long-term track record, a too rapid expansion plan that did not seem realistic, and poor documentation for some very broad assumptions (concerning competition and market demand, for example).

The plan was simply not convincing in its structure or scope. The lender was not given a summarized explanation of the research (if any) that backed up the assumptions supporting rapid expansion. The plan was simply too optimistic. It did not seem realistic.

There are many case histories of businesses that did expand rapidly, creating millionaires out of relative upstarts. In many of those cases, there was no plan, no premise, no assumption base. In the lender's world, however, you cannot expect to be the next *big* success story. The plain truth is for every amazing success story there are hundreds, if not thousands, of failures.

It does not matter how earnestly you believe in your own expansion plans. Chances are you will achieve triple-digit growth in a very short period of time. If you will need financing to get there from here, back away from the full presentation. Settle for a thoroughly supported and researched position, showing sales and profit growth of 25 percent— instead of the 250 percent you *think* you will do.

Remember that a "realistic" plan means one thing to you and a completely different thing to the lender. The standard for judging your assumptions will be the lender's experience. The *norm* will be applied to judge how realistic a plan you have prepared. If you know you will outperform that norm, that does not mean it is prudent to lay out the entire plan for the lender.

WHAT THE LENDER NEEDS TO HEAR

Lenders react poorly when would-be borrowers take the negative approach to asking for a loan. This is not to say that a true negative should be cloaked in positive language, but rather than the successful loan applicant will look for and discuss the truly positive reasons for borrowing.

Example: A business owner tells the loan officer the reason for seeking a loan is to "consolidate debts." What does this really mean? The business owner is admitting to having gotten into debt well beyond the operation's capacity to manage. The lender will then wonder whether the owner has the management skill and foresight to ensure prompt and timely repayment of the *new* loan.

The alternative is to develop a plan that shows how debt will be managed properly. This includes any existing loans, as well as a new loan. It also includes the recurring costs and overhead of the operation, purchase of equipment, investment in inventory or a larger average balance of accounts receivable, and a higher level of permanent spending resulting from expansion.

Borrowers also make the mistake of assuming very rapid growth in a short period of time. The belief might be that the greater the potential for growth, the more compelling the case for loan approval. However, bankers tend to be more conservative than the average business owner or entrepreneur. They probably do not see market potential to the same degree nor with the same amount of appreciation that you will. So your expansion plans must be expressed in conservative terms—perhaps more conservatively than you want.

The third point concerns increased income versus coverage of costs and expenses. You can tell the lender that proceeds will be used to pay direct costs and operating expenses while you expand sales. That will probably not reassure the lender, because the question remains: Where will the money come from for repayment? The answer might be obvious to you, but the *risk* of granting a loan based on that argument might be too great for the lender.

An alternative: Demonstrate how the use of proceeds will increase profits. This is saying the same thing as "covering costs and expenses," but it stresses the bottom line. To the banker, greater profits mean greater cash flow—and reduced risk.

The fourth argument is on the issue of internal controls—the nuts and bolts of managing of your company. The small-business owner might be perceived in the more conservative lending establishments as a renegade and impulsive risk taker. That stereotype is not interested in administration and financial analysis, so you have to convince the lender that you *are* able to wear that hat and to succeed in putting controls in place and keeping them alive.

Do not make the mistake of telling a lender that a loan will solve cost and expense control problems. Not only is that claim untrue; it will set off an alarm bell that could cost you the approval you want. Instead, show the lender how you have instituted controls to track and reduce cost and expense levels—in anticipation of expansion. That will reassure the lender. The four positive and negative approaches are compared in Figure 6–3.

MAKING THE LENDER'S JOB EASY

Improve your chances of loan approval by taking steps to make the lender's job easy. When you walk into the bank and hand over a properly completed application, along with a business plan and all the other

FIGURE 6–3
Approaching the Lender

POSITIVE APPROACH	NEGATIVE APPROACH
debts will be managed within the plan	money is needed to consolidate debts
growth will occur methodically, within the plan's limits	a loan will help the business grow rapidly
money will be spent to increase profits	money will be used to cover existing costs and expenses
controls have been instituted to track and reduce cost and expense levels	cost and expense control problems will be solved by borrowing

paperwork the lender needs, it shows that you are organized, clear thinking, and well-prepared.

These positive traits portray you as a good risk in several respects: The lender will naturally assume that a well-organized, complete application will be submitted by the business owner who is equally as thorough in every other respect, such as preparation and research for the business plan, awareness of risks, and timing of a loan request.

Anticipate problems the lender might see, and prepare by answering them as part of your application. This can be achieved in a cover letter, in the business plan, or with a supplemental schedule, cross-referenced to the appropriate line on the institution's application form.

Example: A business owner applied for a loan and made a footnote reference on the application in the liabilities section. On a separate page, she explained that a very large note payable had three years to run; she described the purpose of the loan and how the current business plan included provisions for cash flow and repayment—both of the existing loan and the proposed new one.

Show the lender that you are completely aware of risk from both sides of the issue. Directly confront the question of the lender's risk, and design your cover letter and business plan to demonstrate not only how *your* risks will be reduced, but also how the *lender's* risks are addressed in your assumptions. Anticipation. That is what pleases and reassures a lender.

Include these papers:

1. **Business plan.** This should be an updated version of your plan, one that explains how the proposed loan fits into your blueprint.
2. **Current financial statements.** Include a balance sheet, income statement, and a summary of cash flow. Ask your accountant to help. If the loan you seek is for a substantial sum of money, present an audited, reviewed, or compiled financial statement, complete with the auditor's opinion.
3. **Updated forecast and budget.** Present an income forecast and expense budget for the current period. If your plan's budgeting information is out-of-date, bring it up-to-date by way of supplement or replacement of the applicable pages.
4. **Three years' tax returns.** Include returns that show business income or loss for the last three periods. Some lenders will ask

for only one or two years; but be prepared, and get copies of all three.

5. **Credit references.** Include complete names, addresses, and phone numbers of vendors who have extended credit to you. Also include credit cards used strictly for business purchases. Write down your account number on the application for each reference.

6. **Completed application.** Fill in the application thoroughly. If you do not understand any of the sections or questions, call the lender before submitting the package, and find out what they want.

7. **Cover letter.** Even if you hand deliver your application and other documents, always include a cover letter. Even if it is brief, it will establish the preliminary purpose in submitting the application and can be used to summarize the major strengths you want the banker to be aware of and to take into consideration.

Present all of the documents the lender will need in order to evaluate the loan. Before even starting the application process, visit with the banker; make sure that institution does approve the kind of loan you are looking for, and ask for a list of paperwork that must be submitted with the application. Get a blank copy of the application. Each institution might have its own additions to a list of paperwork; however, the standard documents you must always plan to include are shown in Figure 6–4.

When you deliver your completed application and other documents, ask the lender when you can expect a decision. Assuming you have included everything needed to evaluate your request, the banker should be able to give you a fair idea of how long it will take. The credit check and review and verification of the information you list takes a relatively short period of time. However, if the bank has a particularly heavy load of applications, yours will go to the bottom of the pile.

Another factor in the time required for approval is whether the loan officer has the authority to approve loans and lines of credit. Some institutions allow their executives to make decisions on their own, up to a ceiling. However, many other banks—especially very large ones—will require review by a loan review board. If that board meets only once or twice per month, your application could take a few weeks to process. Ask your banker how the loan review process works. If the banker has the authority to approve your application without oversight from a committee or higher officer, you can expect an answer fairly quickly. In some banks,

FIGURE 6–4
Application Package

---

1. business plan

2. current financial
   statements

3. updated forecast
   and budget

4. three years' tax
   returns

5. credit references

6. completed
   application

7. cover letter

---

approval can take place in less than a week. The important element to fast approval is the completeness of your application.

In the next chapter, we will examine the process of preparing for and getting loans from *your* perspective. The preparation you put into the planning phase will determine how well you complete an application and explain to the lender how you will use the money to create profits.

CHAPTER 7

LOANS: YOUR PERSPECTIVE

When the foundation of a pyramid
erodes, the top can still be
supported on nothing but money.
—*Laurence J. Peter*

The way that you preceive borrowing money reveals how realistically you are approaching the question of how to capitalize your business. Just as the lender must be aware of their risks, you must also be able to evaluate the direction of your business, the degree of risk you take by borrowing money, and whether or not you can afford to go into debt.

One point of view is, "If someone would loan me the money, I could make this business work." This implies that without additional funds, you will not be able to stay in business or, at least, to achieve satisfactory or timely growth. The problem with this outlook, though, is that it places the burden of success on borrowing. That will not be reassuring to a lender.

A second point of view is, "I can take advantage of an opportunity. I have the management skill, the market is strong, and I know where I am going. All I need to do is fund the expansion." With this attitude, borrowing will make much more sense.

This chapter examines your approach to borrowing. We will address the questions of timing, risk, debt and equity analysis, tax issues, and planning.

TIMING THE LOAN

The reasons you request a loan, the risk-reduction strategies you demonstrate to the lender, and the intended use of borrowed funds, should be so compelling to the lender that the loan will be granted without hesitation.

That is an ideal outcome, of course, and you must expect the lender to move more cautiously than the typical entrepreneur.

Timing is critical in creating a situation in which your loan will be approved. If your business is struggling, a loan will not help, it will only aggravate the income and cash flow problems you are already experiencing. Once you have had enough time to build a base and to demonstrate your management abilities, however, loan approval will be much more likely.

Some people attempt to borrow money before even starting their business. Although some lenders will take a chance, most will see this as a problem. How can an intelligent decision be made without any market or management track record? First, the would-be owner has not shown that he or she is capable of running the operation. Second, there is no history of sales volume or even of demand for the product or service.

Even an already-established business owner has a disadvantage without a year or more of sales and profit history. Be prepared to prove several points to the lender, including

1. **Management ability.** Prove that you have a plan and that you are aware of the future. Prepare and follow a forecast and budget; set goals for yourself; document the outcome. Run your operation by the plan, and be ready to show the lender that you depend on planning as a management tool.

   Also be prepared to show that your books are kept in organized and professional form, that you can manage your cash, and that you have a good credit record with your suppliers —that you are aware of your responsibilities and take them seriously.

2. **Sales history.** Lenders are reassured by a consistent and growing level of sales. That indicates that demand for what you sell is out there, that you know how to tap it, and that it is not unpredictable. If your monthly level of sales and cash receipts are consistent, the lender will have confidence in you and your operation.

3. **Profit history.** If you are planning to ask for a loan, be prepared to summarize monthly or quarterly profits. Think of an unplanned loss as an unacceptable outcome. You may create a well-capitalized loss when future profits are created by way of investment in inventory, advertising and other selling expenses,

and increased levels of accounts receivable, but you *must* also be able to show the lender that you are in control.

4. **Cash flow history.** As part of your business plan, plot your cash flow and follow it—just as you track an expense budget or income forecast. Be ready to show that you are aware of the importance of working capital and that you monitor and plan it.

   If you have had cash flow problems in the recent past, identify the causes and be prepared to explain how the problem has been eliminated or how a loan will help reduce the problem. Remember that the lender will see a history of cash flow problems as a danger signal. It may imply poor planning and management, and the lender will wonder, "If this operation can not raise enough cash to pay its bills each month, how will it be able to repay the loan?" This is a serious question that you must be able to address, even if it is not asked directly.

5. **A profit plan.** Your business and marketing plan must demonstrate how sales, net profits, and cash flow will be created and controlled, at least for the length of time that your proposed loan will remain outstanding. Your cash flow projection must include repayments and show that you have thought ahead so that the risks of default are minimal.

   Plan your profits on two levels. First, estimate what you will earn without a loan. Second, prepare a summary of profits with the loan, including the interest expense involved. If you have planned correctly, the second forecast will produce a greater net profit than the first—your plan will generate a profit greater than the interest expense.

THE RISKS OF BORROWING

The lender will evaluate your application with one major risk in mind—that you will not be able to afford repayments. From your point of view, there are many more risks.

Being unable to make repayments is a significant form of risk. If you are having cash flow problems today, you cannot expect a loan to erase them. It only enables you to get rid of older debt and replace it with newer debt at a higher level. Other risks include

1. **Reduction in market demand.** If your competition takes away part of your business or if demand falls for any other reason, you risk losing the volume to support your cash requirements—permanent overhead *and* loan repayments.

   Several factors beyond competitive changes can make this happen. For example, your operation might depend on population increases that do not come to pass. Perhaps a major employer in your area relocates so that unemployment rises and many people move away. Your product or service might be subject to governmental regulation, and new rules could curtail your ability to grow. Perhaps growth itself might affect your ability to continue generating a profit, just due to the demand for greater commitment to overhead expenses.

2. **Economic changes.** If business demand changes due to outside economic factors, such as a rise in interest rates, you must be aware of the risk due to circumstances beyond your control. Your contingency plan might include diversification of product or service or of customer base.

3. **Obsolescence.** Is there a chance that what you sell could become obsolete? It so, that is another form of risk. If you borrow money today, but your market has disappeared a year from now, you risk being forced to either close your doors or find an entirely new market.

4. **Personal factors.** A serious but invisible form of risk is what might happen to you. Poor health, disability, or death of any business owner will usually mean having to close up, because one-person operations are highly individual and can not be easily assumed by a spouse or other new owner. You cannot make those risks disappear, but you can insure against them. By purchasing the right insurance policies, the unexpected loss will not be prevented; but the economic consequences will be offset.

The lender is certainly aware of these forms of risk, even if you do not address them. They must be confronted and dealt with in your business plan, or the lender will have to evaluate your application on the assumption that you have not planned completely for the risks you face.

Another risk is that growth itself will have a negative consequence for your business. Many small, well-run operations have gone broke by trying to grow too quickly without proper planning and capital or into markets they could not control nor penetrate. Your business plan must establish a methodical, manageable, properly timed rate of growth.

That growth must be achieved on your terms. Too many overly optimistic small-business owners think of growth as something that just happens if they are in the right place at the right time; and the more growth, the better. It should be a controlled factor in the development of your enterprise, something that you allow to happen when you are ready for it. One of the planning elements you must incorporate is control over expansion. Identify an appropriate level of growth, given your present capitalization and the borrowed funds you seek. Be aware of your limitations, and plan to control not only sales, but costs, expenses, profits, and cash flow as well. Address the issue of growth by specifying the level you will allow.

Too many business plans take the wrong approach to the growth issue. The owner does not make a specific assumption about growth levels, but shows the proposed outcome on one or more premises. Gross income might increase by 50, 100, even 200 percent. The projected net profit grows on the same scale. What is not addressed in that approach is the question of management. How will the owner remain in control? How will a higher stake in overhead be managed? What happens if overhead commitments are made and volume then drops?

Never assume that growth "just happens." Never assume that it will result just because you get a loan. The plan must dictate how you will *create* growth and at the same time prepare for the many forms of risk every business owner faces.

TRACKING DEBT AND EQUITY

The successful loan package must include a combination of financial information and explanation. The methods for combining these in a concise and easily followed way will be explained in Chapter 10—Business Plans for Borrowed Money.

Besides historical and pro forma financial statements, the plan should include two ratios designed to control working capital and the level of debt in your operation. The more you borrow, the greater the demand on your working capital, due to the need for recurring payments on principal, and the greater the drain on profits, due to interest expense. Thus, every business owner must establish a policy for controlling debt levels.

This control should be based on a realistic analysis of how much debt is required to maximize profits, as well as how much debt would be considered excessive. In some marginal operations, no debt can be profitable. The degree of profit potential is too narrow to also carry the burden of interest expense. In other businesses, just continuing in operation requires a very high level of recurring debt with turnover in short-term loans, frequent use of lines of credit, or substantial long-term borrowing plans. The factors influencing the debt level decision must include required inventory levels; volume of sales related to inventory replacement; investment in equipment, machinery, and other capital assets; and the need to invest in advertising and other selling expenses.

We will introduce two ratios that will help determine the level of debt right for your operation. A ratio is a worthwhile analysis tool, but only if it is used correctly Reviewed by itself and in isolation, a ratio is meaningless. It must be tracked and compared over time, so that a trend is established. Some ratios will reveal a progressive trend—percentage increases, improvements in profit or equity percentages, or other moving results. Other trends are level and, as long as the results remain within an acceptable range, your controls are working.

The turnover in working capital is an example of a changing ratio. Working capital is the difference between current assets and current liabilities. A current asset is cash or assets that are convertible to cash within one year (receivables, inventory, and investments, for example). Current liabilities are those due and payable within the next 12 months, including the next 12 payments due on long-term loans.

When total sales is divided by working capital, the resulting ratio shows how many times, on average, your working capital was "turned over" to generate the level of sales. This ratio will change, perhaps drastically, as sales volume grows. Because working capital is the net *difference* between current assets and current liabilities, a large number could end up with the same net amount.

Example: During the second year in operation, you have $50,000 of current assets and $20,000 of current liabilities. Working capital, the difference, is $30,000. During the tenth year in business, everything has

FIGURE 7–1
Turnover in Working Capital

$$\frac{\text{total sales}}{\text{working capital}} = \text{turnover}$$

$$\frac{\$762,000}{\$195,000 - \$90,000} = 7.3 \text{ times}$$

changed. You now have $250,000 in current assets, and $220,000 in current liabilities. Working capital is still $30,000.

If volume is much greater in the tenth year of this example, working capital will be turned over many more times than when the numbers are smaller. So the turnover ratio is an ever-changing one. The greater the number of turns, the more effectively working capital is being put to use.

Example: Last year's total sales were $762,000. As of the end of the year, current assets are $195,000 and current liabilities are $90,000. The computation of turnover in working capital is shown in Figure 7–1. Working capital was turned 7.3 times during the year to produce the level of sales. This ratio assumes the average. The entire amount of current assets was not actually exhausted 7.3 times to pay liabilities and produce the sales level; it's only an average. When this ratio is performed quarterly or annually, a trend will emerge.

Be sure you use ratio values consistently. For example, the turnover comparison can be based on year-end working capital or on the figures at the beginning of the year. You may even take the beginning and ending totals and average them. If working capital levels change frequently, you can compute the average of quarterly or even monthly totals. The important point is the ratio is only dependable and accurate if comparisons are made and trends developed consistently.

Here is an example of how turnover in working capital might be tracked to reveal your control over working capital. Using the same results as above in comparison to the same figures a year and two years later, we have the following.

Year	Sales	Current Assets	Current Liabilities	Ratio
1	$ 762,000	$195,000	$ 90,000	7.3
2	984,000	285,000	130,000	6.3
3	1,341,000	405,000	175,000	5.8

In this example, we see an increased investment in current assets, probably representing higher levels of inventory and accounts receivable, and a corresponding growth in current liabilities. Note that sales have grown significantly and are about 75 percent greater than two years before. In this higher-volume environment the turnover ratio has declined only slightly—a sign that the owner is managing working capital well during expansion.

The ratio shows management effectiveness. In periods of growth, there is a tendency to allow accounts receivable to climb too high, to accumulate too much inventory, or to allow liabilities to outrun the volume of sales growth. All of these have a negative effect on cash flow and can lead to problems, such as the inability to afford loan repayments.

A second ratio is a comparison of debt level to total capitalization. In a growing operation, notably one that depends on increasing borrowings due to expansion, it is important to identify a limit on the degree of debt you can afford. Thus, if borrowings exceed the standard, you know that you are overborrowing.

Example: A business owner believes that continuing a current period of expansion will require borrowing money. A loan is approved and granted. A few months later, the owner sees an opportunity for still more growth and plans to seek an additional loan. However, a comparison between debt and equity reveals that debt levels already represent more than half of the total capital.

Identifying the appropriate degree of debt depends on many factors, most important of which is the nature of your operation. An accountant familiar with your capital asset requirements, selling expenses, inventory levels, and type of product or service can help you to identify this level. For the purposes of example, we will assume that you set the following standard: No more than one-half of total capitalization may be represented by debt.

FIGURE 7–2
Debt/Equity Ratio

$$\frac{\text{liabilities}}{\text{tangible net worth}} = \text{ratio}$$

$$\frac{\$90,000}{\$235,000} = 38.3\%$$

To prepare a debt/equity ratio, the first step is to compute *tangible net worth*. This is the net worth of your operation (assets less liabilities), adjusted downward for any intagible assets, such as goodwill or covenants not to compete. The ratio must be computed based only on tangible net worth.

Total liabilities are divided by tangible net worth to derive the percentage. For example, one operation currently reports $90,000 in liabilities and $285,000 in total net worth. That includes $50,000 for goodwill. Tangible net worth is $235,000 ($285,000–$50,000). The debt/equity ratio in this example is shown in Figure 7–2.

THE DEBT/EQUITY TREND

Remembering that the assumed standard is 50 percent, incurring additional debt will affect this ratio. For example, if the owner borrowed $30,000, both tangible net worth and liabilities would immediately increase:

	Net Worth	Liabilities
Before loan	$235,000	$ 90,000
Loan	+30,000	+30,000
After loan	$265,000	$120,000

Working capital is identical in both cases, $145,000. Yet, the debt/equity ratio is changed to

$$\frac{\$120,000}{\$235,000} = 51.1\%$$

The need to control the relative percentage of debt to total net worth is an important planning mechanism and one that should be incorporated into your business plan. A proposed loan should be explained in the context of the debt/equity ratio and a developing trend over time, if only as a premise to establishing a case for increasing profits through borrowing.

A study of the debt/equity trend over time will reveal how easily debt can become a growing portion of total capitalization. For example, an operation reports liabilities and tangible net worth over four quarters on the following schedule:

Month	Liabilities	Tangible Net Worth	Ratio(%)
March	$ 90,000	$235,000	38.3
June	115,000	260,000	44.2
September	122,000	263,000	46.4
December	131,000	268,000	48.9

Looking only at the numbers, increases in liabilities and in tangible net worth do not appear dramatic. Yet, the debt/equity ratio is quickly approaching the assumed maximum. This trend can also be analyzed and demonstrated on a graph, such as the one in Figure 7–3.

This shows how debt approaches the 50 percent mark, while the equity portion deteriorates over time. Without minitoring the debt/equity trend, a significant trend might appear in a relatively short period of time. A decline in the portion of equity from one year to the next, from the lender's point of view, represents a negative in the review process. As an owner, you should also be aware of how growing debt affects cash flow and future profits.

A second way to view the debt/equity picture is to divide profits before interest expense between shareholders and lenders. For example, your profits last year were $45,000 and total interest expense was $17,000. If the two are added together, the total yield from the operation was

	Amount	Percentage
Net profit	$45,000	72.6
Interest paid	17,000	27.4
Total	$62,000	100.0

Now let us assume that you borrow additional funds during the coming year. Profits are increased by $20,000 and interest expense goes up by $15,000:

	Amount	Percentage
Net profit	$65,000	67.0
Interest paid	32,000	33.0
Total	$97,000	100.0

In this example, even though profits were *higher* than interest expense, total preinterest yield has shifted. Net profits previously were 72.6% of the total and have fallen to 67.0%. This is not completely negative in the sense that profits exceeded interest expenses by $5,000. However, you should set a standard for controlling the yield to equity owners and to lenders as part of your business plan. The analysis must also be expanded

FIGURE 7–3
Debt/Equity Trend

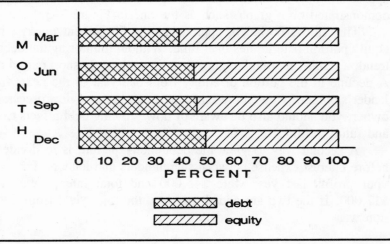

to examine what degree of increased profits were created by borrowings and what degree would have occurred even without a new loan.

Example: Your business plan forecasts future profits on two assumptions: with and without an additional loan. You conclude that without a new loan, profits will grow by $12,000. With the expansion you plan from loan proceeds, the revised forecast estimates $20,000 in additional profits. Thus, for increased interest of $15,000, you produced profits of only $8,000 above the first estimate.

Another concern must be that the one-year review could be too limiting. If your plan calls for use of borrowed funds in such a way that you build in permanently higher levels of growth *beyond* the terms of the loan, then you must consider whether the temporary loss is worthwhile.

Example: Borrowing money this year is estimated to increase net profits by $8,000, while interest will cost $15,000. Over a three-year term, you expect interest to exceed profits by a total of nearly $18,000. However, your business plan calls for expansion of product and territory, and you estimate that net profits will more than offset the interest costs over the years following. You could not achieve a similar pattern of growth in the same time without borrowing.

In this instance, a comparison must be made between two alternatives:

1. Absorbing the three-year loss due to interest expense in exchange for long-term growth.
2. Taking a more methodical approach to growth over a longer period of years.

To make the decision, the long-term net profits must be compared in consideration of risks to you and to the lender, both in the short and the long term. You might conclude that the expense of financing growth is too risky over the more immediate future, that a modified expansion plan and less debt is in order, or that the investment is well worth the future profits you expect to earn.

The analysis of debt and equity, when demonstrated within your plan, shows that your perspective is in line with the lender's, that you are aware of the many risks you both face when borrowing, and that you have a clear idea of how you will control debt and equity and ensure that cash flow and profits meet your expectations.

In the next chapter, sources for borrowings will be explained. A clear understanding of why and when to borrow money is the first step. From there, you next must identify the best source for financing your expansion plan.

CHAPTER 8

LOAN SOURCES

Nowhere is a man's imagination so fertile
as in the discovery of new ways to say no
to a man who asks for money.
—*Joseph H. Shapiro*

Most small-business owners do not realize how many sources for loans exist. The local bank is probably the best place to start, though many government programs and other sources are available in addition to conventional lenders.

In this chapter, we will explain many of the programs offered by the federal government, provide guidelines for approaching your local bank, and discuss alternative sources for business financing.

GOVERNMENT LOAN GUIDELINES

A thorough explanation of the range of government sources for small-business loans would require a completely separate book. The best starting point for any small-business owner interested in locating likely loan sources is to write to departments and agencies and ask for specifics of loan programs offered.

Whenever researching loan programs, follow these guidelines:

1. **Find out what is offered.** There is a wide range of government loans, loan guarantees, and grants. The purpose of many programs is quite specific, however, and many applications are received from individuals who clearly do not meet the criteria for

the program. Before spending a lot of time filling out an application, be sure you know exactly what standards apply and whether or not an agency is right for you.

2. **Make sure you qualify.** The easiest first step is to find out whether or not you qualify for a particular program. A good deal of time will be wasted applying for applications, corresponding, and asking questions about programs designed for a narrow range of applicants based on the type of business, location, or economic strength. Before you ask for any materials, ask what type of business owners an agency helps.

3. **Find out the rules and follow them.** Ask the agency or department how to apply for financial assistance. Get a list of the information you will be asked to supply, application forms, and documentation. Before sending anything to the agency, make sure you have met all the rules.

4. **Follow every lead.** Do not limit your search to one or two sources. Agencies and departments of the federal government are constantly expanding, and new programs might be added at any time. Research thoroughly, and ask each contact for referrals to other programs.

5. **Check state government resources.** Although the federal government might cut back on some loan programs, state agencies and departments also provide assistance, guarantee plans, and grants. Some are funded by federal agencies, while others are operated strictly by the state. Contact Small Business Development Centers and state Chambers of Commerce as a starting point.

6. **Ask to see other applications.** Many agencies will allow you to review applications from other individuals that were approved. This right may be granted under the Freedom of Information Act. Seeing how successful applications were put together will help you succeed with the same agency.

We will list several agency and department sources later in this chapter. However, you must remember that the possible sources for small-business loans will range far beyond the scope of our list. To research beyond what we will describe, send for updated versions of the most comprehensive listing of federal programs, published once per year by the Office of Management and Budget:

Catalog of Federal Domestic Assistance
$32.00, 1,000 pages, published annually
> Superintendent of Documents
> U.S. Government Printing Office
> Washington, DC 20402   202-783-3238

The same information is available through a computerized data base called the *Federal Assistance Programs Retrieval System* (FAPRS). For more information about how to access the system and prices, contact

> Federal Program Information Branch
> Budget Review Division
> Office of Management and Budget
> 17th and Pennsylvania Avenues, NW
> Washington, DC 20503   202-395-6182

THE U.S. SMALL BUSINESS ASSOCIATION

The best-known government source for financing help is the U.S. Small Business Association (SBA). Many people think this agency only gives loans directly to small businesses when, in fact, they provide many additional services through several different programs.

Much of the SBA activity involves loan guarantees rather than direct loans. The average loan guaranteed by the SBA is approximately $100,000. The agency will guarantee repayment of 90 percent loaned, up to $155,000, and 85 percent when loans are higher than $155,000, up to $750,000.

Before the SBA will consider an application for their loan guarantee program, you must either be turned down by a commercial lender or you must be able to produce a letter from your banker explaining that you would not qualify without a guarantee.

The process is run entirely through your banker. Your application is reviewed and then forwarded to the closest SBA office. If approved, your monthly payments will be made directly to the bank, operating under the loan guarantee program. However, the application procedure is paper-heavy and might require several months of review. This is not a fast process. Following is a list of SBA-guaranteed loan forms that usually must be completed when applying for a loan:

1. SBA Form 4. Loan application form with supporting schedules and exhibits.
2. SBA Form 4–1. This is completed by your lender and included in the application package. It includes the lender's conclusions about your ability to make repayments and manage your business and the collateral you have to offer. The form also includes pro forma financial statements.
3. SBA Form 159. This form tells who completed documents in and attached to the application package.
4. SBA Form 413. Individual financial statements for principals in your business.
5. SBA Form 912. Your personal history.
6. SBA Form 1261. Disclosure of federal laws affecting you and of which you must be informed.
7. Credit report.
8. Business plan, including current financial statements and a forecast and budget.
9. Financial information, including current financial statements, statements for the last three years, a schedule of accounts receivable and payable, other debts, and a listing of other capital in the business.
10. Nonfinancial information, which includes resumes of all principals in the business, three years of personal income tax returns, business history, intended use of borrowed funds, contracts and agreements in affect (leases, franchise documents, and so forth), a listing of owners and their shares, articles of incorporation or a partnership agreement (if applicable), an asset schedule, and federal employer identification number.

The SBA may also refer you to local Small Business Development Centers (SBDC) for counseling. To find the address of the SBDC closest to you, call the SBA at 202-653-6768.

You can also contact the SBA district office closest to you or contact SBA for information about free consultation services. Call SBA for information at 800-368-5855 (in Washington DC, 202-653-7561).

District offices of the SBA are

National headquarters
1441 L St., NW, Room 317
Washington, DC 20416   202-653-6365

Region I
60 Batterymarch St., 10th Floor
Boston, MA 02110   617-223-3204

Region II
26 Federal Plaza, Room 29-118
New York, NY 10278   212-264-7772

Region III
One Bala Cynwyd Plaza, West Lobby
Bala Cynwyd, PA 19004   215-596-5901

Region IV
1375 Peachtree St., NE
Atlanta, GA 30367   404-347-4999

Region V
230 South Dearborn St.
Chicago, IL 60604   312-353-0359

Region VI
8625 King George Dr., Building C
Dallas, TX 75235   214-767-7643

Region VII
911 Walnut St., 13th Floor
Kansas City, MO 64106   816-374-3163

Region VIII
1405 Curtis St., 22nd Floor
Denver, CO 80202   303-844-5441

Region IX
450 Golden Gate Ave.
San Francisco, CA 94102   415-556-7487

Region X
2615 Fourth Ave., Room 440
Seattle, WA 98121   206-442-5676

The SBA publishes a number of books and pamphlets dealing with financing for small businesses. These include

Booklets

15	*Handbook of Small Business Finances* Stock No. 045-000-00208-0	$4.50
25	*Guides for Profit Planning* Stock No. 045-000-00137-7	$4.50
44	*Financial Management: How to Make A Go of Your Business* Stock No. 045-000-00233-1	$2.50
103	*Small Business Incubator Handbook: A Guide for Start-Up and Management* Stock No. 045-000-00237-3	$8.50

Self-study series

1001	*The Profit Plan* Stock No. 045-000-00192-0	$4.50
1002	*Capital Planning* Stock No. 045-000-00193-8	$4.50
1003	*Understanding Money Sources* Stock No. 045-000-00194-6	$4.75
1004	*Evaluating Money Sources* Stock No. 045-000-00174-1	$5.00

Pamphlets

MA 1.001	*The ABC's of Borrowing*	free
MA 1.004	*Basic Budgets for Profit Planning*	free
MA 1.016	*Sound Cash Management and Borrowing*	free
MA 2.007	*Business Plan for Small Manufacturers*	free
MA 2.008	*Business Plan for Small Construction Firms*	free
MA 2.020	*Business Plan for Retailers*	free
MA 2.022	*Business Plan for Small Service Firms*	free
MA 2.028	*Business Plan for Homebased Business*	free

Loan programs offered by SBA include more than just a generalized small-business loan guarantee program. As of the end of 1988, the list includes

1. Management Assistance

Contact:

Associate Administrator for Management Assistance
Small Business Administration
1441 L Street, NW
Washington, DC 20416   202-653-6881

   a. Direct loans and guaranteed or insured loans to a maximum of $350,000.

2. Disadvantaged Business Loans

Contact:

Administrator for Minority Small Business
Small Business Administration
Room 317
1441 L Street, NW
Washington, DC 20416   202-653-6407

   a. Grants from $15,000 to $306,250 for disadvantaged business owners or owners located in areas of high unemployment.

3. Physical Disaster Loans

Contact:

Disaster Assistance Division
Small Business Administration
1441 L Street, NW
Washington, DC 20416   202-653-6879

   a. Direct and guaranteed or insured loans to a maximum of $500,000 to restore conditions for disaster victims.

4. Small Business Investment Companies

Contact:

Office of Investment
Small Business Administration
1441 L Street, NW
Washington DC 20416   202-653-6584

   a. Direct and guaranteed or insured loans from $50,000 to $35 million for equity and venture capital for small businesses.

5. Business Loan Programs

Contact:

Office of Business Loans
Small Business Administration
1441 L Street, NW
Washington, DC 20416   202-653-6570

  a. Direct and guaranteed or insured loans from $1,000 to $500,000 for small businesses unable to qualify with conventional lenders.
  b. Handicapped assistance direct loans and guaranteed or insured loans from $500 to $350,000.
  c. Energy-related construction, start-up, and conversions, direct loans and guaranteed or insured loans.
  d. Veteran assistance program, direct loans from $1,000 to $350,000.

The SBA also provides individual counseling, consulting, and assistance programs through each regional office.

OTHER GOVERNMENT PROGRAMS

Following is a list of government departmental programs offering various assistance plans for individual business owners. These divisions and departments are listed because they offer loans, loan guarantees, or grants to individual owners of small businesses.

Department of Agriculture

Agricultural Research Service
Washington, DC 20250   202-447-3656

Agricultural Stabilization and Conservation Service
Agricultural Marketing Service
Washington, DC 20250   202-447-4423

Competitive Research Grants Office
West Auditors Building, Room 112
15th and Independence Avenues, NW
Washington, DC 20251   202-475-5022

Higher Education Programs
Administration Building, Room 350-A
14th and Independence Avenues, NW
Washington, DC 20250   202-447-7854

Department of Commerce
Economic Development Administration
Room H7844, Herbert Hoover Building
Washington, DC 20230   202-377-5067

Export Promotion Service
Washington, DC 20230   202-377-8220

International Trade Administration
14th and E Streets, NW
Washington, DC 20230   202-377-5005

Minority Business Development Agency
14th and Constitution Avenues, NW
Washington, DC 20230   202-377-8015

Department of Energy
National Bureau of Standards
Washington, DC 20234   301-921-3694

Office of Energy Research
Mail Stop G-256
Washington, DC 20545   301-353-4946

Office of Minority Economic Impact
Room 5B-110, Forrestal Building
1000 Independence Avenue, SW
Washington, DC 20585   202-252-8383

Department of Health and Human Services
Bureau of Program Operations
Meadows East Building, Room 300
Baltimore, MD 21235   301-594-9000

Health Resources Services Administration
Parklawn Building, Room 8-38
5600 Fishers Lane
Rockville, MD 20857   301-443-1173

National Institute of Health
Bethesda, MD 20205   301-496-2241

Department of Housing and Urban Development

Office of Multifamily Housing Development
Housing and Urban Development
Washington, DC 20410   202-755-6223

Office of Single Family Housing
Housing and Urban Development
Washington, DC 20410   202-755-6720

Office of Urban Rehabilitation
Housing and Urban Development
451 Seventh Street, SW
Washington, DC 20410   202-755-6336

Department of Labor

Employment and Training Administration
601 D Street, NW
Washington, DC 20213   202-376-7335

Department of Transportation

Maritime Administration
Washington, DC 20590   202-382-0369

Urban Mass Transportation Administration
400 Seventh Street, SW
Washington, DC 20590   202-426-0080

Other Agencies

Export-Import Bank
811 Vermont Avenue, NW
Washington, DC 20571   800-424-5201

Overseas Private Investment Corporation
Washington, DC 20527   202-653-2800

Before writing to a particular agency to request loan information, determine the services each one offers. This can be most easily discovered with a telephone call or by using the *Catalog of Federal Domestic Programs* mentioned earlier in this chapter.

Misunderstandings concerning an agency's services will only delay the time required to find the government program right for you. For example, the Department of Commerce's Economic Development Administration (EDA) does *not* offer direct loans or loan guarantees, but does coordinate such programs administered by local governments or development organizations. They may provide referral information and eligibility requirements. In a letter from the Economic Development Administration received in March 1989, in response to research for this book, the EDA commented:

> Unfortunately, there seems to be a great deal of misinformation circulating at this time regarding EDA programs. Several books and at least one prerecorded advertisement for a book give the impression that EDA has a program providing grants for small businesses.

This is typical of the problems that government agencies and departments face in attempting to communicate what they offer and how applicants can qualify for their services.

On the opposite side is the situation in which services are available, but the word does not seem to get to the right people. For example, the Export-Import Bank, which is an independent government agency, offers a range of financial assistance programs to businesses exporting to foreign countries, including loans as well as loan guarantee and insurance programs up to 85 percent of export value.

The Export-Import Bank offers a range of services to small-business owners, including export credit insurance, working capital guarantees, direct loans, an advisory service, and briefing programs. Yet, few small businesses that do business overseas are aware of this specialized service.

WORKING WITH LOCAL BANKS

You have some flexibility in the type of financing you seek when working with a local bank. Find a bank that has a business loan department and that actively seeks business loan activity. Establish a relationship with the loan officer. Consider a line of credit as an alternative to a loan.

The advantages of working with a bank include

1. They are in the lending business. A bank is more likely to want to give you a loan, in comparison to savings and loans and other financial institutions.
2. A full-service bank will be able to offer you a wide range of services, including loans of various terms, lines of credit, and other alternatives to suit your specific requirements.
3. In the event that you have trouble making repayments, a bank will probably be willing to work with you to reschedule your

debt. Banks do not want their borrowers to default, and many business loans are arranged on an unsecured basis. Thus, when problems do arise, you may be able to renegotiate the terms of your loan. This will not always be the case when a loan is secured by real property, through a savings and loan association, for example.

Disadvantages of seeking a loan through a bank include

1. Establishing a permanent relationship with a loan officer is difficult, because bank personnel may move to another institution, be reassigned, transferred, or promoted.
2. The bank may require a very detailed business and marketing plan as well as a lot of other documentation, meaning a lot of paperwork for you.
3. Banks might be very conservative when working with small businesses, due to the high percentage that fail during the first five years. They tend to prefer lending money to well-established concerns.
4. A loan agreement might include a provision for periodic financial statements during the time the loan remains unpaid. This often means having to pay higher accounting fees than you are accustomed to.

The local bank is still your most likely source for borrowing money. Even having to deal with the paperwork and conservative outlook of the banker, it is wise to start there. Even if you end up seeking a loan guarantee program from a government agency, you will first have to establish the fact that you do not qualify for a loan from the bank.

ALTERNATIVE SOURCES

You may become frustrated if a local bank refuses to approve your loan application, even after you submit a complete business plan, copies of tax returns, and financial statements. In addition, you might not qualify for many of the government-sponsored programs due to your economic strength. In other words, it is possible that you are perceived as lacking the financial strength for the bank *and* at the same time being viewed as financially too strong to qualify for government guarantees or direct loans.

In that case, you must consider other alternatives. These include

1. **Private loans.** You might be able to convince a family member or even a friend to loan you the money you need. Be prepared to make a convincing case through your business plan in the same manner that you approach any other lender.
2. **Home equity.** Although your home equity should be carefully preserved, it can provide funding for a small business. Of course, this involves quite a bit of risk, because losing your home would also mean jeopardizing your personal shelter and your family's security. However, do not overlook refinancing or a second mortgage as one good source of capital.
3. **Lines of credit.** Some lenders will grant lines of credit to small-business owners, often with short-term repayment schedules. The advantage of this form of financing is that you are charged interest only when you draw against your line of credit. Thus, if you need to finance a series of capital expenditures over the next 12 months, a line of credit could be cheaper than borrowing all of the money today.

   Lines of credit may be secured by business property or even unsecured. Some small-business owners arrange lines of credit secured by their home equity, which today is probably the easiest of all credit lines to obtain. Again, misusing home equity is a dangerous trap for every homeowner. Be certain that the use of funds will ensure future profits adequate to repay the debt.
4. **Credit cards.** You can create your own line of credit through spending limits granted with various credit cards. It is not unusual for individuals with a clean credit history to obtain $50,000 or more in spending potential. As long as the debt is repaid and not allowed to accumulate over time, this is another excellent source for temporary financing.

   It is much more difficult for a self-employed person to accumulate big spending limits on a number of cards than for employees whose income can be easily verified. If you are planning to start a new business, set up your credit lines *before* leaving your present job. For annual fees ranging from zero to $25 per account, you should be able to arrange several $5,000 or more limits through mailed-in applications. Some companies allow you to write checks to draw against your limit and will charge relatively high rates of interest from the day you write a check to yourself.

Regardless of the loan source, it is imperative that you remain in control, repay debts on a planned and orderly schedule, and avoid more debt than your business can manage. This is the topic of the next chapter.

CHAPTER 9

LOANS: STAYING IN CONTROL

It's better to give than
to lend, and it costs
about the same.
—*Philip Gibbs*

Before even applying for a loan, you must plan ahead—not only for the way that proceeds will be spent, but also to ensure that your operation produces cash flow adequate to afford repayments.

If cash flow is marginal or insufficient, even after calculating additional profits loan proceeds are meant to create, then the risks of borrowing might not be worth taking. However, if this exercise confirms the fact that borrowing money will be a profitable move, then you will have created a mechanism for projecting cash flow and controlling it.

In this chapter, we will explain the method for calculating the future use of funds and resulting cash flow. This will enable you to determine whether or not the timing is right to borrow money. Then, once loan proceeds have been put to use, you will need to monitor monthly cash flow to stay on the schedule you have established.

EVALUATING BORROWINGS

The first step is to decide whether or not your operation can support the debt service or monthly repayments of a loan. It must be assumed that, in some way, a loan will increase future profits. However, the initial test must be to determine whether or not *current* cash-based profits can support loan payments.

This is a necessary test. Even though you assume that future profits will rise as the direct result of the way you use borrowed funds, the risk that this program will be delayed (or that it will not work at all) must be taken into account. There are two questions to ask. The first is, "Can I afford to repay this loan from profits I am now earning?" Only after satisfying this question should the second one be asked: "Will borrowing money be a profitable move?"

Remembering that we will assume to immediate change in monthly cash-based profits, the first question can be answered by preparing a cash flow projection. This should be based on a conservative estimate of current income, costs, and expenses.

Example: The owner of a construction firm wants to borrow $20,000 to purchase a new truck. His estimate is that with the additional equipment, he will save money on deliveries and be able to expand his operation above its current volume level. However, to be on the conservative side, he estimates no increase in gross receipts or in net profits for the first year. The question he must answer is, "Can I afford loan payments from cash flow being generated today?"

A cash flow projection is first prepared without the loan payments. This represents an estimate of results as the business is operating now. The second step is to expand that analysis for cash flow results if the loan is approved, and proceeds are immediately put into a new truck purchase.

To project cash flow, begin with the previous month's balance forward; add cash receipts, and subtract costs and expenses. Remember that all of this must be reflected on a *cash* basis. Thus, if next month's sales will be $12,000, but you expect to be paid only half of that amount, only $6,000 should be included in that month's projection. The first phase of cash flow is shown in Table 9-1.

TABLE 9–1
Cash Flow Projection before Loan Proceeds

	Jan	Feb	Mar
Balance forward	$4,300	$4,600	$4,900
Cash receipts	8,500	8,500	8,500
Subtotal	12,800	13,100	13,400
Direct costs	$4,700	$4,700	$4,700
Expenses	3,500	3,500	3,500
Total payments	$8,200	$8,200	$8,200
Ending balance	$4,600	$4,900	$5,200

Note that each month's ending balance is carried forward and becomes the next month's beginning balance. This simplified test of monthly cash flow is only an estimate of the near future and should be based on a fair and even purposely low estimate of income, along with a realistic and level allowance for overhead expenses.

In this case, available cash flow from operations is about $300 per month. This does not allow for seasonal variations, which will undoubtedly occur. That part of the full analysis comes later. For now, the next step is to estimate the effect on cash flow that loan proceeds will have, which is shown in Table 9-2.

In this test of cash flow, monthly estimates decline by $400 each month rather than growing by $300. This could indicate trouble, for several reasons:

1. If the business is seasonal, the monthly deficit amount will become worse when gross income falls.
2. If the estimate of cash flow is overly optimistic now, then negative cash flow could be worse than it appears in the estimate.
3. Depending on the number of months in the repayment term, future cash flow problems could be even more severe than today's realistic projection shows.
4. If the use of borrowed funds does not bring income level up quickly, the decision will prove to be a poor one. This adds risk and pressure to the owner to produce results quickly, perhaps more quickly than can be reasonably expected.

TABLE 9–2
Cash Flow Projection after Loan Proceeds

	Jan	Feb	Mar
Balance forward	$4,300	$3,900	$3,500
Cash receipts	8,500	8,500	8,500
Subtotal	12,800	12,400	12,000
Direct costs	$4,700	$4,700	$4,700
Expenses	3,500	3,500	3,500
Loan payments	700	700	700
Total payments	$8,900	$8,900	$8,900
Ending balance	$3,900	$3,500	$3,100

For these reasons, it is suggested that one conservative approach is to first ensure that current cash flow will, in fact, support loan repayments. That might be overly conservative in your business, however, if the cash flow margin is already slim. You can offset the risks of borrowing under the conditions described, if you are fully confident that borrowed funds will produce greater results—soon enough to avoid the risks of having to make loan payments every month.

THE EXPANDED PROJECTION

The cash flow projection can not be limited to only a few months. In fact, you must test it for as long a period as possible. However, going beyond one year with your estimate is not possible with any degree of accuracy or certainty. The further out you project cash flow, the less accurate the numbers will be. A reasonable test of cash flow extending over a one-year period should indicate the likely annual cycle you will experience. This assumes that future years will run at about the same volume and profit levels with seasonal variation.

Example: The owner of an auto rental company bases cash flow projections on historical income levels. Spring and fall income in the past outpaced receipts in summer and winter. Using the assumption that this pattern will repeat in the future, a one-year projection is prepared. Based on estimated levels of cash flow, the negative months are estimated to occur in midsummer and in the November and December period.

The owner ran the projection and then reduced it to a graph, which is shown in Figure 9-1. In this example, you can see the estimated cash income level (dotted line), current cash payments (black area), and estimates of cash payments including the loan (shaded area).

This exercise shows where potential problems will arise. The owner must be able to set aside funds needed to make loan payments in those periods when receipts will be slow. Second, it will be necessary to estimate future receipt and payment levels to make certain that the loan remains affordable in future years. If the trend is toward ever-decreasing margins, that could indicate that debt service is an excessive strain on the operation.

A conservative estimate of how loan proceeds will affect cash receipts must be included. It may be necessary to revise the projection on that basis. However, it is not realistic to simply add a number to the

FIGURE 9–1
Future Cash Flow

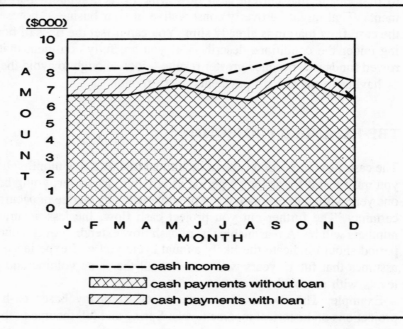

bottom line as an estimate of how much more will be earned. Adjustments must be included for direct costs and for variable expenses.

Example: A manufacturer must allow for a 60 percent factor for direct costs and another 12 percent to cover variable expenses. Thus, any income generated above current levels as the result of borrowing money must be carried through these reductions. That will produce a realistic estimate of increased net income and cash flow.

CALCULATING NET CASH INCOME

Several possible factors will affect how much of your increased potential income will actually be realized in additional cash flow. For example, if proceeds of a loan are expected to increase gross sales volume, will accounts receivable or inventory levels also rise? If so, you must allow for that in your cash flow projection. In addition, a portion of gross sales will be absorbed by direct costs and by variable expenses.

Example: A retail store owner is considering borrowing money to expand the current inventory level. Accounts receivable will rise as well. She expects total monthly income to increase as a result of the change. However, the higher commitment to both inventory and accounts receivable will demand a portion of the cash received as volume grows. The owner is also aware that direct costs will grow as a percentage of gross sales and that certain variable expenses will also change.

A worksheet like the one shown in Figure 9-2 can be used to calculate the cash-based operating profit. This assumes that loan proceeds will, in some manner, be applied so that total sales are increased. Upon completion of this worksheet, revised cash-based income must be compared to current cash-based income. The net result is the increase in cash flow.

The worksheet takes you through the calculation starting with an assumed total monthly sales level. This must be reduced for periodic increases in inventory and accounts receivable levels (if those increases are expected to accompany higher sales). The next step is to calculate

FIGURE 9–2
Cash-Based Income Worksheet

1. total monthly income $ _____

2. less: increased accounts receivable
       and inventory $ _____

3. cash–based income
       (line 1 less line 2) $ _____

4. direct costs
       line 1 $ _____
       x costs _____ %   = $ _____

5. gross profit (cash basis)
       (line 3 less line 4) $ _____

6. variable expenses
       line 1 $ _____
       x variables _____ %   = $ _____

7. monthly fixed overhead $ _____

8. cash–based operating profit
       (line 5 less lines 6 and 7) $ _____

direct costs, which must be based not on cash-based gross, but on total sales. Even though you do not receive cash in the same month a sale occurs, you will probably be expected to pay for additional inventory. The net of this calculation is cash-basis gross profit or the remainder when direct costs are subtracted from cash-based income.

Gross profit is reduced by two additional factors. First, variable expenses should be calculated as a percentage of gross sales (total earned, not received). Determining the right percentage for variable expenses is more difficult than for direct costs, because the percentage is not fixed. The best estimate should be drawn from your current expense budget.

The second factor is fixed overhead. If you believe you will be able to control overhead at a relatively fixed level, then this number will be dependable. It might also be necessary to add an amount for higher overhead when volume increases will demand it.

With the cash-based operating profit computed, the next step is to calculate the actual amount of cash flow available *after* making loan payments.

Example: The owner of a small manufacturing company seeks a loan to replace aging equipment. He fills out the cash-based income worksheet to figure operating profit. The assumption is that with increased income, accounts receivable and inventory levels will both increase. The worksheet is completed with allowances for cash increases in current assets, as well as for the changes in direct costs and variable expenses. Another assumption is that fixed overhead will be increased to a higher level than current expenses run, again due to higher sales volume and the need for increased administrative support, shown in Table 9-3.

TABLE 9–3
Cash-Based Income Worksheet

1.	Total monthly income	$92,000
2.	Less increased accounts receivable and inventory	8,000
3.	Cash-based income	$84,000
4.	Direct costs line 1 $92,000 × costs 60% =	55,200
5.	Gross profit (cash basis)	$28,800
6.	Variable expenses line 1 $92,000 × variables 8% =	7,360
7.	Monthly fixed overhead	19,000
8.	Cash-based operating profit (5 less 6 and 7)	$ 2,400

CALCULATING CASH FLOW

To isolate the amount you can expect to have available *after* increasing income due to application of loan proceeds, perform the previous calculation in two ways: first based on current income, cost, and expense levels; and, second, based on your estimate of increased volume as the result of applying loan proceeds.

The example above assumes cash flow that will result *after* the loan proceeds have been applied. It is also necessary to work through to cash-based operating profit based on current levels. This calculation gives you your cash-based operating profit, shown in Table 9-4. The difference between this level and the projected higher level after loan proceeds are put to work is the net increased cash income. With these values calculated, you can now estimate the net cash flow you expect to generate. A worksheet for this is shown in Figure 9-3.

This calculation begins with current net cash-based operating profit. Next, loan payments are subtracted to produce your monthly cash flow. To this, add the increased income you expect to earn from application of loan proceeds. The total is the amount of cash flow after loan payments are made.

Example: The owner of the manufacturing concern goes through this calculation, based on monthly loan payments of approximately $915 per month, shown in Table 9-5.

Note that in all of these calculations, we have ignored the income tax factor. The basis for comparison is net operating profit and cash flow. Interest expense will certainly reduce taxable income, while the total of loan payment will place an additional strain on cash flow.

TABLE 9-4
Cash-Based Income Worksheet

1.	Total monthly income	$52,000
2.	Less increased accounts receivable and inventory	0
3.	Cash-based income	$52,000
4.	Direct costs line 1 $52,000 × costs 60% =	31,200
5.	Gross profit (cash basis)	$20,800
6.	Variable expenses line 1 $52,000 × variables 8% =	4,160
7.	Monthly fixed overhead	15,000
8.	Cash-based operating profit (5 less 6 and 7)	$ 1,640

FIGURE 9–3
Cash Flow Calculation

cash–based operating profit	$_____
less: monthly loan payments	$_____
monthly cash flow	$_____
plus: increased income due to use of loan proceeds	$_____
net cash flow after loan payments	$_____

The purpose in making the comparison must be to determine whether operating profits (shown on a cash basis) will be adequate to support the monthly loan payment. It will also be necessary to compare after-tax profits to the cost of the loan.

Figure 9-4 shows this calculation. In this test, the monthly interest expense (column 1) is reduced for the amount of tax benefit (column 2). This is calculated by multiplying each month's interest by the effective tax rate you pay. Remember to include federal and state tax, if applicable. If you are self-employed, also include the change due to self-employment (social security) tax. The net interest expense (column 3) is compared to the estimated increased income earned as the direct result of borrowing money (column 4). If column 4 is consistently greater than column 3, borrowing money can be described as a profitable decision.

TABLE 9–5
Cash Flow Calculation

Cash-based operating profit	$1,640
Less monthly loan payments	915
Monthly cash flow	$ 725
Plus increased income due to use of loan proceeds ($2,440 less $1,640)	800
Net cash flow after loan payments	$1,525

FIGURE 9–4
Interest/Profit Comparison

MONTH	(1) INTEREST EXPENSE	(2) LESS: TAX SAVINGS	(3) NET INTEREST	(4) INCREASED INCOME	(5) NET (4) – (3)
	$	$	$	$	$
total	$	$	$	$	$

Example: The owner of a consulting firm borrowed money to purchase a word-processing system. This enabled her to produce reports for clients with greater efficiency, and, as a result, she was able to increase gross receipts. During the first six months, income did not increase beyond the net interest level. However, after six months, income did begin to exceed net interest; thus, over the long term, borrowing money to invest in more efficient equipment paid off.

It is not always realistic to assume that newly established levels of profit will be permanent nor that a new level of gross sales will lead to profits. Accompanying your calculations must be a conscious plan for holding down the level of fixed and variable expenses, controlled cost ratios, and direct control over inventory and accounts receivable levels. Without these essential controls, you cannot expect to generate the cash flow to support the operation.

The interest/profit comparison worksheet reveals that for the first six months, the net interest expense does outpace the additional income earned as the result of borrowing money. However, from that point forward, the picture changes. This test establishes that, even after allowing for a period of adjustment, the decision to borrow money becomes profitable. Before calculating the month-to-month outcome on an after-tax basis, we must first develop a schedule of monthly interest and principal payments. For this example, we are assuming that $30,000 was borrowed at 12 percent monthly interest, to be paid in 36 months. The first year's schedule is shown in Table 9-6.

With the monthly interest expense now known, it is possible to calculate the after-tax expense. This exercise assumes an effective overall tax rate of 35 percent, and the interest/profit comparison for the full year is shown in Table 9–7.

ESTABLISHING INTERNAL CONTROLS

When you undertake the calculation of future cash flow, the process either confirms your plan or indicates that you are heading for a problem. If the numbers do not work out, the existing plan must be revised.

There are alternatives. You might determine that your expansion plan is valid, but must be approached within a longer time frame. With

TABLE 9–6
Loan Amortization, First Year

Month	Payment	Interest	Principal	Balance
Balance				30,000.00
Jan	996.43	300.00	696.43	29,303.57
Feb	996.43	293.04	703.39	28,600.18
Mar	996.43	286.00	710.43	27,889.75
Apr	996.43	278.90	717.53	27,172.22
May	996.43	271.72	724.71	26,447.51
Jun	996.43	264.48	731.95	25,715.56
Jul	996.43	257.16	739.27	24,976.29
Aug	996.43	249.76	746.67	24,229.62
Sep	996.43	242.30	754.13	23,475.49
Oct	996.43	234.75	761.68	22,713.81
Nov	996.43	227.14	769.29	21,944.52
Dec	996.43	219.45	776.98	21,167.54
	11,957.16	3,124.70	8,832.46	

TABLE 9-7
Interest/Profit Comparison

Month	(1) Interest	(2) Tax	(3) Net	(4) Income	(5) Net
Jan	300.00	105.00	195.00	0	(195.00)
Feb	293.04	102.56	190.48	0	(190.48)
Mar	286.00	100.10	185.90	0	(185.90)
Apr	278.90	97.62	181.28	0	(181.28)
May	271.72	95.10	176.62	0	(176.62)
Jun	264.48	92.57	171.91	100	(71.91)
Jul	257.16	90.01	167.15	250	82.85
Aug	249.76	87.42	162.34	250	87.66
Sep	242.30	84.81	157.49	250	92.51
Oct	234.75	82.16	152.59	400	247.41
Nov	227.14	79.50	147.64	400	252.36
Dec	219.45	76.81	142.64	400	257.36
total	3,124.70	1,093.66	2,031.04	2,050	18.96

limited cash flow, you might be unable or unwilling to face the risks of borrowing and will simply have to wait. Possibly a loan may be sought with a longer payback period. Finally, you can seek investment capital rather than going into debt, which will be discussed in later chapters.

The point is that proving the accuracy of your projections will validate what you believe is possible and what can be achieved realistically. It also identifies and addresses the business risks associated with borrowing and demonstrates how you plan to meet and overcome those risks. This is worthwhile as an internal exercise and will also help a lender evaluate you as a risk from the institution's point of view. Few applicants go into adequate detail in determining future cash flow, and most are not prepared to establish that they have the operating capital to make repayments.

In the vacuum of uncertainty, the lender must assume the positive or negative aspects of an operation, possibly leading to a rejection of the loan application. When the applicant presents cash flow calculations and profitability summaries for the coming years, that is a sign that you are prepared to exercise responsible management—in fact, that you are already demonstrating it.

There is another aspect of management that must be brought into the discussion of controlling cash flow. You need to establish cost and expense controls, not only during the repayment period, but as a permanent procedure in your business.

With so much emphasis on gross sales, small-business owners can easily overlook the critical importance of holding down costs and expenses. Thus, during a period of impressive sales growth, profits and cash flow are eroded and the owner loses control. In hindsight, such an owner might realize the error of failing to exercise direct controls. Volume itself, without profits and cash flow, is not only pointless, it can also be deadly. Never overlook the fact that

> Control over costs and expenses is more critical to your success than the amount of gross sales generated.

Example: The owner of a one-location retail store brought in gross receipts of $350,000 during the third year in operation. Net profits were slightly better than 10 percent. During the next three years, sales rose moderately and the return on sales were consistently higher than 10 percent—a result the owner accepted as satisfactory. The most important element in maintaining this margin was consistent exercise of controls over inventory and markup, recurring review of budgets, and strict planning and control over cash.

Example: A similar store experienced rapid sales growth during a four-year period. During the first year, gross receipts were $270,000. By the end of the fourth year, the owner had four stores and gross receipts were more than $1.25 million. However, the owner had no time for administrative oversight. No cost or expense controls were formalized, there was no significant budget review, and the bookkeeping chore was completely delegated. The owner was concerned, though, that with such a high sales volume, the operation was *losing* money.

These two examples are revealing. In the first one, the owner was not concerned with expansion on the top line and was able to build a strongly controlled operation. Cash flow was not a problem, because expansion occurred gradually and methodically. Profits were consistent. In the second example, expansion of sales and outlets was a greater priority. Even with $1.25 million in gross sales, the operation was unable to produce a profit. We can only assume that in these conditions, cash flow would also become a chronic problem.

What types of controls should be instituted, and how can they be monitored? An important element of any control procedure must be ease of use. If controls take too much time, you will be forced away from the entrepreneurial aspects of owning a business and tied to a desk. Some part of the analysis function can be monitored, but you must not let go of the responsibility for planning and review. Successful business owners consistently report that they spend between 10 and 30 percent of their time in planning functions (including control procedures, review, budgeting, and business planning).

The control function can become the most enjoyable and creative routine in operating your business, if properly structured. Before opening your doors, the entire process was a series of plans and plan reviews. That same spirit can and should be applied every day. This is not merely an administrative or accounting function, but the core of business planning. It is the essence of devising and reaching goals. It is also the direct, hands-on way that you predict and create future profits.

Control routines should include

1. **Inventory control** (in retail businesses). Investing too little money in inventory will mean missed sales, delayed deliveries, excessive backorders, dissatisfied customers, and too much of your time spent trying to fill in missing goods. Too much investment—a more common problem—will mean cash flow problems, the need for more storage space, and a greater chance of inventory damage, obsolescence, or theft.

   The level of inventory must be coordinated with sales volume, and the trend can be monitored with a periodic inventory turnover analysis. The best possible level might vary by season and should be developed over time. If you sell a variety of products, also track the markup on each major line. This will reveal the sources of profits above and below average. In multiple-line businesses, it is easy to end up losing money on one portion of the total lines offered, because losses are obscured by the averages.

2. **Variable expense controls.** In product or service operations, the variable expense classifications can become the source of losses. They must be realistically budgeted, reviewed, and controlled. This group includes telephone expenses (to a degree), advertising, travel, entertainment, and other expenses that can vary depending on gross volume.

   Example: A marketing company operates with a number of outside salespeople. Travel, entertainment, and transportation expenses are reimbursed twice per month based on expense reports. When the level of these expenses rises, the owner asks the bookkeeper to analyze the trend. This analysis shows that the level of selling expenses is outpacing the rate of sales growth. In response, the owner develops a budget and imposes limits on each salesperson. An expense allowance is established, based on the volume or orders each individual generates.

3. **Overhead expense controls.** Fixed, or permanent, expenses are rarely fixed. They will not stay at the same level each month just because they are not expected to vary with changes in sales volume. Without your direct involvement, overhead expenses can, in fact, outpace the rate of growth in sales and end up absorbing all of your profits.

By concentrating on expense controls, you might create a higher level of profits than would be possible by doubling gross receipts. In fact, without those controls, you cannot expect to realize a profit nor to maintain a healthy level of cash flow.

Control begins with a realistic, well-documented budget. This does not have to become a bureaucratic or time-consuming procedure. If the budget is constructed with intelligent assumptions and if you are willing to review and compare actual and budgeted levels each month, then you will be able to spot emerging problems before they have a negative impact on profitability.

Problem areas can be controlled by enacting procedures to hold down expenses. For example, if your office supply expenses are rising, you might need to review all supply orders before they are placed. A responsible employee can be put in charge of a requisitioning system. If you have a number of employees, minor pilferage might become a problem that adds up to a big number over the course of a year. You might have to lock up supplies and put someone in charge of dispensing them. Monthly or even weekly analysis will further help reduce the problem. The employee in charge must be instructed to shop for the best discount price when ordering in bulk, and even recurring supply orders should be placed with a supplier who does not charge top dollar.

Similar controls can be put in place for a number of other expense items. Some examples:

Telephone. Use a phone log for all toll and long-distance calls. Review monthly billings to identify long-distance calls made by employees. Announce a procedure that no personal calls are allowed, and charge employees for nonbusiness calls made on your phone.

Printing. Make sure your employees are ordering the most cost-efficient quantity of printed material and that prices are compared before orders are placed. Look for a dependable printer who will offer better prices and reduce the frequency of forms orders.

Delivery. Review this expense, looking for excessive use of overnight delivery services. Can some mailings be combined or sent via less expensive services?

The types of internal controls you put into place must be designed based on the type of expense or cost involved. The time spent in review will be worth the effort, not only to reduce expenses in the current month but to hold down the overall level of spending in the future. The attitude that business costs and expenses must be watched constantly will go a long way toward building a responsible attitude among employees.

The same degree of discipline must be applied to yourself as the owner. Even in a one-person operation, you must be able to critically review your spending habits and to eliminate unnecessarily expensive spendings.

Example: The owner of a consulting business realized that too much money was being spent on computer software. All he really needed was a dependable word-processing system and a data file management program. However, over the previous year, he'd purchased a number of other programs, none of which added to his ability to produce profits. An honest review brought him to the realization that he liked automation and wanted a lot of sophisticated programs, but that the real business demands were not extensive. As a result of this review process, the owner decided to not purchase any more programs and to hold down computer expenses to necessary supplies.

Acceptable levels of profit and maintenance of positive cash flow are not the results of luck. They come from diligent, consistent exercise of controls. Your control processes must be efficient, immediate, recurring, and of the highest priority. Planning time often is put off or cancelled completely, because more urgent problems take up the owner's time. You must avoid the pitfall of failing to plan.

Give planning the highest priority in your operation, remembering this key point:

Every hour you spend in planning and control will yield profit and cash flow benefits this month and every month in the future.

If that means you must spend one full day a week in reviewing cost and expense levels, exercising controls, analyzing budget variances, and tracking the progress of your plan, then spend that day. If it means you need to just sit and think for four hours per week, reviewing overall progress and direction and planning where you want to be in one, two, or five years, set a standard for yourself that you will spend that time. You will discover that it is the best use of your time as a business owner and that it is an essential element of management that will keep you on the right track and enable you to directly control profits and cash flow.

The next chapter discusses the detailed business plan designed for presentation to a lender, how to construct that plan, and how to reduce the complexity of your financial information to an understandable and convincing summary that will get you the money you need.

CHAPTER 10

BUSINESS PLANS FOR BORROWED MONEY

Can anybody remember when times
were not hard and money was not
scarce?
—*Ralph Waldo Emerson*

Lenders want to see specific features in the business plans submitted to them. This relates both to the business operation and to the owner's background, experience, and qualifications as a manager. The plan you put together specifically to obtain financing should be more detailed than the preliminary plan that tests your assumptions and sets up the overall course for the coming year. When you approach a lender, you must emphasize why you will need the money, how it will be used, and how the lender's risks will be reduced.

Small business owners make three mistakes in their approach to a lender:

1. **Presenting no plan.** When an employed individual applies for a home mortgage or auto loan, the lender can verify income with a telephone call. Thus, a personal balance sheet and credit history are adequate to answer the lender's questions. However, a small-business owner's application presents a different problem. The lender must be able to evaluate the risk of borrowing against a different standard.

   Not only must historical income be verified, the likely future profitability of the business must also be judged. This means not only that your estimates need to be supported, but that you prove your ability to look ahead, manage your business, and use cash responsibly.

All of that requires a business plan. A good number of the loan applications that are turned down are presented without any plan. The owner merely attaches the latest financial statements and hopes for the best.

2. **Presenting a "nonplan."** You can put a lot of effort into the completion of a document called a "business plan," without giving the lender the information needed to evaluate you and your business. This is a waste of time, money, and effort. Just because a plan is long, organized, or professionally prepared does not mean it has any value.

Do not concern yourself with the length of your business plan, and do not assume that you need to hire a consultant or accountant to prepare your plan. You might want help in putting together financial statements, forecasts and budgets, or other number-related segments of your plan, but organize and write the plan yourself. Use *your* assumptions and not someone else's. Remember that you understand your operation better than anyone else and can write a business plan on your own.

3. **Presenting a plan with the wrong emphasis.** Make sure your plan addresses the lender's concerns. If your plan is designed for internal use or to attract investors, the lender will have difficulty identifying the key points necessary to evaluate you: future sales and profits, cash flow, seasonal changes, your ability to manage a growing operation, marketing strategy, and competitive factors.

ORGANIZING YOUR PLAN

We previously introduced the format for a simplified plan. This should be expanded to add three additional sections dealing with the future. In addition, the sections of your plan should be rewritten to emphasize areas of interest to someone who will be risking money on you and your business. A full sample plan is presented in Appendix A of this book. For now, we will describe the sections in the lender-oriented plan.

A business plan specifically designed with the lender in mind should contain the following sections:

1. **Company history.** Explain the origin of the company—the year it began, specific market it serves, and a description of the

products and services you sell. Also provide a short biography of the principals—you and any other owners or key employees. Include qualifications and background and responsibilities within your own company. Remember that the lender will be interested in finding out who you are, why taking a risk on your company is worthwhile, and how you are qualified to ensure repayments.

2. **Objective.** This is a one-page section consisting of a single paragraph. It describes the company's purpose and standards, the customer served, and the direction in which you are headed.

3. **Purpose.** This section explains how borrowed money will be used. It should be specific. Do not merely state that the money is needed to provide "working capital." List the fixed assets you will buy, the marketing strategies you will finance, or the facilities expansion actions you will take.

4. **Assumptions.** This part of the plan should be as detailed as required. It lists the beliefs under which you are operating. For example, if you assume that your customer base will grow during the next five years, explain that and support your belief. If you assume that the competition will be unable to take advantage of the market as well as you can, tell why.

5. **Marketing strategy.** In this section, you detail the ways in which you plan to grow. Many small-business owners have never taken the time to estimate future sales volume, territories, or potential new markets. Yet, this is a basic management skill that you must be prepared to explain to a lender. It describes how the lender's risks are reduced. Your marketing strategy should contain three elements:

- **Expansion method.** How do you plan to grow? Will it be in terms of sales volume and profits generated by moving into new markets or locations? Precisely how do you plan to penetrate the new territory? What risks are involved, and how will you address them?

- **Support systems.** During your expansion period, how will you ensure that costs and expenses remain at a reasonable level and that cash flow is controlled? Will expansion require additional employees, larger facilities, increased inventory, or investment in capital assets?

- **Deadlines.** Besides knowing what you plan to accomplish and what it will cost, you must also describe *when* your plan will be complete. Will it take six months, a year, or five years? Specify deadlines for the phases of expansion to demonstrate that you will be in complete control of your marketing plan and are not just trusting in fate to reach your goals.

6. **Risks.** Describe the risks that both you and the lender face. By confronting and then explaining the risks, you will reassure a lender, who otherwise must assume that you either are not aware of them or are avoiding the topic.

   Risks should be expressed in terms of solutions. In addition to the market risks you face just because you are in business, also address the risks of timing, competition, obsolescence, and economics. If you need statistical information to support your position, incorporate it into this section of your plan.

7. **Financial analysis.** This section shows the lender how you plan to manage your own future. The key here is that your estimates must be realistic. If you estimate future sales and profits too optimistically, it will call your entire plan into question, not to mention your judgment as a business owner.

   Sections should include a detailed income forecast (broken down by markets, product or service lines, and month), cost and expense budget (with monthly and account details), and cash flow projections (by category of source and expenditure as well as by month).

   Also include a section for analysis of trends. This should include any trend that describes the recent history and likely future of your business. For example, if the emphasis of your plan is on growth in sales, break down the last two to three years of sales growth and then show how you plan to increase volume in the coming two or three years. Also analyze your use of working capital and the relationship between debt and equity (more on these trends later in the chapter.)

8. **Financial statements.** The last section of your plan is for the three commonly accepted financial statements: balance sheet, income statement, and statement of cash flows. The statements should be in summarized form, with details provided by way of attached supplementary schedules and footnotes, as required. Also state whether you prepared the statements yourself or had someone else do them for you. If they were compiled, reviewed,

or audited, the accountant should so state. The lender will want to know what level of examination an accountant performed and how much verification will be required for your statements.

WHAT YOUR PLAN SHOULD PROVE

It is not wise to assume that one format for a business plan can work in every possible situation. Although the meat of the plan will not change, the assumptions, emphasis, and detail level should be dictated by the purpose of the plan. When you are planning to present your plan with a loan application, remember that you are addressing risks and that the lender must be told how you are qualified to manage money and run a business.

Your plan must prove these points:

1. **You have the ability to manage.** Always begin with the assumption that the lender knows nothing about you or your operation. The questions on the lender's mind is, What qualities do you possess that make you a competent business manager?

    This is a critical question because it is lack of management skill that often leads to business failure and the application of skill that enables a small business to earn consistent profits and beat the odds. Most new businesses fail within the first five years, so a lender will be more likely to approve your application if you can establish the fact that you are among the minority that will succeed.

    Your ability is demonstrated when you present a comprehensive and realistic plan. That is a good first step. Within that plan, you further demonstrate management skills by proving that you are thinking about the future, are aware of risks (both for yourself and for the lender), and that you respect the importance of planning. The combination of an income forecast, cost and expense budget, and cash flow projection help establish your planning skills. This is especially true when your estimates are realistic and backed up with reasonable assumptions.

2. **Your financial history supports your contention that you are a good risk.** Including a detailed financial history in your plan is essential. Not only does it establish a summary of capitalization

and profitability, it also directly addresses a major area of risk constantly on the lender's mind. The question the lender must answer is: Does the business operation adequately generate sales, profits, and cash flow to repay the loan?

You must include a financial history, even if it includes weaknesses. However, if you have reported losses in the past, if sales have fallen, or if you have had cash flow difficulties, explain the problems as honestly as possible. Then show how the situation has changed today and—perhaps more critical to the application—tell how you will prevent similar problems from recurring in the future.

A new business will not have the history to show at all; thus, it is easier for someone who has been operating for a few years to get a loan. If you can not show more than one year's historical information, your plan will need more detail concerning similar businesses and their formula for success, existing competitive factors, and your background and experience as a manager.

Your financial history should address three major areas, whether based on your own operation or on a series of assumptions made for a new enterprise: sales, profits, and cash flow. This is not merely a repeat of what is shown on financial statements. The information must be described in a planning context. What was your original plan, and did you meet your own expectations? If so, that helps support the direction you are planning in the future. If not, it helps identify flawed assumptions, past management errors, and market conditions you did not anticipate in the past. This all helps to prove your awareness of management issues and risks.

If you are just starting a business, the initial plan must be especially well supported. Your task is to convince the lender that you have a specific, workable idea, but without the track record to prove it can be done or that you can execute the idea.

3. **You have a specific profit plan that will work.** A lender must be concerned with how realistically you have planned your future. Estimates put down on paper have a way of not coming to pass, and lenders will be wary of an overly optimistic plan. You must support your contention for major increases in sales and profits, based on your knowledge of your market, product or service, customer base, and competition.

With a few years of history, you can make a strong case. Use the past to support what you plan for the future. It is a mistake to ignore your own history, because it can be your strongest argument for assumptions made in your current plan.

If you are just starting out, make sure your assumptions are absolutely correct. Base your forecast on studies of trends in market demand, a complete description of the customer you will serve, and a very thorough summary of your competition. You will have to identify your own market niche and convince the lender that you are postured to take advantage of an opportunity as it exists now and in the future.

Besides providing the lender with a complete forecast and budget, assumptions, and profit picture for the future, footnote your estimates with cross-references to narrative sections. Explain how you developed your budgets and why you believe they are realistic. Be aware that the lender might start reviewing your numbers with the belief that small-business budgeting is rarely a dependable science. You must prove that your budget is the exception to this rule.

THE FINANCIAL ANALYSIS SECTION

The loan-oriented plan must estimate the future outcome of sales, profits, cash flow, and overall financial strength. These are best supported with a realistic analysis of key trends and assumptions.

Some of the trends you should report on will include sales volume, profits, and accounts receivable (if you sell on a credit basis).

A sales trend should report volume by lines of business or by territory. This is especially important if you plan to expand in one primary area. The emerging trend will support your contention that the market demand is there and exists to a degree that makes your forecast a reasonable one.

Example: The owner of an antique shop applied to a local bank for a loan with the idea of opening a second store. The location the owner had in mind was downtown. The lender pointed out to the owner that within a three-square-block area, there were already six antique shops in operation. The owner was attracted to the high traffic potential of the area, but forgot to study the competition.

Example: When the founder of a construction company submitted her loan application, it was accompanied by a business plan that claimed sales volume would grow by 40 percent during the next three years. This estimate was supported by an analysis of past volume trends, as well as by a discussion of competitive factors. Growth in new housing starts in the area was impressive during the past year, and trends in employment and housing demand supported the contractor's contention that volume would grow at the rate forecast.

Profits and cash flow should be analyzed in your plan as well as gross sales. It is always desirable to be able to report a consistent and steady growth in net profits and to be able to demonstrate that you have never had cash flow problems. However, that is not always the way the numbers come out. Thus, if your history shows inconsistency, but your estimates of the future are smooth and even, the lender will naturally view your plan with pessimism. Identify seasonal changes and build changing levels of profit and cash flow into your plan. Try to match future estimates with likely outcomes, based on past experience. Explain how additional capital will help you to strengthen profit and cash flow levels in the future.

Accounts receivable levels should be studied within the trend section of your plan, especially if the majority of your earnings are not paid in cash. Summarize monthly levels of outstanding receivables, as well as the average number of days required to collect money.

To develop an accounts receivable collection trend, start by developing 12-month averages for each month in the last year. Next, perform the same average for sales made on a credit basis (be sure to exclude all cash sales). The average of accounts receivable balances divided by the average monthly credit sales produces the average number of days required to collect.

Example: As of December 31, the average monthly accounts receivable level was $27,230 (amount outstanding at the end of the month). Average monthly sales as of the same date were $62,754 (computed by adding up sales for the 12 months, and then dividing by 12). The collection ratio is

$$\frac{\$27,230}{\$62,754} = 43.4 \text{ days}$$

This reveals that as of December 31, it took 43.4 days to collect the average bill. The ratio, by itself, does not reveal the trend. Only when it is compared to the number of days during previous months does a trend emerge.

Example: Over the past year, the days required to collect the average bill declined from 52 days in January down to 43.4 days at the end of the year. This indicates that you are exercising collection controls to ensure that bills do not remain unpaid for an unreasonably long period of time.

Trends will be more dependable when they are expressed in terms of averages. Monthly distortions from the average will distract a reviewer from the significance of the trend itself. Thus, a moving average should be used whenever reporting a trend, along with the monthly changes in the numbers.

Example: You are preparing a graph to report the monthly level of gross sales. Volume is higher during the spring and summer months and lower than average in fall and winter. In this case, it is important to show the seasonal levels of sales, but it is also valuable to be able to review the trend on the basis of monthly averages.

As long as the average is limited to a 12-month period, the calculation is fairly straightforward. Add up the totals in each month, and divide the total by 12. The result is a year-long average.

An alternative is to develop averages in one isolated year. Thus, the first month consists of a ratio by itself, the second month is the average of two months, and the twelfth month is the average of all 12. This method is appropriate when reporting trends for turnover in working capital or a debt/equity analysis, for example, because those trends are based on a number of events or a percentage over a specific period of time.

In comparison, a dollar-value average (such as the one used for the collection ratio) should always be based on 12 months of activity. Thus, December's average will consist of the January-to-December period, and the March average will involve the April-to-March period. In those cases, the averaging will include results from before the reported test period.

As long as the values you report in your trend analysis are consistent and accurate, the trend will be dependable as well. If the assumptions in a trend are wrong, then the conclusions you will draw will be wrong, too. It does not matter how long a period you use to develop an average. What is important is that the result fairly represents what occurred in the recent past. That is the best way to back up what you estimate will happen in the near future.

ANALYZING WORKING CAPITAL

We have previously stated that turnover in working capital serves as a useful ratio. It demonstrates the degree of use to which working capital is put to work. The higher the number of times working capital was turned over, on average, the more efficiently your working capital is applied to generate sales. However, it must be remembered that this ratio can be misleading unless reviewed as part of a long-term trend.

Example: At the end of the first quarter last year, gross sales were $385,000. Current assets were $96,000 and current liabilities were $37,000 (the difference, $59,000, is working capital). The turnover ratio is computed by dividing sales by working capital:

$$\frac{\$385,000}{\$59,000} = 6.5 \text{ turns}$$

To see how this ratio can be drastically changed, let us assume that the company is planning to purchase new equipment in April, which will reduce current assets by $20,000. If the company paid for that equipment one month early, working capital would be reduced to $39,000. Now the turnover ratio is

$$\frac{\$385,000}{\$39,000} = 9.9 \text{ turns}$$

The opposite effect could be achieved—a lower number of turns—if the company had sold a capital asset before the end of the quarter. The timing of decisions, often by only a few days, can drastically affect the outcome of this ratio. Thus, an analysis should be performed over a long period of time and using both the month-end number of turns and a moving average. In that way, temporary distortions will be absorbed, and a dependable trend can be developed.

Lenders will be aware of the potential for distortion whenever they review financial information in any form. Ratios, even reported net profits and capital levels, can be misrepresented in error or even intentionally. Thus, when financial information has been reviewed by your accountant, that lends credibility to your business plan.

The inclusion of appropriate trends in the plan will help the lender to complete an analysis, especially from their perception of risk.

Example: You are applying for a loan with your local bank. As part of your business plan, you want to prove that you will be able to maintain a consistent degree of control over working capital. You work out an analysis of turnover in working capital as the means for summarizing the past, which will also be used to estimate future turnover. The period studied covers three years, and your analysis is done by quarters. The earliest quarter in the study is called quarter 1, and the latest is called quarter 12. Your financial summary is shown in Table 10–1.

With this summary, you conclude that in the most recent year, the rate of turnover has fallen. You have no reason to believe the rate will continue to fall, but that it reflects a slowdown in expected turnover due to the substantial increase in the rate of sales volume. At the latest level ($507,000 for the 12th quarter), sales have risen 32 percent since the beginning of the period. You plan to make a case for your belief that in the future, the turnover rate will remain in a range between five and six turns per quarter.

This position is supportable as long as you can prove to the lender that continuing expansion will be properly managed. That will require careful control over inventory, accounts receivable, and the amount of debt you carry.

To summarize your turnover analysis, you want to show not only the quarterly levels, but also a moving average for the 12 quarters in the study. You use the method described earlier: isolating the average to only those 12 periods in the study. Thus, the second month is the average of months one and two, and the last month is the average of all 12 periods.

TABLE 10–1
Turnover in Working Capital

Quarter	Sales	Current Assets	Current Liabilities	Turns
1	$385,000	$ 96,000	$37,000	6.5
2	407,000	104,000	44,000	6.8
3	401,000	99,000	61,000	6.6
4	429,000	112,000	45,000	6.4
5	412,000	106,000	44,000	6.6
6	443,000	124,000	58,000	6.7
7	437,000	126,000	61,000	6.7
8	451,000	134,000	68,000	6.8
9	482,000	151,000	65,000	5.6
10	516,000	142,000	59,000	6.2
11	489,000	154,000	62,000	5.3
12	507,000	162,000	72,000	5.6

The purpose of including the average is to demonstrate the overall consistency of cash flow control and also to equate the trend with growth in the volume of sales. The moving average of turnover in working capital is shown in Table 10–2.

Even though the month-to-month turnover shows a decline in the latest year, the moving average shows an overall consistency. This is desirable as it indicates steady management over cash flow, even while sales volume is rising. Your projection of future turnover will be made at a lower rate than the moving average; however, the analysis showing both monthly and moving average totals will help the lender to see a dependable history and will also support your future projections. An analysis in graph form is shown in Figure 10–1.

DEBT/EQUITY ANALYSIS

A second form of trend analysis that will be helpful as part of your business plan is a summary of trends in debt and equity. This ratio compares total liabilities (your business debts) to tangible net worth (net worth less any intangible assets). The resulting percentage is the portion of total capitalization represented by debt.

If a business borrows excessively, debt will eventually overtake equity, and the interest expenses will erode profits. This curtails your ability to increase profits in the future. As the level of debt rises, cash flow will suffer as well.

Example: You apply for a loan and include an analysis of the debt/

TABLE 10–2
Moving Average Turnover in Working Capital

Quarter	Moving Average	Quarter	Moving Average
1	6.5	7	6.6
2	6.7	8	6.6
3	6.6	9	6.5
4	6.6	10	6.5
5	6.6	11	6.4
6	6.6	12	6.3

FIGURE 10–1
Analysis: Turnover in Working Capital

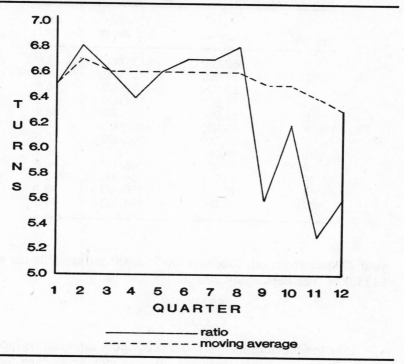

equity relationship. The trend appears to be moving toward increasing debt over time. However, you have also established a policy to keep debt levels at or below 60 percent of total equity for the next five years and to reduce the level to below 50 percent after that.

Even though debts have grown over the last three years and you now want to borrow more money, you can use the debt/equity analysis to prove that you have a plan for keeping a ceiling on the relative level. This will be an important point to raise as part of your plan. The lender will be interested in seeing exactly how you plan to increase profits while holding down debt. If you are able to make a strong case for achieving this, it will back up your marketing plan.

The calculation of the debt/equity ratio involves dividing total liabilities by tangible net worth. For example, during the first quarter of

TABLE 10–3
Debt/Equity Ratio

Quarter	Total Liabilities	Tangible Net Worth	Ratio (%)
1	$52,000	$135,000	38.5
2	57,000	137,000	41.6
3	69,000	149,000	46.3
4	57,000	138,000	41.3
5	54,000	141,000	38.3
6	71,000	150,000	47.3
7	75,000	153,000	49.0
8	84,000	161,000	52.2
9	82,000	166,000	49.4
10	71,000	154,000	46.1
11	75,000	156,000	48.1
12	85,000	164,000	51.8

your 12-quarter period, liabilities are $52,000 and tangible net worth is $135,000. The debt/equity ratio is

$$\frac{\$52,000}{\$135,000} = 38.5\%$$

Like the previous analysis, the debt/equity ratio can be reported in quarter-by-quarter percentages as well as in moving average form. The nonaveraged report can be shown on a line graph or a bar graph. The bar graph will enable you to show relative positions of debt and equity that make up total capitalization.

A summary of financial information for the 12 quarters is shown in Table 10–3. A bar graph of the debt/equity analysis is shown in Figure 10–2.

Like all ratios, the value of the debt/equity ratio is limited when reviewed in isolation. The outcome of the ratio itself can be distorted; thus, a long-term consistency must be established and should be reported on a moving average.

An example of the way that this ratio can be distorted: In the last quarter, the ratio is reported as 51.8 percent. It would make a better impression on the lender if this was lower. This, before the month is closed out, the owner uses $10,000 of available cash to pay off some current liabilities. With this modification, liabilities are reduced to $75,000 and the last quarter's debt/equity ratio is changed to

$$\frac{\$75,000}{\$164,000} = 45.7\%$$

A careful review of the books would reveal this form of distortion, and a declining trend could not be hidden forever. The point, however, is that what could appear as a fair representation of fact could be distorted by timing of payments.

A lender will certainly be aware of this problem and of the potential for misrepresentation. That is why it is important to explain the methods you use to develop trend analysis and to report trends over a three-year period using the moving average in addition to the quarterly summaries.

The moving average, computed using only the 12 periods in the study, produces these ratios is shown in Table 10–4. A graph of the moving average trend is shown in Figure 10–3. In this instance, both debt

FIGURE 10–2
Analysis: Debt/Equity Trend

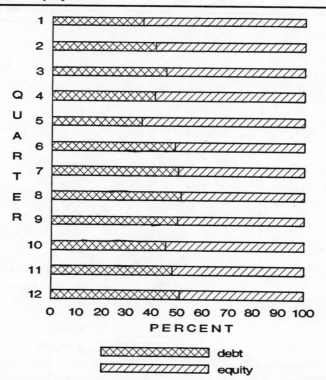

TABLE 10–4
Moving Average Debt/Equity Ratio

Quarter	Moving Average (%)	Quarter	Moving Average (%)
1	38.5	7	43.2
2	40.1	8	44.3
3	42.1	9	44.9
4	41.9	10	45.0
5	41.2	11	45.3
6	42.2	12	45.8

FIGURE 10–3
Moving Average: Debt/Equity Ratio

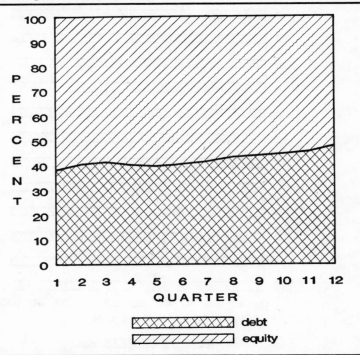

and equity portions of 100 percent of total capitalization can be seen at a glance.

A detailed business plan for borrowed money, including several examples of trend analysis and related comments, is given in Appendix A. In addition to plans for borrowing money, you might want to attract investment capital from a new buyer, a partner or new shareholder, or from a venture capital company. In any of these cases, the marketing assumptions and direction your business takes will contain the same form of information, but the emphasis will be different. The next chapter begins a discussion of equity from the investor's point of view.

CHAPTER 11

EQUITY: THE INVESTOR'S PERSPECTIVE

When a man says money can
do anything, that settles
it: he hasn't any.
—*Edgar Watson Howe*

Just as lenders perceive risk differently than you do, a potential equity investor—whether a company or an individual—must evaluate your business from a point of view and with different priorities than the owner. The choice of investing in your business will be compared to other investments.

This chapter describes the decision to become an equity investor, from the point of view of the person with the money. You will gain insight by understanding how the investor approaches the decision. That insight will help you to better prepare for your presentation, what points to emphasize, and how to address the investor's concerns and risks.

THE INVESTOR'S CHOICES

An investor has a number of choices of where to invest available money. We will begin with the assumption that the investor wants to put his or her money into a business in some way. In other words, they have decided to not buy real estate, rare art, or bonds. They believe the greatest potential for a high return on investment is by purchasing an equity interest in a business. With that assumption in mind, it is important to realize that the investor has a number of choices:

1. **Direct investment.** The investor may purchase part ownership in your operation without becoming involved in its management.

The silent partner will expect to be repaid at a profit at some point in the future. Invariably, the latest possible date for liquidation of the investor's equity position must be known.

2. **Active partnership.** Another alternative is to purchase a share of equity in your business and become part of the management team. The active partner will expect to be compensated for his or her time, just as an owner or employee takes a draw or salary. Thus, even with an infusion of capital, cash flow will be affected when a new owner is on the scene.

3. **Complete buy-out.** Someone interested in investing money in your business might not be satisfied with partial ownership. They might want to buy the whole oepration. In that case, you must consider whether you want to give up control of the operation you have built up. The sale transaction is certainly less complicated than a partnership in any form; but it raises other questions. For example, what will you do next? After risking your time and capital and putting yourself on the line and then succeeding in your own business, are you willing to become an employee or to start over with yet another new business?

4. **Buy a franchise.** The investor might also consider purchasing franchise rights. If the franchise is a well-established organization, this certainly eliminates an element of risk of concern to the investor. However, it is also an expensive way to go into business.

5. **Purchase stock.** An equity investor also has the choice of buying stock in a corporation. Investing in the stock market or in a small, unlisted company might yield a fast return or gradual increases in value over time. It also contains a significant element of risk. Many investors oriented toward venture control will be less attracted to the passive ownership of shares and are more interested in putting their money into a smaller operation with the greatest potential for growth.

6. **Buy limited partnership units.** Those investors who do not mind taking a passive role can also purchase units in private or public limited partnerships. However, depending on the experience of the partnership's management, this is a risky approach. In addition, passive loss limitations under federal tax law have removed many of the past attractions—primarily tax benefits—in this method of investing.

7. **Lend money with equity options.** One way to invest that combines equity with debt is to make a loan to the business owner. The contract includes provisions for equity options. For example, in the event that the owner does not make a scheduled repayment of the loan, the lender acquires a portion of equity. This may be progressive, so that after several repayments are missed the lender owns more than 50 percent. At that point, there's no guarantee that you will have any control—or even a job.

8. **Start a new business.** The individual with money to invest might decide to start a new business. However, many will prefer to pay a premium for a going concern, in which the previous owner has already overcome the common start-up hurdles, market identification, and investment in inventory and fixed assets. In addition, an investor will not necessarily be an expert in a business that offers the potential for future equity growth. A wise investor will also know his or her own limitations in the management of an operation. That is why the equity partner often needs you as much as you need them.

Individuals and companies with money to invest have a number of choices, any of which can affect the way that you will be able to raise capital you need. Before approaching a source for equity capital, be sure that you know exactly what type of arrangement the other person has in mind. Also be aware that the alternative to raising equity capital that you would find most desirable will be viewed with competing ideas in mind. In some instances, your task will be to convince an investor that putting their money in your business is the most sensible choice and that the potential for the greatest profit will be found by investing the money with you.

THE INVESTOR'S DECISION

The investor will look at every aspect of your business with a series of questions in mind. First is the value of the product or service you offer: What is the market demand, competition, and growth potential? Another issue is financial strength. Few investors will be willing to bail out an operation that is losing money or experiencing cash flow problems. Finally, the investor will be very interested in the owner. What management abilities do you possess? How does your talent affect the future potential for profits?

The investor's evaluation must begin with a selection of the way to put money into a business. They must answer these questions:

1. **Should I buy into a business or start a new one?** A potential partner could become a competitor, if an evaluation of your business is not compelling enough to make that the best choice. If an investor believes he or she could do better than you, why go into a situation that you will manage? To succeed in attracting venture capital or partnership interests, be aware of this consideration. Be prepared to show that you are a capable, essential manager and that you are the best resource of the operation.

2. **How do investment risks compare to start-up risks?** Investors might prefer to buy interests over starting their own operation, primarily because there is less risk involved. You have already proven that the idea works. Now the money person might want to share your profits by financing growth. That is proper and valuable to both sides, as long as you are willing to give up part ownership.

3. **How long will it take to generate a positive cash flow?** This question applies whether the investor buys into your business or starts a new enterprise. If the investor gives you the money, when will you be able to repay it, if at all? Can you agree on a maximum length of time after which the partner's interests will be bought out?

   A going concern is already generating cash flow, or so we must assume. Starting a new business, it might take several months to build to the point where costs and expenses are covered by income. The investor might not be willing to put in the time and work to manage a business every day and might not be able to afford financing start-up costs *and* months of negative cash flow. If you are willing to supply the labor and talent, the investor might prefer to pay the cost of acquiring a share of the going concern.

4. **Am I capable of organizing a business?** Organization is another point to consider. The details of identifying a market, finding a location, hiring employees, advertising, merchandising, and all of the other management skills required to create a successful

business might overwhelm the investor. It is much easier to provide the capital and let someone else run the day-to-day operation.

These preliminary questions may well lead a number of would-be entrepreneurs to the decision to invest in your business. It is one thing to take the risks involved with starting a business, which requires a good dose of management ability. However, someone who has money to invest might not be willing to put in the time to assume the risks of starting from scratch.

THE INVESTOR'S EVALUATION

Once the investor has eliminated the idea of starting a new business, the next step is to find a going concern and decide whether or not to make a direct investment. That is where your management ability becomes an issue, and when the financial and market factors affecting future profits must be evaluated.

An investor will probably begin the evaluation by reviewing the financial strength of your company. Although this is only one of many points to consider, it is a good place to start, because a number of companies will be eliminated rather quickly. If the investor applies a minimum standard of financial strength, profits, cash flow, and growth potential, a financial review is largely a process of elimination.

In many respects, the investor's evaluation and decision is similar to the steps you took when you first thought about going into your own business. You needed to determine whether or not you would cover costs and expenses, achieve growth, remain independent and in control, and, ultimately, profit from the hard work you would have to put into your new enterprise. For the investor, the same questions must be asked, but the hard work you invested is replaced with money.

Some of the financial questions an equity partner will need answered are

1. What is the history of profits and cash flow?
2. How will the market expand in the future?
3. What are the company's current debts?
4. Who are the current owners, and what special skills or talents do they bring to the operation?

5. In what areas has this operation experienced problems in the past?
6. How will more capital increase potential for future profits, to what degree, and in what time frame?
7. What target range of return can I expect to make on my investment? How will it be paid and when?
8. Why will a new partner improve potential to a greater degree than borrowing money? Has the owner applied for a loan, and if so, was the application turned down?
9. Does the owner have a current business plan, and does it include provisions for expansion with new equity capital?
10. What contingency plans has the owner devised in the event the goals of the plan are not realized?

The list of additional general questions could be endless, and each potential investor will also be concerned with details. In addition to financial issues, the investor will need to study the market. What customers are served? How wide a base is there in the existing market? What new markets does the owner intend to go after?

Financial and marketing concerns are separate. On the one hand, the investor needs to develop a thorough understanding of the financial strengths and weaknesses of the business—existing debts, capital assets, sales and profits, and cash flow. On the other hand, the investor must determine how much of a market exists for the product or service, both now and in the future. This includes a study of the competition, likely maximum growth in existing markets, new market potential, and the owner's expansion plans.

Besides financial and marketing questions, the investor must study the third—and perhaps the most important—question. That concerns your management skills. Have you exercised sound principles of management? Have you demonstrated your ability to control costs and expenses, to build a market up to a profitable level, manage cash flow, and plan for the future? Have you hired capable employees? Have you purchased the right equipment, created internal control systems, and brought leadership skills to the organization?

The issue of your management ability should not be overlooked. In preparation for a venture capital or partnership presentation, great emphasis is placed on financial information and, to some degree, on the potential for new markets. In many cases, little if anything is brought up about the owner's ability to manage a growing business. In the mind of the partner-to-be, this could be a critical issue and one that often remains unspoken. Even a demonstrated talent for creating and managing a small business does not always establish that you are qualified to do as well when the stakes are higher.

Example: The founder of a clothing mail-order company started the operation six years ago. He has built the business up from nothing and today publishes four catalogs per year. Revenues are about $700,000 per year. The potential is there to triple gross income, if the proper advertising techniques are used, automated mailing and tracking systems put into place, and staff hired to run the operation.

Everything looks positive. It is obvious to the would-be partner that the founder has succeeded to this point. However, it also appears that he is at his limit. There is no proof that the founder could manage a national mail-order operation at a larger scale.

In a situation like this, how can you prove that you possess the skill to lead a company from small to medium size or from medium to large? Follow these guidelines:

1. **Present a farsighted business plan.** Demonstrating the ability to look far into the future is a good beginning to showing management skill. The vision must be there, accompanied with a realistic road map for achieving well-stated goals. The marketing and expansion plan must be structured with financial considerations in mind. Cash flow, the purchase of needed assets, creation of staff, facilities, inventory, and internal systems must all be taken into consideration as the premise of an expansion plan.

2. **Equate past experience with future growth.** If you have had experience in managing a company or even a division or department, mention that background information in your business plan. All experience helps establish your credentials to manage. The investor takes a risk in financing your expansion and must be aware of the negative consequences if you will end up in over your head. You must give the investor good reasons to assume you are capable of running a larger show.

3. **Anticipate resources you will need.** As part of your plan, include the need for skilled employees. Incorporate the recruitment factor into your expansion ideas, and never assume that you can continue running the whole operation on your own. If current

employees will fill future executive roles in your company, describe their skills, background, and leadership qualities.

4. **Aim for a specific goal and deadline.** From the investor's point of view, the decision to put money in must be finite. A future date must be identified at which interests will be bought out or the enterprise will be liquidated. This might conflict with your ideas, which might include continuing to operate indefinitely. Whether you plan to finance a buyout of the investor's interests or not, include in your plan a provision and deadline for repayment.

5. **Emphasize the importance of management.** Capable and talented business owners are keenly aware of the importance of management. In comparison, less talented leaders are often completely unaware of the application of those skills or even that management plays a part in success. Make management a central theme in your plan and proposal.

These guidelines are summarized in Figure 11–1.

From the investor's point of view, these points address areas of risk. The investor is aware of these issues and must be assured that you offer

FIGURE 11–1
Guidelines: Establishing Management Skill

1. Present a farsighted business plan.

2. Equate past experience with future growth.

3. Anticipate resources you will need.

4. Aim for a specific goal and deadline.

5. Emphasize the importance of management.

the attributes that will lead to success, not only of the operation, but also of the investment. These must include financial, marketing, and management attributes that minimize risks and point toward the greatest potential for future profits.

COMPETING WITH PASSIVE INVESTMENTS

Considering the number and variety of risks—from the investor's point of view—it might seem hazardous to place available money in even the most successful operation. The investor must believe that the potential is there for better than average future equity growth in order to make a decision in your favor.

Although the investor has a wide range of choices, it comes down to two: buying a portion of an existing business or assuming a passive position in some other investment format. The most popular and obvious way to do that is by buying stocks.

There is an element of investment risk involved with the stock market, just as there is with investing in a business. A relatively small investor has no direct control over an organization's future profitability or stock market value. The difference is one of control and the owner's personality.

Control is an attractive feature to the investor. If you are able to prove that by your individual efforts and skills you will be able to create future profits, the investor then has a compelling argument in favor of investing in your company. In comparison, investing in a publicly traded company gives the individual no real control at all. That company is run by a board of directors, overseeing a management group, and no one investor can exert direct control without a huge investment in stock.

Personality is equally as important, if not more so. If two or more likely investments have equal financial strength and market potential, the decision favoring one over another will be made on the basis of the owner's abilities, management skills, and personal traits. Even the best financial and marketing information cannot match the importance of the potential investor's perception of the owner's personality and ability to continue managing the operation.

If the investor meets with you in person, a degree of the decision will be made intuitively, assuming that the financial and marketing information meets the investor's criteria. Like all business decisions, the intuitive sense of what is right will play an important part in the final decision.

This is not as applicable when equity money comes from an institution. A venture capital company, like a bank or other lender, will limit its review to risk evaluation, based on financial and marketing facts in front of them. The owner's management skills will play a part in deciding whether or not to take the risk. But even that is not as intuitive as the decision made by an individual in a face-to-face meeting with the owner.

The intangible sense of a "good" or "bad" risk is a very real part of the decision the individual investor will make. The same rule applies when the investor chooses shares of stock. The fundamental or technical indicators must meet minimum criteria; however, many investors who use the most advanced systems for evaluation will often decide to buy or not to buy based on whether or not they "like" the company.

You will compete with passive investment choices such as buying shares of stock. The investor, we must remember, is probably attracted to the control and personality issues and, accordingly, has already decided against merely buying shares and waiting for them to increase in value. The investor who ends up buying an equity interest in your business is probably willing to take greater risks than the stock market investor, because they also recognize that the future return on that investment will be greater as well.

BUSINESS PLAN ANALYSIS

When an investor considers buying into a company, the business plan will play an important part, even if it involves eliminating unsuitable candidates. The most important first test is

> Does a business plan exist?

Most business owners will agree that there is little chance of convincing an investor to risk money if no business plan has been prepared. Yet, just as many business owners approach a lender with no preparation at all, some will attempt to attract equity capital with no written plan.

An investor who is able to study the plans of several businesses has the preliminary means for picking an interesting prospect. Just as a passive investor must have a prospectus, annual report, research paper, or at least a broker recommendation, an equity partner must be provided with the basic facts to begin the process of risk evaluation.

A second test to be aware of is

Does the business plan clearly explain where the company is going?

A lot of detail might go into the creation of a document that summarizes historical information, presents budgets and forecasts, studies trends in cash flow and profits, and discusses markets at length. However, the essential element of the future may be ignored completely. Your plan *must* exist to prove that you have a direction and clear goal and that you, as the owner, are conscious of that goal. Once the goal is expressed realistically, you are on the way to completing it. From the investor's point of view, this is an essential and guiding premise of the planning process.

Are the plan's assumptions both realistic and clearly expressed?

The danger in any form of planning is that flawed assumptions will lead to flawed and overly optimistic future growth forecasts. Remember that no substantial increase in sales or profits can be sustained indefinitely, at the same rate from one year to the next. As part of your plan, address the issue of how realistic an assumption base you use. Test and prove assumptions with basic financial standards, and avoid overly optimistic growth projections in your plan.

Has the owner shown how stated goals will be achieved within the defined market and capital limits?

It is one thing to state a goal and time limit as part of your plan and another to demonstrate how you will get there. A plan is not complete until the specific steps are identified. You must show that the plan is realistic and that your goals will be reached through a series of actions and decisions—limited by assumptions and controlled by the deadlines and other restraints at work in your operating environment.

One point often overlooked in the development of a plan is that any specific market must be limited. Only so much growth can be achieved over time, given geographic, competitive, and demand factors. Once the saturation point is reached, one of three things must happen. First, growth will stop. Second, markets or territories must be extended. Third, the company must diversify its product or service lines.

Any expansion plan, both in degree and timing, is also limited by capitalization. You cannot afford to expand beyond what you can afford to support financially, even with a significant infusion of capital. A projection of timing and rate for expansion must be restricted to the limited capital resources at your disposal. It also helps to compare likely growth under the current capital structure and with the addition of equity capital. That should demonstrate the degree of additional profit potential the investor can create by making the decision to buy an equity share of your company.

If you analyze your plan realistically, the assumptions and direction will be obvious, compelling, and convincing to the potential investor. Many plans fail to convince an objective reader, because assumptions are either excluded or the results are obviously inflated beyond what is likely to occur. The most convincing plan is one that demonstrates patience and respects a methodical and gradual approach to expansion and growth.

The investor comes to a meeting with a number of risks in mind. These must be addressed in order for the decision to be made. At the same time, you have a different point of view concerning equity capital. That is the topic of the next chapter.

CHAPTER 12

EQUITY: YOUR PERSPECTIVE

> The shortest distance between two
> points is under construction.
> —*Noelie Alito*

The range of possible equity sources is wide. You may approach an individual with a partnership in mind, attempt to sell stock to a number of individuals, or approach a venture capital company. In any case, your preparation and approach will determine whether or not the individual or company will be willing to invest in your future.

The majority of new businesses require capital just to start out. That is not limited to outside investors or lenders, but also includes the use of home equity or savings, loans or gifts from relatives, and loans of various amounts and terms from other lenders. Equity capital raised beyond the start-up must be defined in one of several groups:

1. **Permanent partnership capital.** Raising capital by taking in a partner is a way of replacing one organization with another. A sole proprietorship grows to a point where further expansion is not possible alone. At that juncture, the decision must be made to stop growing or to continue to expand with outside help.

   A partner may be silent or uninvolved in the daily operation of the business. In that case, the method of operation will not change, but the capital base will be greater. At some point in the future, the silent partner will have to be repaid. In addition, silent partners may impose reporting standards on the original owner or even restrict the use of capital with capital expenditure and expense spending oversight.

   A partner may also be active. In addition to bringing money to the operation, the new partner is actively involved in one or more aspects of the business. This might prove to be the most worthwhile form of partnership. Not only is the investor involved in creating profits, but probably brings a talent to the operation that you cannot provide.

2. **Venture capital.** Capital can be raised through an organization whose primary function is acquiring interests in emerging companies. An emphasis among venture capital companies is seen in technology-based firms and, as a general range, will invest $500,000 or more. The range varies from one company to another. However, raising capital through a venture capital source is generally not as possible for a smaller company than it is for one that is positioned to expand in a big way. With that in mind, venture capital is not for everyone.

3. **Limited partnerships.** Private placement partnerships are a means for raising capital through a management group. They are similar to public stock offerings, but use a partnership form rather than the corporate form. By holding down the amount of capital to be raised or by offering units in the partnership in one state only, organizers of private partnerships can escape the complicated regulations for registering an investment with the Securities and Exchange Commission (SEC).

   Private placements require the preparation of a disclosure statement (called the "offering memorandum"), which contains much of the same information found in a prospectus. Units can be marketed through an investment banker or a securities firm, but the fee for that service could be as high as 10 to 15 percent of the total amount raised. In addition, putting together a private placement will require the help of an attorney who specializes in that field.

   In the past, research and development partnerships were very popular, largely for the tax benefits investors received for making an investment. With the series of tax reform bills passed between 1980 and 1986, the tax benefits of investing in limited partnerships have been virtually eliminated. Thus, today's program must contain specific economic advantages in order for investors to benefit in the long run.

4. **Public offerings.** Many people who start their own business assume that within a few years, they will incorporate and sell shares to the public. As a new enterprise, this is not only an

unlikely way to raise money, it is also unlikely to happen at all or at least until your business has expanded significantly above the usual start-up level.

Organizing a public offering is a complex, costly, and time-consuming experience. A public company must report financial information to regulatory agencies, so that what you now consider private information becomes very public to everyone, including both your stockholders and your competitors.

THE GENERAL PARTNERSHIP OPTION

Any discussion of general partnerships must begin with the observation that this method of raising capital is the most expensive *and* the most risky way to go. There are times and situations when a partnership makes perfect sense. Pursuing this alternative might not be necessary in order to achieve your expansion plans.

When does a partnership make sense? If your requirements are strictly to raise cash for the immediate future, you will probably do better to retain 100 percent of your equity and plan to grow with debt—that is, assuming that you can generate adequate cash from operations to afford repayments of a loan. With debt, you will eventually achieve your goals and repay a loan while still staying in total control of your company. That also means that you will earn 100 percent of your future profits.

A partnership is necessary in the following cases:

1. **You cannot raise the money you need in any other way.** If you have financial strength and are earning profits, chances are you will be able to find a source for debt financing. However, in some cases, a business might have the potential for growth but is simply unable to achieve it without additional funds. At the same time, the apparent risks make lenders shy away from taking a chance.

2. **A partner brings something to the business in addition to the money.** When a business owner needs to raise money, it is often difficult to look beyond that immediate concern. The need is urgent and immediate, and any thoughts of long-term growth—five to ten years out—give way to the problems visible today. However, going into a partnership commits you and your

future profits to a shared arrangement that could be expensive to dissolve. A valuable partner is one who adds a nonfinancial element to your operation.

Example: You have a flair for marketing your product and have achieved tremendous expansion over the first three years in business. But today, you are losing money because you cannot manage an expanding administrative staff. You have tried hiring capable managers, but with no lasting success. A partner with solid accounting and administrative experience could take charge of these duties and help the operation to continue to grow. To expand successfully beyond today's level, you seek a partner who can bring those attributes to the operation.

3. **The personal relationship between the partners is a successful one.** Conflict between business owners will prove to be the most disruptive element in a partnership. It accounts for a large percentage of failures. A partnership is the business version of a marriage. If both partners will be active in running the business, you must make sure that you know the other person, that areas of responsibility are well-defined, and that everyone knows who makes the final decisions. Defining the relationship is essential if a partnership is to succeed.

4. **The degree of involvement in the business is clearly defined ahead of time.** Even a silent partner—who puts up the money but is not involved in the operation directly—might not be content to stay away from the business. Remember that once you give up a portion of your equity, you are no longer free to make decisions or to take risks without accounting to your investors.

Example: The owner of a small software manufacturing company gave up 25 percent of her equity to a silent partner. She believed that in the immediate future, the partner would allow her to run the operation as she had been doing all along. However, at the end of the first quarter, when financial statements were sent to the partner, many expenses were questioned, including business travel and subscriptions. The original owner discovered that owning a majority of the equity does not mean the minority owner cannot ask questions or criticize decisions or even to insist on accountability, controls, and preapproval of expenditures.

5. **You do not become a de facto employee.** However an equity deal is structured, it is important to ensure that you do, indeed,

remain an owner. If the partner ends up with more than 50 percent of equity or if that partner gains rights over your actions, you could find yourself working for someone else instead of for yourself.

JUDGING THE POTENTIAL PARTNER

When looking for equity money, remember that the value lies in your business. If someone is willing to take the risks of investing, they will see a potential for future profits. With that in mind, you can afford to assume a critical view. Screen partners in much the same way that a lender or investor will screen you.

It is a mistake to take the view that the partner will ultimately make the decision. If you want the equity so desperately that you will enter a partnership on their terms without checking into the partner's background and personal history, then you risk entering a relationship that could end up forcing you out of the business. This could occur due to legal conflicts, personality clashes, or a partner's fear when returns are not realized quickly enough.

Apply these tests to every potential partner:

1. **Check previous investment history.** Has the individual invested in any other businesses? If so, chances are that the he or she understands how businesses operate and knows that some operations will not emerge profitably for several years. An impatient partner can become demanding and disruptive and can interfere with the smooth running of your business.

   Look for a partner who understands how businesses are operated and managed. Preferably, find someone who is familiar with your type of business and who knows what profit margins to expect.

   Example: A restaurant owner wanted to expand to a second location and took on a 40 percent partner to finance the expansion. Even though the business plan estimated that the second location would not be profitable for the first year, the partner was nervous after the first three months. He hired an attorney and sued the restaurant owner. Although the owner was able to neutralize the attempted lawsuit, it was an expensive and disruptive experience.

2. **Speak with previous partners.** Will the potential partner refer you to other business owners with whom he or she has been in business? If not, that could be a danger signal. It might be that previous relationships have gone sour and that the investor is not in the game for growth, but to eventually take over and control operations, using capital to squeeze out the founder.

   Call or write to previous business partners and ask for the details. If they have had positive experiences, ask what elements they believe helped the partnership to succeed. Also ask for their observations about pitfalls to avoid.

3. **Get to know the partner on a personal level.** Remember that you are considering sharing your professional life with someone else. It is essential that you both follow the same business philosophy and that your goals are coordinated. For example, if you plan to remain in business for the rest of your life, but a partner wants to sell out at a big profit in two years or less, there is an obvious conflict in goals.

   You should also be familiar with a partner's life-style and personal habits. Successful partnerships may depend more on personalities than on financial arrangements. For example, if the other partner does not manage money well, has a drug or alcohol problem, gambles excessively, or has been married and divorced several times, you must be aware that these problems are expensive. Inevitably, the cost will probably come out of your business.

   Although personal habits, problems, and life-style might have nothing to do with a person's business ability, they will make a difference to your partnership. There is very little as destructive to your business as when a partner constantly needs more money. The more you know about your partner, the better. Remember, when you buy a horse, you do not make the decision based only on color. You must also check his teeth.

4. **Discuss future liquidation.** It is a mistake to form any partnership without talking about how the relationship will finally be resolved. The ideal partnership is one in which each partner intends to work full-time in the business for the indefinite future

and in which common interests and goals are completely shared. In some cases, the partner is strictly an investor and will want to take out future profits at some point—perhaps as quickly as possible and in such a way that continuing to operate will be impossible. You probably do not want to be forced into liquidation.

You must ensure that the new partner understands how long it will take to produce the profits he or she expects to realize. There is also the chance that the level of profits you estimate will not come to pass by that time limit. In fact, you cannot guarantee that the business will succeed at all.

Questions to be addressed include: Will you have the first right to buy out the partner? How will the actual amount of payment be determined—as a percentage of equity, based on sales or profits, or by some other method? What demand rights will the partner hold for payment? What happens in the event of disability or death, and will the partners need to buy insurance policies to protect against the consequences? How will disputes be settled—will you each hire an attorney, or can you agree to binding arbitration?

5. **Identify income requirements.** In cases where a new partner will be an active participant in the business, he or she will expect a draw or salary. This means that additional profits created by an infusion of capital must be adequate to support two income requirements rather than just one. In some instances, this will place a severe demand on cash flow as well as on overall profitability.

You will have to judge the proposed active partnership idea not only with an eye to long-term expansion, net worth, and profitability, but also in terms of what you can afford next month and next year. Both you and the partner must carefully define exactly how much money will be drawn or paid by way of salary—all within the restrictions of available cash flow. Future increases in owner salaries or draws must be determined and agreed to on some reasonable basis. The moment you take on a partner, you are no longer free to raise your own pay whenever you want and whenever the money is there. Also it will prove equally difficult to miss paying yourself when money is tight, as you might have done in the past. Your new partner, a minority owner, might not be as willing as you are to survive without a regular draw.

By raising these questions, considering how much your business life will change and judging the partner's response, you will gain a fair idea of whether or not the two of you will be able to reach a meeting of the minds. In many respects, both of your lives will change. You will give up many of the freedoms so important to you when you broke away from the responsibilities and restrictions of corporate life. In many respects, your new partner must also be willing to accept the changes and limitations of working with someone else.

If any major disagreements or misunderstandings are to arise, it is better to resolve them before signing the papers. It is much less expensive that way and will help both sides to avoid a costly mistake. Like the newlywed who must adjust to the toothpaste being squeezed in the middle, new partners must resolve differences ahead of time and will have to go through a period of adjustment.

DECIDING ON THE FORM OF ORGANIZATION

Besides your concern about the partner's level of interest, experience, and motives, you must also think about how a partnership will affect your income taxes. If you have been operating as a sole proprietorship, another form of organization might be more appropriate, depending on anticipated levels of profit; other income of either partner; and long-term plans for expansion, investment, and growth.

As a sole proprietor, you must file a federal schedule C (an income statement), and you are taxed on your annual net profit. In addition, you must file schedule 1040-SE (self-employment tax) to contribute to the social security system for your retirement income, disability, and health benefits.

Partners are also taxed on their proportionate share of net profits from self-employment, as well as self-employment taxes. Thus, if you pay yourself and your partner a salary, any additional profits will be taxed even on money that was not withdrawn. Another complication is that a partnership information return form 1065 must be filed once per year.

Forming a corporation might present a solution to many of the tax problems and reporting complications that partnerships face. However, like a partnership, the corporation will be taxed for profits each year, and the rate may be higher or lower than individual tax rates. The best method depends on each individual's tax status, other income, and current tax laws (which may also be modified in the future). Recordkeeping for corporations is more complted and formal than for proprietorships or partnerships, another point to be remembered in deciding how to form your venture.

One form of corporation worth considering is the S Corporation. By making the election to adopt this form, taxes are computed as though the organization was a partnership. Rather than paying a corporate tax, each owner is taxed on their portion of profits. This might be advantageous and, at the same time, provides each owner with protection not available to partners. For example, in the event of disability, personal liability, or other financial losses, an S Corporation stockholder will not be exposed to the other owner's debts, which could happen in a partnership.

To make the S Corporation election, you are restricted in the total number of shareholders you are allowed to have. All must be U.S. citizens, and the election must be agreed to by each one. Upon reversing the election, you are not allowed to revert to S Corporation status for a period of years.

The advice of an attorney is advisable whenever a partnership or other business venture is being discussed. A tax accountant should also be consulted to decide the best form of organization, with tax and reporting consequences in mind. If your state also assesses a state-level tax, that will also be an issue in deciding how to organize your new company.

DEVELOPING A COMMON VISION

If a partnership is to work out to everyone's benefit, you must be able to view your operation from the investor's point of view as well as your own. Certainly, whenever negotiations begin for any financial transaction, there are two sides and two points of view. The successful enterprise is one that starts out with both sides aiming for the same goals. What you might view as a certainty could be seen more skeptically by a would-be investor. To convince the investor that you have a solid operation geared to achieving long-term growth, follow these guidelines:

1. **Present a realistic business plan.** In preparing the business plan you will present to the investor—which is essential—take an

especially critical point of view toward your own projections. Anticipate doubts, raise them, and show how risks will be confronted and eliminated.

Document every assumption with the most solid facts available. If you project sales growth, explain where every dollar will come from—new markets, territories, products or services, or increased demand due to a rising population, growing affluence, or changing customer needs. Be specific. Never forecast income or profit expansion with an unexplained percentage increase. That is the least convincing form of projection and the most difficult to support. Unfortunately, the unsupported and generalized growth assumption is also the most common one reported in business plans.

Every part of your plan should be put together with the investor in mind. It is not enough to display a positive attitude and self-confidence in your plan. Set significant goals, but be prepared to examine them from the most critical point of view. Prove that your assumptions are reasonable and that your goals can be reached with diligent management and intelligent marketing.

2. **Identify the ideal equity arrangement.** In all discussions that could lead to a partnership agreement, venture capital investment, or other form of equity arrangement, specify what you want. If you are only willing to enter an agreement with an active partner, state that up front. If you want to stay in operational control and can only work with a silent partner, specify that as well. State the percentage of equity you are willing to give up. You will save a lot of time by eliminating ideas that others simply will not accept and by disclosing your limits at the beginning of the negotiating process.

As part of this definition, also specify what rate of growth you anticipate realizing with additional capital, when you expect a return on the investment to be paid out, and how you plan to finance liquidation of the equity position. If you do not plan to liquidate, explain how the equity partner will be compensated on an on-going basis.

3. **Do not overlook the nonfinancial benefits.** Some people want to invest money in certain types of industries or in companies that provide social benefits of one kind or another. If you are target-

ing this type of investor, be sure to address these issues as part of your proposal.

Example: One investor believes that specific areas of technology will lead to social innovations in the future, will supply new jobs, and will be the most profitable companies of the future. These are nonfinancial points; however, the investor responded most favorably to companies that emphasized the attributes she found appealing.

4. **Compare career and financial advantages.** If the would-be investor is interested only in the financial potential of placing equity in your business, that will define the type of relationship the investor is seeking. However, if the investor also wants to be an active, working partner, you should be sure to discuss the career opportunities both of you will have by working together.

   For example, an investor is considering placing equity money in your company and also wants to work with you on a full-time basis. Each of you possesses a particular talent and has experience that compliments what the other knows and does best. The emphasis in your negotiations should be on the career potential of working together, with the financial arrangements playing an important, but secondary role. Even if you will be able to come to financial terms, it is more important that your personal and career goals are coordinated, that both of you are heading in the same direction, and that you can both reach those goals by working together.

5. **Confront the cash flow issue.** The equity investor will expect to earn back their capital at some point in the future. Thus, you must develop a plan for buying out their interests, either with outside financing or by gradual repayment on a predetermined schedule. Anticipating this requirement and devising a schedule for satisfying it is essential to the success of your proposal and to addressing an important investor consideration.

   Even those equity partners who are not concerned with eventual liquidation of their interests will expect to receive dividends, salary, or draw—if not at once, then at least in the future, when profits begin to accrue within the company. You must plan for this disbursement and show that your plan has considered the investor's needs. Timing, amount, and affordability from operating cash flow must all be specified in your plan and budget.

Some small-business owners assume that the bigger the company, the less severe the cash flow problem will become. In reality, as companies grow, their need for cash grows as well. You should not expect growth to solve cash flow problems. Instead, expansion demands more diligent controls over cash. When an investor must be repaid in the future, that is just one more cash outlay for which you must plan carefully. You must be able to demonstrate your ability to anticipate and plan for that repayment—often in an environment where expenses are higher, margins are lower, and cash flow is a critical and daily issue for management.

COMPARING EQUITY AND DEBT

There may be compelling reasons to seek an equity partner instead of the more temporary and less expensive debt alternative. However, before accepting as inevitable the idea of giving up part ownership, compare the year-to-year costs of borrowing money and of raising additional equity.

One reason that some growing businesses look for a silent partner is from concern for short-term cash flow. For example, you may find a partner who is willing to advance a sum of equity capital and let it work for five years or more. In theory, you will be "left alone" during this period of time, and the investor will be paid off later.

In reality, a silent partner might not be all that silent. He or she may become impatient before the indicated time span expires or might want to exercise oversight or control over your management style and business decisions. The equity arrangement with a silent partner is usually not as free of trouble as the owner would like to believe. Even when a written contract states that you will retain full control over business decisions, you cannot automatically assume that a silent partner will leave you alone.

Bringing in an active partner will not free you from repayments, because that partner will expect to be paid each month. Be sure to compare the cost of paying another owner to the cost of repaying a loan that provides you with an equal amount of capital. You might conclude that debt is a less expensive alternative without the long-term equity sharing that is inevitable when another owner is brought into the picture.

An active partnership makes sense only when your combined efforts and talents magnify profit potential and cash flow substantially. This might be the case when two existing competitors join forces, for example, creating a single company that no longer needs to reduce profit margins to struggle for a limited market. The combined talent and effort of each side must be stronger than the sum of each of your efforts alone.

The comparison between debt and equity should take into account both the short-term and the long-term cash flow and profit issues. For example, if you are able to put together a deal calling for no repayments of equity interest for the first five years, that will free up your cash flow. This provides an obvious and immediate cash flow advantage, but it might also be shortsighted to look ahead only to the short term. In the long term, you must expect to provide a significant level of return to the equity partner. Thus, for short-term purposes, you might end up sharing a greater portion of future growth.

If, as an alternative, it is possible to structure debt so that loan repayments can be made from operating cash flow—while you still are able to achieve your expansion plans—then the long-term goals can be reached without having to give the lion's share to an equity partner.

The loan alternative might mean having to exercise greater patience. For example, if your growth plans will be restricted because you cannot borrow all that you would like today, you might need to reorganize your goals over a longer period of time. That could mean missing a growth opportunity that exists today; it could also mean that, in the long term, your profits will be higher and will remain 100 percent yours.

The decision must be made by each owner individually. There is no absolute answer for every condition, and your own personality and willingness to work with another owner will determine whether or not you should pursue the equity alternative. The next chapter tells where to find the equity money you will seek.

CHAPTER 13

EQUITY SOURCES

Never invest your money in
anything that eats or
needs repainting.
—*Billy Rose*

If there is a secret to successfully raising equity capital, it must be this:
Before applying to a company, make sure that it deals in the type of
investment you seek. The same is true when approaching individual
investors or potential partners.

There is no shortage of venture capital, according to Andrew J.
McWethy, executive vice president and general manager of Irving Capital Corporation. He reports that from the mid-1970s to the mid-1980s,
assets of venture capital companies grew from $2 billion to approximately
$12 billion.

The question is not whether or not money is available, but what
sources are best for your particular operation. This is determined by the
type of business, purpose of raising equity capital, growth potential,
and—perhaps most important—the specialization of a venture capital
source. Many venture capital companies distinguish their operations by
the type of business in which they will invest, geographic location of your
operation, volume of sales, or the amount of capital you need to raise.
Some prefer to arrange capitalization programs combining lending and
equity features. For example, some venture capital firms will loan money
to a business with provisions for acquiring stock—either in lieu of loan
repayments or as an option for the lender.

FINDING THE BEST SOURCE

A number of associations and networking sources are available for locating sources of equity capital. Because there are so many possible sources,
it might be a hit-or-miss approach to approach a venture capital com-

pany directly. Rather, using an association to narrow the field is a smart first step.

Geographic location of the venture capital company often plays an important role in determining whether or not you will get the money you need. Small Business Investment Companies (SBICs), for example, are the major providers of equity capital. Many prefer to invest in small companies operating in the same region in which they are located. The same may be true of venture capital companies affiliated with banks, insurance companies, brokerage firms, and other financial service companies.

In addition, before applying to a venture capital company, find out what requirements they apply to small businesses and what information they want to receive. For example, Continental Illinois Venture Corporation lists the elements they want to see in a business plan, including section titles and sequence. Thus, an applicant would be wise to arrange his or her plan in the sequence the company specifies. In their brochure, Continental recommends the following sections:

- The company.
- Funding history.
- Product lines.
- Research, development, engineering, and design.
- Operations.
- Management, directors, and organization.
- The market and competition.
- Financial summary.
- Legal considerations.
- Miscellaneous.

Even when your business plan does not follow the order recommended by the venture capital company or when it excludes some of the named sections, your plan should conform to the list specified. If a different company wants information in a different format, be prepared to reorganize your plan according to their specifications.

Picking the best source depends on what you are willing to give up. If you set limits on the amount of equity you are willing to exchange, be sure the guidelines of the venture capital company conform to your standards, or there is no point in wasting time pursuing that source.

A common method for raising equity among small corporations is through convertible debt or preferred stock. Many firms are willing to advance money through convertible notes or debentures. Although terminology will vary from one company to another, a note generally runs 10 years or less, whereas a debenture is a long-term, unsecured corporate debt.

Example: An equity capital company lends you $100,000 in the form of a debenture. This can be converted to 20 percent of your common stock at any time and at the option of the venture capital company. The two possible outcomes are

1. You will eventually be required to repay the debenture in full and with interest.
2. The venture capital company will exercise its option and exchange the debenture for equity in your corporation.

Another loan/equity combination involves an option to buy stock. Although this is not as popular as the convertible debenture, it might be proposed to you. Under this arrangement, you are required to pay interest only for a specified number of years and then principal and interest on a prearranged schedule. The lender has an option to buy stock at any time, up to a stated limit, often 30 to 40 percent or more.

Yet another alternative is to issue convertible preferred stock to the venture capital company. They have the right to convert to shares of common stock at any time, often gaining a controlling interest in your corporation.

Initial equity capital often is raised in the most widely understood manner. The venture capital company advances money in exchange for shares of common stock. The company might require as much as 35 to 40 percent of equity plus participation on the board of directors.

REFERRAL SOURCES

The following associations offer direct referrals to members, information regarding location of equity capital, or networking and advertising outlets.

National Venture Capital Association
1655 North Fort Myer Drive, NE, Suite 700
Arlington, VA 22209   703-528-4370

The NVCA includes over 200 member venture capital firms. Collectively, these organizations invest an estimated $3 billion per year in equity capital. A free membership directory is available.

Venture Capital Network
P.O. Box 882
Durham, NH 03824   603-743-3993

VCN is a not-for-profit corporation managed by the Center for Venture Research at the University of New Hampshire. It offers a computerized network to match entrepreneurs with high net worth individuals interested in investing money. Two brochures are available: *Dealing with Investors* and *Venture Capital Network* (this includes an application and information regarding fees).

National Association of Small Business
Investment Companies (NASBIC)
1156 15th Street, NW, Suite 1101
Washington, DC 20005   202-833-8230

This organization's membership includes approximately 400 SBICs and Minority Enterprise Small Business Investment Companies (MESBICs), which supply nine-tenths of the sources for equity capital. These companies offer loans and equity investments, but specify investment policies and guidelines by amount, industry, and region. Write for a current membership directory (which includes each company's guidelines) and information about NASBIC-sponsored executive training seminars.

American Association of Minority Enterprise
Small Business Investment Companies
915 15th Street, NW, Suite 700
Washington, DC 20005   202-347-8600

This organization specializes in referrals to equity capital sources and loans to business owners and entrepreneurs classified as socially or economically disadvantaged. Write for additional information.

Association of Venture Founders
521 Fifth Avenue, 15th Floor
New York, NY 10175   212-682-7373

This association provides educational networking services for its members and publishes *Venture Magazine*.

Center for Entrepreneurial Management
83 Spring Street
New York, NY 10012   212-925-7304

This organization offers educational materials, referrals, and guidelines for obtaining venture capital and publishes a newsletter, *The Entrepreneurial Manager*.

Institute of Certified Business Counselors
3301 Vincent Road
Pleasant Hill, CA 94523   415-945-8440

This is an association whose members are professional brokers in the buying and selling of businesses. The institute may provide referrals to members.

In addition to associations, several organizations affiliated with banks, insurance companies, brokerage firms, and other financial service organizations offer venture capital to small businesses. Write or call for brochures and guidelines for qualifying for venture capital investments. These organizations include

Allstate Venture Capital Division
Allstate Plaza North E-2
Northbrook, IL 60062   312-402-5681

BancBoston Ventures Inc.
100 Federal Street 01-31-08
Boston, MA 02110   617-434-2442

Bankamerica Ventures, Inc.
555 California Street
12th Floor, Department 3908
San Francisco, CA 94104   415-622-2230

William Blair Venture Partners
135 South LaSalle Street
Chicago, IL 60603   312-853-8250

BT Capital Corporation
280 Park Avenue, 9W
New York, NY 10015   212-850-1920

Chase Manhattan Capital Corporation
One Chase Manhattan Plaza, 13th Floor
New York, NY 10081   212-552-6275

Chemical Venture Partners
277 Park Avenue, 11th Floor
New York, NY 10172   212-310-4949

Citicorp Venture Capital, Ltd.
Citicorp Center
153 East 53rd Street
New York, NY 10043   212-559-1127

Continental Illinois Venture Corporation
231 South LaSalle Street
Chicago, IL 60697   312-828-8021

First Boston Corporation
12 East 49th Street
New York, NY 10017   212-909-4588

Hambrecht & Quist Inc.
235 Montgomery Street
San Francisco, CA 94104   415-576-3300

Hancock Venture Partners
One Financial Center, 39th Floor
Boston, MA 02111   617-350-4002

Irving Capital Corporation
1290 Avenue of the Americas
New York, NY 10104   212-408-4800

The Lambda Funds/Drexel Burnham Lambert
55 Broad Street, 15th Floor
New York, NY 10004   212-363-4002

Montgomery Securities
600 Montgomery Street
San Francisco, CA 94111   415-627-2000

Morgan Stanley Venture Partners L.P.
1251 Avenue of the Americas
New York, NY 10020   212-703-8485

Ampersand Ventures
(Painewebber Venture Management Company)
55 William Street, Suite 240
Wellesley, MA 02181   617-239-0700

Piper Jaffray Ventures, Inc.
Piper Jaffrey Tower
222 South 9th Street
Minneapolis, MN 55440   612-342-6310

Prudential-Bache Capital Partners
One Seaport Plaza, 30th Floor
New York, NY 10292   212-214-5420

Republic Venture Group, Inc.
325 North St. Paul Street
Tower II, Suite 2820
Dallas, TX 75201   214-922-3500

Robertson, Coleman & Stephens
One Embarcadero Center, Suite 3100
San Francisco, CA 94111   415-781-9700

Rothschild Ventures Inc.
One Rockefeller Plaza
New York, NY 10020   212-757-6000

Salomon Brothers Venture Capital
Two New York Plaza
New York, NY 10004   212-747-7900

Sears Investment Management Company
Xerox Center
55 West Monroe Street, 32nd Floor
Chicago, IL 60603   312-875-0463

Security Pacific Capital Corporation
650 Town Center Drive, 17th Floor
Costa Mesa, CA 92626   714-556-1964

Sierra Ventures
3000 Sand Hill Road
Building 1, Suite 280
Menlo Park, CA 94025   415-854-1000

Weiss, Peck & Greer Venture Partners, L.P.
555 California Street, Suite 4760
San Francisco, CA 94104   415-622-6864

INCORPORATING YOUR BUSINESS

If your small business is operated currently as a sole proprietorship or
partnership, you should plan to incorporate before contacting a venture
capital organization. There are several reasons for taking this step:

1. **Stock purchase.** Invariably, the venture capital source will be interested in acquiring corporate stock, rather than a partnership interest. Stock is easily transferred from one owner to another without disrupting operations and the complications that can arise in the event of an original owner's death, disability, or ill health.

2. **Continuous operations.** When the ownership structure of a corporation changes, stock is transferred from one owner to another, but the operation continues without any changes. However, when you take on a new partner who invests money (or when an existing partner leaves), the organization must be dissolved and replaced by another. The same is true in the event of an owner's death. The company must be dissolved.

3. **Reporting convenience.** Requirements for partnership tax reporting are complex when compared to corporate requirements. The partnership must file an information return, form 1065; in addition, each partner receives a schedule K-1 showing proportionate profit or loss, capital gains, and other tax information. The partners then include the information on their own returns.

4. **Formality.** With a board of directors overseeing operations, the corporate form is likely to provide a more formal documentation flow than other organizational forms. This will be desirable in the eyes of a venture capital company. The investor may also want a seat on the board. That will be possible only if your business has been incorporated.

5. **Liability protection.** The corporate shell protects owners in several ways. First, in the event the company is named as defendant in a lawsuit, it is difficult (but not impossible) to also name individuals in a suit. Perhaps more significantly, each partner in a partnership may incur risk for the personal liabilities of other partners. In the event of death, ill health, disability, or a lawsuit, you could find yourself responsible for your partner's debts. This is an undesirable risk from your point of view. From the venture capital company's side, it is an unacceptable risk.

6. **Insurance.** The corporate form protects your equity in a company. Your financial risk, in most instances, is limited to the value of your stock. With a partnership, key employee life and disability insurance, as well as buy-out plans, may be essential.

Deciding to choose a different form of organization is an important step in the life of a growing company. Before making the decision, you should consult with your accountant and attorney. In addition to the decision to dissolve a sole proprietorship or partnership, you must also determine whether to adopt the standard corporate form (called the C Corporation) or elect to be taxed as a small business corporation (called the S Corporation). Under this form, taxes are assessed to each partner in a manner similar to the partnership. However, you also enjoy the liability protection of the corporate form. A venture capital investor may require you to abandon the S Corporation as a prerequisite to investing money, if only to shelter their portion of profits for the period during which they own stock.

Individual investors might be more flexible and willingly enter into a partnership arrangement with you. However, even then the risks of partnerships might lead you to the conclusion that incorporation is preferable.

FAMILY AND FRIENDS AS INVESTORS

Many small-business owners approach family members or friends as potential investors. Although this might seem an obvious source for equity capital, you should also be aware of the special dangers you face when going into business with a close friend or relative.

Objectivity is the issue. An outsider will evaluate you and your company strictly on the merits of the investment: growth and profit potential, management strength, competitive position, cash flow, historical financial data, and so forth. However, friends and relatives are less likely to take a professional approach. In addition, owners of small businesses often appeal to friends and family members in a manner different than the approach to a venture capital company.

Although many small businesses have been financed without the involvement of outside companies and have succeeded, you incur special risks when the investment bond is both financial and emotional. Many people have concluded that the *worst* investor is someone too close. So many factors could enter the equation beyond the black and white of financial data. This is not to suggest that you must never invest with a friend or family member. However, you must be aware that the relationship will change when money is involved. Exercise great caution, and

ensure that the terms of your agreement are precise, written down, and
agreed to completely by everyone—before you take the money.

The next chapter discusses the importance of staying in control when
you accept equity capital. Unless you are willing to give up your business, some forms of equity investment actually may become phased
takeovers.

CHAPTER 14

EQUITY: STAYING
IN CONTROL

All progress is based upon a universal
desire on the part of every organism
to live beyond its income.
—*Samuel Butler*

Whenever you accept capital in exchange for an equity position, you will give up a degree of control, if not complete control of your business. This is a dilemma for the owner who wants to call the shots but needs money today.

You might overlook this problem now, hoping to somehow find a way to repay the equity capital before the question of control becomes an issue even if the level of repayment exceeds your long-term business plan's limitations. It is essential to understand all of the terms of the agreement before you sign and to coordinate the terms of your agreement with the plan itself.

THE TAKEOVER PLAN

Although the majority of equity sources are interested in investing money for future profits, some actually want to take over businesses with growth potential and approach owners with offers of debt or equity capital with that in mind. They have the money and simply want to make your business thrive—but with you out of the picture.

If you have started a business offering an innovative product or service, taken it to a plateau and realized profits, but can no longer grow, you might be a candidate for the planned, phased takeover. The problem, of course, is that you cannot grow any more because your capital is strained to its limit. Some people reach this point and will sign anything just to get the money they need. What they do not realize is that they could be unintentionally giving up their business while receiving little or no profit.

Example: Two brothers had an idea. They could manufacture their own furniture and sell it at retail, keeping the marked-up profit without a middleperson. They started out without any capital by placing a series of ads in newspapers and magazines. When they received over 200 orders within the first month, they approached a bank and obtained a short-term loan. This enabled them to set up both a manufacturing and a retail outlet.

Within a year, the operation was thriving. Sales exceeded their expectations, and the brothers opened a second store. They paid back their original loan with no trouble. Then they were approached by a company with an offer to finance growth on a big scale. The company proposed lending them $1 million to finance several new retail outlets and national advertising. The opportunity was so appealing that they agreed to proceed.

At first, the offer seemed too good to be true. However, it was not that simple. The agreement gave the new investor decision and veto power even though capital was called a loan. Thus, it was possible for the lender to approve or disapprove all expenses and capital expenditures and even to dictate spending available cash in ways they wanted. The agreement also stated that repayments were to be made in a series of payments over ten months, a schedule that could not possibly be met even with the most rapid growth in sales. The most important provision of the agreement stated that for each missed payment the brothers would forfeit one-tenth of their equity.

The agreement was designed with takeover in mind. As long as the lender was able to control the level of spending, repayment of the loan might never occur—and it did not. Six months later, the lender held 60 percent of the stock. At that point, the two brothers were removed from the payroll. Four months later, they had no equity and no recourse. They had given up their entire business without receiving any compensation.

The problem here was that two relatively inexperienced owners met with unexpected success and wanted their business to grow. They realized that growth would be limited, unless they could raise a large sum of money. However, they ended up losing everything. Some guidelines to follow to avoid this from happening to you:

1. **Check out the equity source.** What is the track record of the lender or potential partner? Do they, in fact, lend or invest money with the expectation of being repaid? Or are they in the business of advancing money just to take over promising your enterprises? The brothers who started the furniture manufacturing and retail operation never even visited the office of the lender, even though it was less than an hour's drive away. You should know what business your equity source is in. Are they lenders, venture capital companies, or just someone with money available to pick up profitable young companies?

2. **Talk to other companies.** Who else has been given loans or equity capital by the organization? Ask for a list of names, addresses, and phone numbers. Check them out. Make sure you understand exactly what kind of agreement you are entering before you sign. Find out how others in your situation have fared. If the organization will not give you this information, walk away from the offer. A legitimate investor will gladly refer you to other successes in which they have been a part.

   One critical test: Are those other companies still in business? If the original owners are now out of the picture, that only means one thing: The equity you will receive will not help you to grow, but will be used to take your business away from you.

3. **Be careful when they come to you.** It is possible that a legitimate equity investor will approach you. It is much more likely that you will have to go out and seek the capital you will need for growth. When someone approaches you and states that they want to invest in your business or lend you money, be sure you know what you are getting into.

   If someone is willing to buy in or make a loan without seeing a business plan or without the definition of planned and orderly growth, you should question the arrangement and look at it from the other side. Ask yourself, "If I had money to invest or lend, would I be willing to put it into a company without seeing a detailed business plan and without having the right to participate in management and control?"

4. **Read the contract thoroughly.** No contract should ever be signed in haste, under pressure, or without a thorough reading. You might think you understand the terms and the spirit of the agreement. The real bottom line is what will happen when some-

thing goes wrong. That is when the real terms of the contract come to the surface, no matter how fine the print.

The brothers who lost control of their furniture operation had a written contract, but they never read it. Their understanding was strictly verbal, and they trusted in what they heard— largely because they were told exactly what they wanted to hear.

5. **Get a legal review.** After reading the contract but before signing it, have your attorney look at it carefully. Find out what it really says, and examine all of the contingencies. Do not be charmed by a supportive, friendly lender or equity source, who seems to come along at just the right moment to help you succeed. Apply the basic principles of sound business management, and do not sign anything until you know what it says.

6. **Make sure you can afford repayments.** When small businesses meet with sudden or unexpected success, the immediate problem becomes, "How can I afford to continue this rate of growth?" A higher volume of sales does not solve cash flow problems, it intensifies them and raises the stakes all around. So when equity money suddenly appears, it is easy to overlook the future and to take the money.

Not only should you know what will happen if you miss a payment. You should also make sure that the repayment schedule itself is realistic. If a $1 million loan must be repaid in a year or less, what will you need to generate in net profits to afford the schedule? Chances are you will not be able to make those repayments in a timely manner, and that is where the problems will start. A legitimate equity source or lender will not require you to repay the money on an impossible schedule.

7. **Do not give up more than you want to.** Before seeking or accepting additional equity investments in your business, decide what limits are acceptable to you. For example, you might insist on keeping no less than 51 percent of the equity under your personal control. Or you might be willing to give up more, meaning the decision-making power could end up on someone else's desk.

Do not allow yourself to become so desperate that you give up more than you want to. Remember that your own equity has value; if you take additional equity money in exchange for control, you might end up losing all of your business and all of your equity.

You could be a target for the takeover lender, if you have great potential to earn profits but capital is limited. If demand is high and growth has exceeded what you expected, and if you desire expansion beyond today's level, remember

Rapid expansion might pose the greatest threat to continued success. More than ever before, you need a plan, and that plan should include provisions to manage and control new capital.

STANDARDS FOR GROWTH PLANNING

To stay in control of your business when you accept equity investments, you will need to set standards for cash management and growth planning.

Just as loans must be accepted with profits in mind, equity capital should enable you to achieve financial success for everyone involved. In our discussion of loans, it was stated that the potential for growth should exceed the cost of borrowing money; the same is true for equity investments.

You can test the viability of taking on partners or investors by applying this test. Does your plan support the idea that higher future profits will be adequate to repay the investor? Can the investor earn an acceptable profit (as they define it) on the money put into your business? As a result, will you be better off as well?

Growth has time and profit limits. Given enough time, you could make your business as profitable as you want, given that cash flow will be adequate. Your plan should prove that the profits can be created so that everyone wins.

Questions you need to address in setting standards for growth should include

1. What does the investor expect to earn from putting money into my business? How long does the investor plan to leave the investment intact? Have you identified a liquidation date and method.

   Example: An investor is willing to put $200,000 into your business in exchange for 40 percent equity. You ask these questions:

   How much growth do you expect from your investment?

   How many years will you leave your money in my business?

What is the intended final liquidation date of your equity interest?

How do you expect to take your money out? Will you want all cash in one payment or a series of payments with interest, or are you willing to negotiate liquidation when the time arrives?

2. How does the plan match with the investor's expectations? Is the growth plan adequate to meet that goal?

Make these comparisons to test how well your business plan will be coordinated with what the investor expects:

What growth rate is called for in the plan versus what the investor wants?

Are the two goals compatible? Is the rate of planned growth, including the added capital, reasonable?

Now that you have defined the investor's goals, what about yours? Will meeting the investor's expectations mean you will have to force more rapid growth than you would like?

What additional risks must you accept in order to satisfy the investor? Are those risks acceptable, or do they mean you will have to put the entire operation in danger?

3. Am I willing to allow the rate and degree of growth necessary to match what the investor wants?

Do not make the mistake of believing that growth finds its own level. Remember that permanent and profitable growth is the result of planning and management. Ask these questions:

Are the investor's goals and my goals a match? Or does getting the money mean I have to abandon my plan?

Will I be comfortable with the timing of growth that will be required according to the investor's goals?

How will my operation change as the result of expanding to a size needed to yield an acceptable return on the investor's money?

Make sure that your plan rules and that the limitations of timing and rate of growth, as well as profits and cash flow, dictate exactly what you are willing and able to accept. The extra money might be desirable and even necessary. You can only afford to take it if you do not have to abandon or compromise your plan.

REPORTING STANDARDS

If you do allow someone else to take an equity position in your business, you must also expect to have to keep them up-to-date on your financial condition. They will want to keep an eye on their money, which also means keeping an eye on you and the way you operate.

For some owners, this creates a point of resistance and, possibly, a major problem in the relationship. You broke away from corporate life to start your own business so that you would not have to report to someone else. The greater the amount of money involved and the higher the percentage of an equity position, however, the greater the reporting demand will be. It should be listed and specified in your written contract.

In some cases, an equity partner—even one with less than 50 percent ownership—might gain the right to approve or disapprove of expenditures before you can make them. For example, you might want to invest in new capital equipment, but the equity partner says no. If you have a contract giving up that right, that is the end of the discussion. You might even need to have reimbursement of your own out-of-pocket expenses approved before you can cut a check—a situation that you will probably find restrictive and distasteful. So before entering any form of equity or lending agreement, be sure you first define exactly what and how you will report and whether or not the reporting terms take away any of your rights to make financial commitments for yourself.

Even without extreme restrictions on spendings, you will probably be required to fulfill some or all of these reporting requirements:

1. Preparation of an annual sales forecast, expense budget, and cash flow projection and six-month revisions.
2. Monthly or quarterly budget variance reports with explanations of significant variances.
3. Comparative financial statements on a monthly or quarterly basis with annual external audit.
4. Periodic reports summarizing significant financial ratios and trends for the current and previous year. These may include working capital, collections, and return on sales summaries, among others.

It is not unreasonable for equity partners to ask for any of these reports, and it would be unrealistic for you to expect to enter an equity capital agreement that did not call for a level of financial reporting. If you are not accustomed to preparing reports for outsiders or if that makes you feel like a junior partner, then the requirement for a formalized report will change the way you operate. This extends not only to the time you will have to schedule to prepare the reports, but also in the fact that you must be prepared to explain trends and variances that were not expected. Your new partner might be much more concerned about unexpected losses than you were when it was just your money at risk. From your point of view, the extra reporting could become a demanding and exhausting fact of life.

Before signing an agreement, you should come to a precise understanding about reporting, including

1. Format of the report.
2. Content.
3. Frequency.
4. Auditing involved, including the extent and frequency of the audit (which will probably have to be paid completely by you).

All of these issues should be included in the contract you enter, including sample formats of the reports you will prepare.

One critical question you and your new equity partner should answer before signing the contract is

What information will represent a fair test of business performance?

That is the information that should go into the report. For example, if you enter an agreement only to discover that the equity partner expects a monthly detailed budget comparison, comparative financials, and four pages of ratio analysis, you will have taken on a tremendous reporting burden.

It is possible that the test of performance can be reduced to a smaller body of information with the frequency of reporting changed to a quarterly level. The point is that before finalizing the deal you should define and specify how and what you will report. Otherwise, you will set yourself up for a disagreement with your new partner—a situation that can be easily avoided.

Example: The owner of a secretarial service purchased the accounts of a similar business when the previous owner retired. The purchase was financed by a silent partner, who acquired a 30 percent share of equity. The agreement specified that the new owner was to submit a complete set of financial statements every month. Preparing these proved to be a burden as the due date arrived at the busiest time of the month. The owner was late with the report several months running, and the silent partner turned out to be very inflexible—both in enforcing the contractual due date and in refusing to modify the reporting requirement.

DESIGNING REPORTS FOR INVESTORS

If equity investors have not already designed reporting formats, you can work with them in arriving at an agreement. Try to reach a compromise between what the investor would like to see and the time required for you to prepare and submit information.

Example: An investor wants to see a detailed budget and variance report every month. You propose a summarized version each month that highlights the largest variances, and a more detailed version at the end of each quarter.

Example: After a contract has been signed, the investor expresses concern when variances show up in the budget. As a solution, you modify the agreement, so that an acceptable *range* of variances is identified, given that the budget is only an estimate. When the actual results fall outside of the range, variances are explained.

Example: During negotiations, the investor states that she would like to receive a series of ratio summaries and detailed financial statements every month; you would prefer to submit detailed reports quarterly. As a compromise, you design a monthly summary of the information the investor wants with a quarterly detailed report and budget comparisons.

A monthly budget report can be prepared on one sheet with the most significant variances explained in notes. You and the investor may agree to define what represents a "significant" variance, and this should be specified in two ways: by amount and by percentage.

Example: Your expense budget for the coming year adds up to $275,000. Because each account contains budgets for varying amounts between a few hundred and several thousands of dollars, a significant variance cannot be consistently defined in every case. Thus, you and the investor agree that a "significant" variance, one requiring an explanation, will occur when two conditions are present:

1. The amount of variance is $100 or more.
2. The percentage that expenses exceed the year-to-date budget must be 5 percent or more.

The report prepared each month can summarize major categories with the explanation for causes of variance listed below. A form for this is shown in Figure 14–1. This form shows the estimated and actual totals in each group, with the variance isolated and compares those numbers to the previous year. What may appear in line in total might be made up of several offsetting variances. For example, total expenses could be within 3 percent of the budget. Within the totals, however, you might have a number of significant variances, some favorable and some unfavorable. The explanation below these summarized figures should break out the details with additional sheets attached as needed.

The purpose of this form is to reduce your workload on a monthly basis, while also satisfying the investor. The concern will be to ensure

FIGURE 14–1
Summary of Variances

Budget Status Report

Date_____

	THIS YEAR TO DATE	LAST YEAR TO DATE	+ (−)
Sales Forecast	$	$	$
Sales Actual			
Variance			
Cost Budget	$	$	$
Cost Actual			
Variance			
Expense Budget	$	$	$
Expense Actual			
Variance			
Profit Forecast	$	$	$
Profit Actual			
Variance			

that you are diligently controlling the budget and working to achieve the terms of the business plan to which you have both agreed.

A second form of reporting can involve one or more graphs. When you and the investor agree to report budgets within an acceptable range, the graph will show that range with actual results added to the graph each month. Do not make the range so wide that your actual results will always fall within the acceptable range; that makes the entire process worthless. If you have defined a 5 percent variance as acceptable, the range between the budget and the goal should not exceed 5 percent.

Example: Your sales forecast has been prepared for the year, as well as your cost and expense budget. You agree to submit an explanation whenever the actual results vary from the forecast and budget. This is further defined in terms of significance. Each month's total forecast and budget is expanded to include a "goal" total. This is the amount within what you consider an acceptable range. The goal for sales is lower than the forecast; and the goal for expenses is higher than the budget; as shown in Table 14–1.

The separation between the forecast or budget and the goal is not a consistent percentage of the original estimate; the degree of variance was determined partially by the seasonal factors. If your business volume and expense level varies in the same way, the definition of significant should be flexible enough to allow for the realities of your operation.

TABLE 14–1
Sales and Expense Forecast.

	Sales				Expenses	
	Forecast	Goal			Budget	Goal
Jan	$100,000	$ 95,000	Jan		$ 85,000	$ 90,000
Feb	110,000	100,000	Feb		90,000	95,000
Mar	110,000	100,000	Mar		90,000	95,000
Apr	100,000	90,000	Apr		80,000	85,000
May	110,000	100,000	May		87,000	90,000
Jun	125,000	115,000	Jun		96,000	100,000
Jul	145,000	120,000	Jul		103,000	110,000
Aug	150,000	130,000	Aug		105,000	112,000
Sep	140,000	120,000	Sep		100,000	108,000
Oct	130,000	120,000	Oct		100,000	108,000
Nov	120,000	110,000	Nov		96,000	103,000
Dec	110,000	100,000	Dec		90,000	95,000

This exercise can be expressed in graph form, as shown in Figure 14–2. The graph can be prepared once at the beginning of each year, and an updated version sent to the investor each month. Whenever the "actual" line falls outside of the defined acceptable range, an explanation should accompany the report.

Variance explanations should identify the precise cause of the prob-

FIGURE 14–2
Budget Range Reporting

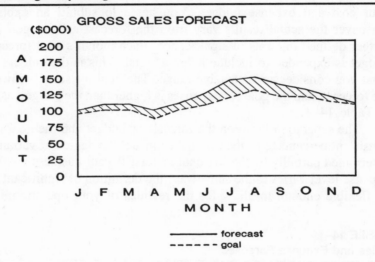

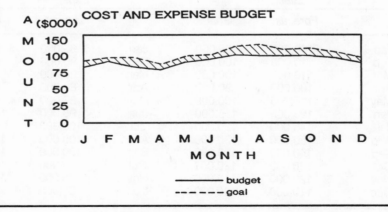

lem and not merely repeat what the numbers already show. For example, compare these explanations:

> *Vague.* Year-to-date sales were 7 percent lower than forecast, due to a slower than expected level of early summer orders.

> *Precise.* Year-to-date sales were forecast on the assumption that our new store would be open and operating by May 1. The opening date was moved to July 15, due to delays in completing store site improvements.

In the first example, the degree of variance is written out even though the report already reveals it; the cause is not really identified. In the second, an exact cause for the problem is specified. In order for your variance explanations to convey meaningful information, forecasts and budgets must be based on a series of well-documented assumptions. Then, when each variance is analyzed, it will be possible to compare what has actually occurred to what you estimated would occur.

Taking on an equity partner invariably means having to also improve your internal budgeting procedures—if only so that your reports will be worthwhile. Even without an equity partner, sound budgeting is essential if you want to control and plan growth.

A final report—summarizing key financial information—is appropriate when a quarterly, more detailed report is to be supplemented with monthly, abbreviated versions of the same information.

Example: You and your equity investor agree that you will summarize working capital ratios, collections, and key profit and loss information each month with a more detailed quarterly report. One possible reporting format for this requirement is shown in Figure 14–3. This provides a comparative summary on a year-to-date basis in three sections. The current ratio (current assets divided by current liabilities) might not be completely revealing by itself. So the report includes not only the ratio, but the amounts for each group. For example, you might report a ratio of 2 to 1. If assets are $100,000 and liabilities are $50,000, however, that is a lot different than when each figure is twice those amounts.

Total accounts receivable are broken down by the percentage that is current and past due. Average days outstanding is a valuable trend, as it shows whether your cash flow is improving or deteriorating with any seasonal factors in mind. To compute the average days, the total of year-to-date credit sales is divided by the *average* monthly balance of accounts receivable.

FIGURE 14–3
Status Report for Equity Partners

Financial Ratio Report

Date _____

	THIS YEAR TO DATE	LAST YEAR TO DATE	+ (−)
1. WORKING CAPITAL			
Current Assets	$	$	$
Current Liabilities			
Working Capital	$	$	$
Current Ratio	══	══	══
2. COLLECTIONS			
Total Accounts Receivable	$	$	$
Percentage: 0–30	%	%	%
31–60	%	%	%
61–90	%	%	%
over	%	%	%
Average Days Outstanding	══	══	══
3. SALES AND PROFITS			
Gross Sales	$	$	$
Direct Costs			
Gross Profit	$	$	$
Expenses			
Operating Profit	$	$	$
Federal Income Taxes			
Net Profit	$	$	$
Return on Sales	%	%	%

Sales, costs, expenses, and profits are also shown on a comparative basis, along with the return on sales percentage. The investor will be able to compare from one year to the next, as well as from month to month.

The investor can compute ratios beyond what is shown on the report, making it even more revealing. For example, a comparison of accounts receivable to total sales might show that collectibles are growing at a faster rate, which could be a sign that better collection procedures should be put into place or that credit policies should be reviewed and revised.

The purpose of all reporting going from you to the investor should be to satisfy a defined requirement and not just to complete a series of blank forms. As every business owner who used to work in a big company already knows, the procedure can easily become the end in itself without any follow-up, control action, or study for relevance. You may want to achieve growth and you may be willing to take on an equity partner, but you do not need to create a bureaucracy in the process.

The degree of flexibility an equity investor or venture capital company is willing to exercise might also tell you how much bureaucracy is involved in dealing with an outsider. For example, a very large, procedures-conscious venture capital company might impose a series of requirements on you, many of which do not actually address the requirements for testing solvency, quality of management, financial health, or appropriate planning. If that company insists on compliance, without being able or willing to work with you to design a reporting format applicable to the actual situation, you may want to ask yourself, "Do I want to be in business with them?" You could end up filling out forms each month without any useful purpose being served. You cannot afford to ignore the fact that, when you accept an equity partner, you are no longer the sole owner.

That purpose will be defined partly by the type of operation you are running and partly by the nature of your business plan. The next chapter deals with building a business plan to successfully find and acquire equity capital.

CHAPTER 15

BUSINESS PLANS
FOR EQUITY MONEY

Strategic planning is worthless
—unless there is first a
strategic plan.
—*John Naisbitt*

The requirements of an equity investor are completely different than those of a lender. So the business plan you prepare to raise venture capital or attract a partner should be tailored so that different features are emphasized and expanded.

Lenders are interested in the use of borrowed money and the risks involved in making a loan. Investors will look at your business from another perspective. They will want to examine details of

Competitive posture. Where you stand in your industry, region, and capital structure compared to others in the same business.

Your marketing strategy. First, whether you even have one, and, second, how realistically it has been prepared.

How additional invested capital will improve profit potential. Whether putting equity into your operation will or will not increase net worth and profits in the future.

It is a mistake to assume that one business plan format will work in every case. Some mistakes worth avoiding in the preparation of a plan for an equity investor are the following.

1. **Overselling the idea.** No one believes an unrealistic plan. Avoid the temptation to make your business sound like an emerging big-time conglomerate or even to estimate potential profits beyond a realistic level. Present your plan with your best and most realistic estimate.

A very effective technique is to prepare future projections in two ways: without an infusion of capital, and with additional, invested equity. If your assumptions are reasonable and if this approach shows that both you and the investor could profit by joining forces, your plan will achieve its intended purpose.

A second version of the unrealistic plan is one that assumes stable overhead even with vastly improved sales volume. Thus, the projected profits grow to enormous size, and the margin increases with each year. The experienced investor will know that overhead must increase as the volume of business increases.

2. **Downplaying negatives.** Every operation has strong and weak points. A useful plan will discuss and expose both and demonstrate how the future will be managed. Strong points will be used to exploit the available market and to maximize controlled growth. Weak points will be carefully managed and, hopefully, overcome. If extra capital is needed for this (a common situation), then the argument will be a compelling one.

The negatives should not be dwelled upon too much; but they should be revealed in the plan. That is the best way to show how they will be solved. If a plan does not even bring up the negatives, they can not be addressed. That means the plan is incomplete and inaccurate, leaving it to the investor to assume the worst.

3. **Placing emphasis on the wrong information.** Never forget *who* will be looking at your plan. The investor holds a specific point of view and will be interested in seeing precisely how your operation addresses it. Thus, your marketing strategy, competitive posture, and projections of the future are of great interest. Although your background, management style, and track record are also critical, that information is not at the top of the investor's priorities list.

4. **Forgetting the investor's perspective.** Remember, the most important question on the investor's mind is: "What can I realistically expect to earn as a return on my capital by buying an equity share of this business?" Chances are that question will be applied to a number of different operations at the same time. A wise investor may decide to go with the company that offers the greatest potential for growth, even if the track record is not the best. Or, if a lot of potential can not be identified, the investor may select the business with the least amount of risk.

The potential for profitable growth is established in your projections and is closely tied to how you plan to approach your market and which future markets offer the greatest chances for expansion. If the equity money will enable you to pursue that plan successfully, the investor will be interested.

SOURCES FOR INFORMATION

Your assumptions concerning future growth are critical if your investor will be convinced. A growth plan cannot always exist on its own; you will have to support what you believe with economic projections, trends, and estimates. Several sources for supporting information and for step-by-step plan preparation can be used to strengthen your presentation, including

American Institute of Small Business
7515 Wayzata Boulevard, Suite 201
Minneapolis, MN 55426   612-545-7001

This organization offers a package called "How to Write a Business Plan." It includes a detailed sample plan and step-by-step guidelines. The cost is $85.00.

Dialog Information Services, Inc.
3460 Hillview Avenue
Palo Alto, CA 94304   415-858-2700 or 800-334-2564

Dialog is an automated information data base. It allows subscribers to access magazine articles, corporate news and trends, economic research, government publications, and consumer information. A computer and modem are needed to use this service. Rates include a $35 start-up fee and on-line searching at $24 per hour. Articles and documents can be copied for between $7.50 and $10.

NewsNet
945 Haverford Road
Bryn Mawr, PA 19010   215-527-8030 or 800-345-1301

This is another business-oriented data base service. It provides business news and developments, including important trends and a library of business newsletters. The service provides access to the major newswires, including AP, UPI, and Reuter. Subscription cost is $120 for the first year, $75 for six months, or $15 per month.

Other data base services can be used to research trends in your industry, although they tend to offer information more generalized in nature or emphasize stock market and other investment-related information. These services include CompuServe, the largest computerized data base, and Dow Jones News/Retrieval.

In addition, you may purchase software to prepare your business plan with automation. Most affordable programs will not allow you to design your own format, however, so that a tailored business plan will still have to be prepared manually. You can use one of the many spreadsheet programs to cut down the time required for future projections and then incorporate the results into your plan. This allows you to perform many "what-if" projections, including comparisons of future growth with and without equity capital or with equity in varying amounts. A computerized support system is no substitute for the hard work and thought you will have to put into preparing your plan, but it can supplement your efforts.

ORGANIZING YOUR PLAN

Whether you supplement your plan with an information data base or use only your own historical facts and future projections, it should always be prepared with the investor's interests in mind. Using the format previously introduced for a simplified plan, this means you emphasize and expand certain sections. A completed sample plan is included in Appendix B. Following is an outline of the plan's sections for raising equity capital.

1. **Company history.** Give the investor a brief overview of your business—how long it has been in operation, the service or product it offers, the customer base, and biographies of the principals. Allow one to two pages for this first section, at the most.

2. **Objective.** This should be a one-paragraph definition of your operational standards, employees, customers, and long-term direction. The objective tells the investor how you view your

company and what is important to you. While negotiating with a potential investor, having the objective in clear and precise language can help avoid future misunderstandings. For example, you might express a high standard for working directly with every customer. The infusion of capital might enable you to expand, but what does that mean in terms of the objective? If expansion will create a conflict in your management style, it should be resolved before proceeding with an agreement.

3. **Purpose.** This section is often left out of the business plan, and that is a mistake. Here, you will explain how additional capital will be used. No investor will willingly put money into your business to bail you out of a poorly managed cash flow situation. If you do not explain exactly how extra money will help achieve permanent and profitable growth, the investor will have no information on which to make a decision.

   Explain how expansion will require additional facilities, employees, advertising, and capital assets. Show how a better-capitalized company will also become a more profitable, expanded company. Do not assume that the investor will fill in the blanks. Anticipate questions and answer them in this section.

4. **Assumptions.** This is the section where any outside research on business and economic trends can support your best case. Assumptions are your list of beliefs that are behind your projections.

   For example, you might believe that future demand for your product or service will increase substantially, but that you can take advantage of it only if you are better capitalized. You might have an idea for a new approach to selling, a highly specialized service, or a product that anticipates new technology. All of these beliefs are also assumptions. If the investor subscribes to your assumptions and believes you are able to move in the direction you want, you are on the way to an agreement.

5. **Marketing strategy.** This is one of the sections you will want to expand considerably when preparing a plan to attract equity capital. You must be able to show how you plan to proceed with that extra capital and how it will make a difference. This section can be made most effective by showing projections with and without the investment.

Describe your strategy and approach to the future in three parts:

(a) Expansion method. Do you plan to penetrate new territories or markets or offer new product or service lines? How will this be accomplished, and what special risks are involved? Describe the potential for expansion without new capital, and then explain how invested capital will change the picture.

(b) Support systems. Growth invariably means you will have to make significant changes in your overhead level. You may need a bigger office or store; more employees, both at management and line levels; higher inventory of goods; and increased budgets for advertising, promotion, travel, and other variable expenses. You might also need to invest in an automated system and other capital assets.

These changes should be described as you expect them to occur with the current level of capital and how that schedule can be changed with an additional investment from someone else.

(c) Deadlines. When will you achieve the growth you have described? Remember that a goal is valid only when you place a deadline on its completion. This should be specified on both conditions: with existing capital levels and with an infusion of new money.

6. **Risks.** This section is worth expanding considerably. The investor, of course, is extremely aware of risks, and it is refreshing for that person to read a plan that raises the question and addresses it—from the investor's point of view.

Discuss the investor's risks in the following categories:

(a) Timing. Any expansion plan's success depends on proper timing and, perhaps, a bit of luck. Why do you think the time is right to begin your expansion now? What are the risks in the event the timing is poor, and what contingencies have you built into your plan?

Address the problem of timing by citing trends you have experienced in demand for your product or service and where you believe that demand is heading in the future.

(b) Competition. An investor might be favorably impressed with what you offer, but equally concerned about how you can stand up to competition, especially if a larger, better-financed company enters the same market. How will you address this risk?

Point out the opportunity to specialize within the market, to take advantage of a larger competitor's size, and to offer a distinctive form of service that no one else is addressing.

(c) Obsolescence. What are the risks that your product or service will be obsolete within a few years? If you do not allow for this, chances are you will end up going out of business.

Include provisions in your expansion plan for change and diversification in product or service, especially if you do face the risk of obsolescence. Adopt a farsighted point of view.

(d) Economics. If your operation is sensitive to changes in the economy, your investor will be especially cautious. For example, if you sell a product the consumer buys only in certain economic conditions, then volume and growth is beyond your control, at least to an extent.

Your plan should include a contingency strategy. If economic risk becomes a factor, how will you continue to support overhead? What additional product or service lines can you offer? How will you defuse the economic risk?

7. **Projections.** This section, which may also be called "Financial analysis," deals strictly with the future. Your pro forma income statement and cash flow estimates should be based on your assumptions and should not extend beyond a reasonable rate of growth. Too many business plans "prove" that an investor will get rich, because each year's sales and profits will grow on a geometric scale. That rarely comes to pass.

Break down your sales and direct costs by specific service or product lines; list details of expenses and profits by calendar or fiscal quarters for the next three to five years. Include a detailed monthly budget and forecast for the next 12 months. Also show cash flow projections for at least the next year. These analyses should be prepared on the assumption that no additional cash will be invested and then compared to the estimated outcome *with* additional equity.

Also estimate the most revealing financial trends. If your emphasis is on sales growth in a single product or service line, show how that will occur, based on a well-explained series of assumptions (if you employ direct salespeople, base estimates on recruitment and average order volume per salesperson, for example).

Show how overhead expense levels will be controlled, leaving room for higher overhead levels with an expanded business. Also show how cash flow and working capital will be controlled, both with and without new equity capital.

Avoid projecting into the distant future in overly specific terms. The farther out your projections extend, the greater the variance. Emphasize short-term growth in the specifics, and long-term directional growth—what you want to achieve in terms of market share, product or service lines, and overall profitability.

8. **Financial statements.** Include a balance sheet, income statement, and statement of cash flows. These standard reports should be included on a comparative basis, showing the latest full year next to the previous year. If the current year has gone a full quarter or more, interim statements should be included as well.

When dealing with investors, an internally prepared statement may be naturally suspect. There is no easy way to check on the fairness of statements you complete on your own, so it is a wise idea to pay an independent accounting firm and include externally audited statements as part of your business plan.

WHAT YOUR PLAN SHOULD PROVE

A business plan should be tailored for the situation. If you want to borrow money, certain types of information will be emphasized; and for investors, some sections contain more detail than others. This is not a deceptive practice, because the same series of assumptions, risks, projections, and marketing strategies are involved. It is just that you are trying to satisfy a different series of concerns and address a different listing of risks. Your plan should prove these points to the investor:

1. **Your vision of the future is accurate.** Your business plan should be a reasonable estimate of what is likely to happen in the future, assuming that

   * You are able to manage your operation to achieve what the plan expresses.
   * The demand exists and can be answered with the capital available.
   * The level of costs and expenses you list in the plan is realistic.

2. **You will achieve your goals with new capital.** The greatest oversight in plans for investors is the failure to prove that new capital will increase future profits and future business net worth. That is why comparative estimates are so important. Show the investor that both of you will profit by putting the money to work in your business.

3. **It will be possible for the investor to get the money out in the future.** Investors will eventually want to receive their principal back and will also want periodic dividends or draws. Just as lenders must be convinced that you have the ability to repay a loan, investors must be shown how you plan to return their money.

   It is unlikely that you will find an investor who is willing to simply put money into your operation and leave you alone without eventually wanting his or her money back. Surprisingly, some business owners never stop to consider this point. When you take on equity, you are sharing ownership, and your part owner will have certain rights. You will want to describe in your plan how you will buy out equity shares, what the target growth range is, and *when* that will occur.

   These projections might require identifying a date for complete liquidation of the business. Your investor could be interested in helping to make your operation profitable enough to sell. If that goal conflicts with what you want, then you are talking to the wrong investor. As an alternative, you should be prepared to give the method, timing, and approximate amount of a repayment, based on the degree to which you expect the investor's share to increase in value.

4. **The investor's money is safe.** Even the most speculative in-

vestor will be concerned about how well you will manage capital. If the investor will be an inactive partner, you will have to prove that you are capable of achieving the growth described in your plan. If the investor will be an active part of your management team, you will still want to show that you will care for the new money just as much as you have cared for your own. This can all be established in the way you prepare the plan. Raise the risks and explain how you anticipate them. Bring up your own weaknesses and show how the investor's involvement and capital will help reduce them. Show that your well-managed growth plan will work.

5. **You and the investor will be able to work together harmoniously.** It is easy to concentrate on the numbers alone and to overlook the personality issue. If the investor will be actively involved in the operation, you should each bring a specific and nonconflicting talent to the picture. Otherwise, you will be competing with one another and, quite likely, you will have different management ideas. Active involvement of two or more people in the ownership of a business is always a considerable risk. It is a business marriage in which each individual must be willing to compromise, communicate, and work together to achieve common and well-expressed objectives.

   Even when an investor will stay out of the management activity, you will have to establish a clear understanding of *how* you will work together. How often will you prepare reports? What information will be submitted? What approval or veto rights will the investor have?

USEFUL TREND ANALYSIS

You can help support the future estimates made in your plan by citing recent trends. Financial analysis does establish and support projection, but remember that its value is limited. The future is always difficult to project, even with strong past indicators, because

1. There is no guarantee that future performance will be a repeat of what happened in the past.
2. Outside factors (the economy, competition, changing market

demand, for example) might radically alter your operating environment, making past trends inapplicable.

3. If you do raise new equity or debt capital, the entire picture changes. Thus, a trend that worked in a relatively small, low-volume company might not continue.

4. Rates and degrees of growth are naturally limited in terms of time and demand. You might be able to grow very rapidly when you first start out; but as volume increases, the rate of growth will slow down. The margin of profit could be smaller when volume is higher, so that a profit trend will have to be modified.

Combine trend analysis with future projections to round out your plan. Do not make the mistake of estimating the future entirely on what has happened in the past. It is important to keep in mind that any change you make today will alter your course. This includes higher volume of sales, expanded geographic influence, a higher competitive stance, and new equity capital.

Curve your trends to present the future in moderate or even conservative terms. Even when you believe your sales and profit lines will continue upward at the same rate as in the past, exercise some caution. Present a "worst case" projection to establish the maximum risk level. Then if results exceed what you project, everyone will be pleasantly surprised. That is a more desirable alternative than having to explain to an investor why the plan you believed to be realistic did not come to pass. It also increases the trust level on the investor's part, portraying you as a responsible, realistic owner whose view of the future is cautious.

THE PROJECTIONS SECTION

Supplement historical trend analysis with realistic and applicable projections of the future. The types of projections you make should depend on the emphasis in your marketing strategy. If expansion will be the result of opening a number of stores or other locations, that requires one form of management and planning. If you plan to remain in one location and expand your product or service lines, the analysis should be concerned with a different emphasis.

Consider how differently you will project the future in these types of business operations:

1. A retail clothing store.
2. A household goods mail-order operation.
3. A computer consultation business.
4. An insurance sales office.

The attributes of each type of business will limit and dictate the type of planning you will do, the speed and amount of growth you can achieve, and the use of invested capital. Your business may need money for capital assets, advertising, or a reinforced support staff and larger facilities. A product manufacturer will need inventory and equipment; a retail operation demands capital for organizational costs and advertising; and a sales company must pay the cost of recruitment, training, and administrative support.

To identify the most valid projection trends to study, first define the factors that influence growth in your operation. Then decide how to reduce those factors to easily understood trends.

Example: A retail clothing store will support its growth projections by identifying the typical buyer, the average purchase, traffic patterns by location, inventory requirements, and possible new markets.

Example: A mail-order operation will support estimates of future growth with past sales trends, tied to catalog pricing, style, and distribution; may need automated tracking systems and investment in larger lists; and will be able to compete in terms of price through volume purchasing.

Example: A consultation company is limited by the available time of its principals. Thus, profit growth must be tied to staff expansion. This means that growth will require additional payroll expenses, accompanied by a series of internal control systems to ensure quality at an acceptable level.

Example: A sales operation will grow by being able to recruit the most successful salespeople. Capital will be invested in the expenses of locating these people and providing orientation; continuing training and support programs (including staff and facilities); in paying a competitive commission rate, meaning reduced gross profit margins; and in product development necessary to reduce attrition of the best sales resources.

These varying factors should be expressed in financial terms, reduced to trend forms, and shown on graphs whenever possible. All of that helps the investor to understand how your business plan is constructed, how you expect to deal with growth, and what that will mean in terms of future profits and greater net worth.

The financial aspects of your plan certainly tell the investor what you expect to achieve (either with or without the additional equity). Your projections show how you will achieve your goals and how profits will be created and managed. Besides the strictly financial side to your plan, you should include a discussion of the less tangible, but more human element.

Many plans are preoccupied with the numbers to the extent that a review must be limited. The truth, though, is that any considered joint venture involves a dose of intuition, a sense of whether or not a business owner has the ability and motivation to succeed, and a feeling about the product or service. These isues should be raised in your plan and can be mixed in with the financial sections. They are not in opposition to what you state financially; the human element rounds out what the numbers show, rather than creating a conflict. They add reality to a plan that otherwise is completely hypothetical.

As the owner, you are more aware of the intangible elements at work in your business than anyone else can possibly be. Thus, you're the best person to add the human element to your plan.

Example: The owner and founder of a mail-order operation wrote her own plan. By discussing both financial and human elements, she was able to convey her enthusiasm and belief in her product and marketing strategy. She discussed (under "Marketing Strategies") the buying patterns of her customers, factors that were addressed through catalog design and artwork. A potential investor was able to sense from this description that the owner was committed to creating a permanent, established, and loyal mailing list and that the operation did involve an intangible quality generated through the owner's enthusiasm.

Example: The president of an insurance sales office contracted with a number of insurance companies as an independent agency branch office. He had very strong views concerning the importance of providing support to a sales staff. These views were explained in the business plan. It was this element of the plan, more than the financial projections, that convinced an investor to contribute equity capital to finance planned growth.

Whether you attempt to raise money through debt or equity, always remember that the other person—lender or investor—will have a series of concerns that are not always in line with yours. Be ready to talk about risks and to show that you have anticipated and planned for them. Prepare a realistic business plan that proves you will make *more* profit by raising and using capital and not use up the money to get out of debt or to support existing working capital. Always include a specific future date when the investor will get back the money as well as a respectable profit—just as a lender expects a contractual commitment to repayment of principal and interest.

There is no mystery to raising money. If you have a solid idea, if you manage your operation well, if you bring a sense of confidence and enthusiasm to the investor, and if you select worthwhile and affordable risks, you will find a source for the additional capital you need. Be willing to show that you view expansion realistically, that you are patient and able to wait for the right time, and that you know all forms of demand have limitations.

Of the many skills you need to successfully operate your business, one of the most important is to see issues from the other person's point of view. You have demonstrated this already, in the sense that you know what your customer will pay for what you sell. That took marketing ability and insight. You will prove that putting money into your business is a sound and safe investment—just by calling upon the same ability and insight when confronting and solving the problem of financing your growing business.

GLOSSARY

A

accrual method   An accounting method in which sales are reported as earned, regardless of when paid, and costs and expenses are reported when incurred, even when payment takes place later. The accrual method is more accurate than the cash method, as receivables and payables are included in financial statements.

active partner   An individual who invests capital in an organization and also becomes directly involved in day-to-day management.

assumption   The basis for developing a sales forecast, cost or expense budget, or cash flow projection. The assumption should be a measurable factor or belief that will accurately determine the budgeting result. For example, a sales forecast is based on recruitment assumptions; an expense budget is based on assumptions of peremployee spending; and a cash flow projection is based on assumptions concerning new loans and acquisition of capital assets.

audited financial statements   Financial reports that have been prepared in accordance with Generally Accepted Accounting Principles (GAAP) with transactions checked and verified by an independent accountant.

B

balance sheet   One of three financial statements. See also **income statement** and **statement of cash flows.** The balance sheet reports the book value of assets, liabilities, and net worth as of a specific date.

budget   An estimate of levels of costs and expenses for the coming 6 to 12 months, broken down by month and by category. The budget for each cost or expense should be supported by detailed assumptions.

budgeting The process of developing and reviewing income forecasts, cost and expense budgets, and cash flow projections.

business plan An operational and strategic document outlining the goals of an organization for future growth, cost and expense controls, cash flow, budgeting, and marketing expansion.

C

capital budget A budget used for the planning and timing of the acquisition of capital assets or for the investment of business assets.

capitalization The money used to finance operations and investments of a company, consisting of debt capital (borrowed money) and equity capital (net worth).

cash-based income The profits earned during a specified period of time, adjusted for changes in cash position and reported on a statement of cash flows. Cash-based income is net sales reported for the period minus increases in current assets (such as inventory and accounts receivable) minus direct costs, variable expenses, and overhead.

cash flow test A test applied to determine whether an infusion of additional capital is advisable. In order for the decision to make sense, the addition of capital should improve long-term cash flow rather than place an additional strain on working capital.

cash method An accounting method in which no entry is made in the books until cash changes hands. Sales are reported when payment is received, and costs and expenses are reported when paid. Although the cash method is acceptable by Generally Accepted Accounting Principles standards as long as it is consistently used, it does not report the true current status of equity value or sales and profits.

collection ratio A ratio used to test and follow the trend in collections of accounts receivable. The average accounts receivable level is divided by the average daily sales made on credit. Because these levels may vary from one period to another, the ratio may be calculated on a moving average basis. The factor that results from the calculation represents the average number of days required to collect outstanding receivables.

contingent liability A liability that might or might not become an actual debt, such as the amount that will be due if a company being sued loses a judgment.

corporation A business entity separate from the individuals or other companies that own stock. Ownership of specific assets cannot be identified, as each stockholder owns shares of the whole. In the event one or more owners sells stock, the corporation continues without interruption. The corporation is liable for income taxes based on its net profits. In comparison, a partnership must be dissolved and a new company formed whenever a partner is added or dropped. The partnership does not pay income taxes directly, but files and information return reporting each partner's share of taxable income.

cost of goods sold   A category on the income statement including direct costs and the net change in inventory levels. When the cost of goods sold is subtracted from sales, the remainder is the company's gross profit.

current assets   Assets of a company that are in the form of cash or that are convertible to cash within 12 months, including accounts receivable, marketable securities, short-term notes receivable, and inventory.

current liabilities   Debts of a company that are due and payable within 12 months, including accounts payable, taxes payable, and the next 12 months of payments due on notes.

D

debt capital   Capital derived from borrowed money in the form of loans, notes, or bonds. When debt capital and equity capital are combined, the two represent total capitalization.

debt/equity ratio   A ratio that tests the relative debt capital of a company. To compute, divide total liabilities by tangible net worth (net worth less any intangible assets). The resulting percentage is the portion of tangible net worth represented by debt, and the remainder is equity capital.

direct costs   Expenditures that vary and are directly influenced by the level of sales, including merchandise purchased for sale, direct labor, and other costs that are necessary to (1) create a finished product, (2) generate volume, or (3) support the existing level of sales.

E

equity capital   The net value of a company; the owner's book value. Equity capital equals total assets minus total liabilities. When equity capital and debt capital are combined, the two represent total capitalization.

expansion capital   Funds raised for the purpose of financing growth in volume and activity beyond original or existing levels.

extraordinary item   Any unusual, nonrecurring amount on a financial statement. The effect on equity and profits is not expected to continue into the future. Examples include changes in accounting method or asset valuation, judgments against the company, profit or loss from currency exchange rates, or exceptionally high gains and losses resulting from the sale of capital assets.

F

financial statements   The balance sheet, income statement, and statement of cash flows for a company with supplementary schedules, footnotes, and disclosure or auditor's letter.

fixed assets   Capital assets of a company. See also **long-term assets.**

fixed overhead   A classification of expenses that does not vary with minor changes in sales volume, such as rent, clerical salaries, and equipment lease payments. As sales volume levels increase, fixed overhead may grow as well, due to the requirement for a larger support staff, office and warehouse space, and other fixed expense categories.

footnote   A note attached to a financial statement for the purpose of explaining or clarifying what the numbers reveal. Footnotes may include a disclosure of pending litigation, contingent liabilities, changes in accounting methods, explanation of extraordinary or nonrecurring items, or a summary of un-reported assets (such as a current appraisal of real estate shown at purchase price on the balance sheet).

forecast   An estimate of sales for the next 6 to 12 months, supported by a series of detailed assumptions detailing those elements that will affect the out-come. Assumptions may be based on degrees of volume growth, production trends, sales activity, recruitment, and other factors.

G

GAAP   Acronym for Generally Accepted Accounting Principles, a series of opinions and guidelines for auditors and accountants in the interpretation and reporting of financial information for a company.

general partner   An investor who participates directly in day-to-day manage-ment decisions. See also **active partner.**

general partnership   A form of partnership in which two or more general partners participate directly in the day-to-day management of the company. In comparison, a limited partnership has two categories of owners: general partners and limited partners (who are not directly involved in manage-ment).

goal   A specific end result a company or its owner wants to achieve in the future. A goal should be written and defined clearly, should identify action steps, and should be given a precise deadline.

good risk   A term used by lenders to describe an individual or company most likely to repay a loan; one whose financial strength and credit history are positive.

gross profit   The dollar amount remaining when the cost of goods sold is subtracted from sales; the amount of profit before deducting general expenses and the provision for income taxes.

I

income statement   One of three financial statements. See also **balance sheet** and **statement of cash flows.** The income statement summarizes sales, costs of goods sold, gross profit, expenses, operating profit, other income and expense, provision for income taxes, and net profit for a specified period of time.

intangible asset   An asset that does not have physical or specific value, such as covenants not to compete, goodwill, or assumed value of patents and rights.

L

limited partner   An investor who is not involved in day-to-day management. See also **silent partner.**

limited partnership   A form of partnership with two classes of partners. The general partners manage the company on a day-to-day basis, whereas the limited partners have no voice in management decisions.

living expenses   A category of start-up capital used to pay a company's founder during a start-up period in the form of a draw or salary.

long-term assets   The capital assets of a company, reduced by periodic depreciation over a recovery period, also called "fixed assets."

long-term debt   Debts payable beyond the coming 12 months, including the balance of payments on notes above the amounts due during the coming year.

long-term liabilities   Debts payable beyond the coming 12 months. See also **long-term debt.**

M

margin of profit   The percentage of gross profit compared to total sales.

marketing plan   Part of a company's business plan expressing the goals, action steps, deadlines, competitive strategies, and financial aspects of future market expansion.

marketing strategy   The collective action steps a company plans to take to expand its customer base, geographic influence, product or service lines, or method of selling.

moving average   An average computed by using a field of changing factors over an extended period of time. As each new factor is added to the average field, the oldest factor is dropped. The moving average smooths out current variations and stabilizes trends.

N

net interest expense   A calculation of the cost of debt capital on an after-tax basis. Because interest payments are tax-deductible, the true net cost to the company is calculated by reducing interest expense by the amount that income taxes were reduced due to interest paid during the year.

net worth   The owner's equity (in a sole proprietorship or partnership) or shareholders' equity (in a corporation), representing total assets minus total liabilities. Net worth may be subdivided into capital stock or paid-in capital, retained earnings, and current profit or loss. The value of intangible assets is usually excluded.

O

objective   A brief statement expressing a company's purpose, standards, and priorities.

organizational capital   Funds raised and used to pay for costs, expenses, and owner's draw or salary during the period of time prior to opening for business and generating sales.

overhead test   A test of management's control over expenses applied to determine whether or not expansion is occurring profitably. The test can be applied in two ways. First, any increase in sales volume should exceed the rate of increase in overhead expenses. Second, any additions of capital should decrease or stabilize overhead rather than leading to growth in the level of general expenses.

P

partnership   A form of organization in which two or more individuals, other partnerships, or corporations own portions of the whole. Partnerships assign proportionate income to each partner and file an information tax return only. When any partner is added or dropped, the existing organization must be dissolved and a new one formed.

profitable volume   Increased levels of sales that are accompanied by a corresponding increase in the level and percentage of net profits; a growth in sales volume when an acceptable level of net profits is maintained.

profit and loss statement Alternative title of the **income statement,** one of three financial statements of an organization.

pro forma statement A financial statement, most commonly an income statement, that shows estimated future activity levels. The pro forma results are based on current budget and planning assumptions.

projection An estimate of sources and applications of cash for the coming 6 to 12 months, based on known and estimated revenues, costs, expenses, and cash commitments (such as loan repayments).

S

selling expenses Expenses that vary based on the' level of sales activity, but that are not directly connected to the sale (a direct cost). Selling expenses include advertising and promotion, salespersons' travel and entertainment, and sales-related telephone expenses. See also **variable expense.**

short-term debt Debts payable within one full year, including the total value of 12 months' payments on long-term notes.

silent partner An individual who invests capital in an organization, but who does not actively participate in day-to-day management.

sole proprietorship An unincorporated form of organization owned and operated by one person.

statement of cash flows One of three financial statements. See also **balance sheet** and **income statement.** The statement of cash flows reports the sources and applications of working capital during a specified period of time.

T

tangible net worth The net worth of a company minus any intangible assets.

total capitalization The combination of debt capital and equity capital; the sum of all invested and borrowed money in the organization.

turnover in working capital A ratio that tests the effective use of working capital (current assets less current liabilities). The ratio can be interpreted and given significance only when reviewed comparatively as the latest step in a trend. To compute, divide total sales for a specified period by working capital. The result is the average number of working capital turns or the times that working capital was replaced to generate reported sales.

U

unprofitable volume   A form of increase in gross sales accompanied by deterioration in the percentage or amount of net profits; volume achieved when an expected increase in the return on sales does not also occur, due to higher than expected levels of costs and expenses.

V

variable expense   An expense that varies in response to approximate levels of sales, but not as specifically as a direct cost; a selling expense.

venture capital   Funds raised to finance business operations and growth in the form of debt or equity positions taken by outside individuals or companies. In some instances, a debt position may be convertible to a predetermined equity share.

W

working capital   Current assets less current liabilities.

APPENDIX A

BUSINESS PLAN

A sample business plan designed to raise debt capital is shown on the following pages. The fictitious company is called Financial Consulting Group, an incorporated marketing company.

FINANCIAL CONSULTING GROUP
BUSINESS PLAN

(Date)

Contents

FINANCIAL CONSULTING GROUP

Contents

Introduction

1

Introduction

This business plan has been prepared by the management of Financial Consulting Group (FCG) to demonstrate that existing marketing opportunities justify outside financing.

The company is a leader in the financial services industry, offering the highest quality products and services; a thorough screening process; and recruitment of only the most experienced, successful, and capable sales professionals. Recent trends show that consumer interest in financial planning is on the rise. We predict that in the future the financial services consumer will demand the level of personal care and quality we offer.

The company is organized as a home office serving a number of remote field sales branches. This relationship, however, does not involve an employer–employee relationship. Each branch office is an independent business entity. Financial Consulting Group holds a regulatory duty to supervise field activities in two capacities. First, it acts as securities broker–dealer and is responsible for ensuring compliance with laws and regulations of federal and state securities agencies. Second, FCG is the master agency for insurance companies contracted with the company. In the regulatory sense, branch offices are employees of FCG.

Company History

2

Company History

Financial Consulting Group (FCG) was formed 12 years ago by Harold S. Green, a certified financial planner with more than 35 years of experience.

Mr. Green, CEO of the corporation, was the president of a major national life insurance company for 15 years before founding FCG. He previously worked as a financial counselor and has written three books on financial subjects.

Mark Walters is executive vice president and is in charge of operations. He supervises the managers of home office departments and is responsible for budgeting and controls. Mr. Walters has an extensive background in the financial services industry, having served for more than 10 years as treasurer of a national brokerage firm.

William R. Jacobs is marketing vice president and is responsible for recruitment, training, and monitoring of our growing sales force. He has demonstrated his ability to attract the most experienced professionals, support their needs, and ensure that motivation remains high. Mr. Jacobs also organizes our regional and national sales conventions and seminars.

James Miller is chief compliance officer. He is responsible for ensuring that all products offered for sale are economically sound and of the highest quality. Mr. Miller previously was a compliance examiner with a state securities agency.

The home office staff consists of seven managers and 31 employees. The total staff has doubled in size over the last two years, and anticipated future growth will require adding another seven employees in the next 36 months.

FCG was incorporated three years ago and owns its headquarters building. The company serves the middle- and high-income consumer by consulting on long-term financial goal setting and the sale of products designed to meet those goals.

Objective

3

Objective

Financial Consulting Group is a full-service broker–dealer providing financial planning and related services to the consumer. Our purpose is to ensure that all advice and sales are suited to the individual's financial status, comprehension, and risk tolerance level. We believe that a motivated, professional sales force is essential to realizing this goal and that the field effort must be completely supported by an experienced and responsive home office staff.

Purpose

4

Purpose

The company is applying for a line of credit in the amount of $500,000. Although we intend to draw the entire amount, we will complete repayments within 36 months.

Our marketing expansion plan, which has been developed over the past year, will vastly expand the markets and volume of Financial Consulting Group (FCG). We are well aware of the dangers in rapid expansion and intend to control our internal environment, as well as costs and expenses. We believe that expansion is worthwhile only when standards for quality and excellence are maintained. The financing will be used to achieve the following goals:

1. Expansion from the current 22 offices in three states to 120 offices in 45 states. Deadline: three years.

2. Emphasis during this expansion phase on
   (a) Advertising. We have discovered that consistent advertising and promotion are essential to keeping our positive and high profile in the minds of the consumer and sales professional.
   (b) Conventions and seminars. We sponsor five meetings per year, including two national and three regional meetings. These meetings provide our sales force with continuing education required for professional advancement, as well as orientation to new products and management techniques.
   (c) Training. All new salespeople are required to undergo a 10-hour training and orientation course we have designed. In addition, every representative must attend a refresher course no less than once per year.

3. Acquisition of computers for every branch office. We believe that communication in a marketing organization is essential, because we deal with several regulatory agencies and with products that change and emerge on a daily basis. We will own all computer hardware and software and require branch offices to use the network we develop. Cost per branch: $7,000. Deadline: Installation and training to be completed within six months for all existing offices and within 90 days for all newly recruited offices. Total cost: $850,000.

4. Completion of licensing in 42 new states within our three-year

Purpose

5

target period. The licensing process varies with each state and involves legal fees, deposits, and filings of financial statements. An additional licensing cost is incurred to transfer registration for newly recruited salespeople.

5. Expansion of existing staff. The headquarters building is owned by FCG and will provide adequate space for the planned expansion. We will recruit two new executives (increasing annual overhead by $140,000 per year) and five new support staff members (additional overhead of $120,000 per year).

Assumptions

6

Assumptions

Our marketing plan calls for extremely fast expansion into new areas and at a volume level far above current levels. We have chosen this course based on several observations, beliefs, and projections, including

1. A slower, more methodical course of growth will take away competitive advantage. Existing, larger firms are expanding in terms of volume, but are not providing the same level of quality we intend to maintain.

2. We will be able to maintain the control and professional standards in the home office by recognizing the importance of quality support. This task will be the greatest challenge in an expanded environment.

3. The high standards we have set for our sales representatives will ensure that higher volume will also increase our annual profits. We will not allow the standards for experience and knowledge to deteriorate, and we will not relax our rules for continuing education.

4. Future demand for our consultation and sales activities will increase. In the past decade, the consumer has shown increased interest in obtaining responsive professional help for investment, insurance, and financial planning needs. This demand moves far beyond the mere sale of a product and extends to individually designed financial advice.

5. The financial services industry will soon take steps to impose minimum professional standards on individuals. This trend has already begun. We believe that in the near future, anyone representing themselves as a financial planner will need to first obtain a professional license and establish their qualifications. In anticipation of this new development, we already screen newly recruited salespeople and accept only those who meet the standards we expect to become the rule within the next 10 years.

6. Our successful expansion will require an efficient, easily used communications network. By installing automated systems in every branch office and training personnel in its use, we will be able to communicate on a daily basis without incurring excessive mail and telephone expenses.

Marketing Strategy

7
Marketing Strategy

Our expansion plan will depend on one key element: recruitment. By attracting professional salespeople to the organization and then providing them with support services they expect and deserve, volume growth will continue.

Recruitment is possible when several elements are present. These include

- Diversity in the approved products offered, both in securities and insurance lines of business.
- Competitive commission schedule. We pay our sales representatives 50 percent of gross concessions received for investment sales in most cases. Our contracts with insurance companies include competitive commission rates for our representatives.
- Commitment to screening standards. Those representatives who meet the education, experience, and licensing requirements we impose will expect us to continue this policy.
- Maintenance of home office support facilities and services, and development of new service programs.
- Training and orientation programs that are designed to help salespeople succeed.
- Regional and national conventions that provide remote branch offices with practice management, product, and regulatory ideas.

We have projected our recruitment of new salespeople on a quarterly basis. During the three-year expansion phase, we will recruit a total of 144 people, and we project that of this group, 28 will leave within the first year. This attrition rate is based on trends observed in the past. We also project that the typical newly recruited sales representative will generate $6,000 in gross sales revenue per quarter, also based on historical trends.

We currently have 98 sales representatives under contract in 22 field offices. We have estimated that of this group, an average of three individuals will resign or be terminated per quarter. Historical trends show that once a new salesperson has been with the company for more than one quarter, average gross sales are $9,400 per quarter. This average has been used to project future sales volume for existing salespeople and for newly hired individuals after the first quarter.

Our marketing strategy will require extensive advertising, travel,

Marketing Strategy

8

meetings, and organizational effort. We have defined three elements for the planning and control of this marketing effort.

1. Expansion Method

Sales volume forecasts are based on our recruitment goals. These figures will be tracked on a monthly basis. We will achieve our goals by ensuring that each salesperson meets the monthly level established in the past or exceeds it. We will also track attrition rates and identify the reasons that people leave the company.

With diligent monitoring of internal costs and expenses, we will ensure that profits grow along with sales volume. We believe that sales growth is worthwhile only when the company ensures that profit standards are also met.

As we expand, we will identify new markets and sales opportunities. As a national organization, we will be better positioned to approach institutional markets, such as savings and loans, credit unions, and banks and to enter into new and more diversified contracts with investment and insurance companies.

We intend to continue operating from our headquarters office. The location is convenient for a national organization, and space is adequate even after our planned expansion. With branch offices in most states, we will be able to play a leading competitive role in the industry.

2. Support Systems

Expansion will be successful only because we will emphasize the need for excellence in our support systems. We cannot expand so rapidly that this support system cannot keep up.

We will ensure that internal costs and expenses do not exceed our budgets. Monthly variance reporting and monitoring will lead to investigation and corrective action for any negative variances that are discovered.

Cash flow will also be monitored carefully. We are in an excellent position for expansion, because we recently repaid a previous loan. With the planned cost and expense controls and new sales volume, we are keenly aware of the need for diligent control over working capital.

We also recognize that our own internal staff must be provided with a working environment, opportunities for career advancement, and a voice in development of the company. By building an

Marketing Strategy

9

involved, motivated professional staff, we will ensure profitable and permanent expansion.

Facilities must be adequate to support our expansion plan. We have upgraded our commission reporting system and plan to support the field effort with our new automated network system.

Capital investment in the network will be substantial. Beyond that, we anticipate the need to purchase office furniture and equipment for staff expansion and a higher volume of transactions.

3. Deadlines

We have divided our expansion plan into a series of phases, each with a deadline. Recruitment will be tracked on a monthly basis with management review and marketing actions to ensure that recruitment and sales volume goals are met. Our plan for the purchase and installation of automated networking hardware and training of field personnel is coordinated with planned development of new field offices. Management travel and advertising for recruitment is also scheduled over the three-year period.

Based on our recruitment goals, investment in networking hardware will take place on the following schedule:

Quarter	Amount
1	$200,000
2	0
3	50,000
4	50,000
5	150,000
6	50,000
7	50,000
8	0
9	150,000
10	50,000
11	50,000
12	50,000

We have scheduled installation of the network system in our existing 22 branches over the first six months of the three-year period. As each new branch office is added, the network will be installed within three months, and training will be completed at the same time.

Risks

10

Risks

We have identified the major risks involved with our expansion schedule, and have planned to confront and overcome them. Our entire plan is premised on the belief that we will be able to recruit additional salespeople, that they will be able to generate the volume we have forecast, and that the market demand will exist for the level we estimate will result. Our risks include the following.

Cash Flow Will Not Support Loan Repayments

Our goal is to use and repay a line of credit in the amount of $500,000 within three years. This is an aggressive repayment schedule, and it represents a significant demand on cash flow. To overcome this risk, we have established several internal guidelines:

1. If working capital falls below our projected level, we will slow down our plan deadline until the problem has been resolved. This contingency will include not withdrawing additional funds from the line of credit.
2. If cost and expense levels exceed the budgeted levels, we will freeze additional spending plans until the negative trend has been brought under control.
3. If sales levels fall below our forecast, we will identify the source of the problem and take immediate corrective action. If the speed of expansion dictates, the plan will be revised to allow for an orderly pace of growth.

Market Demand Will Not Support Growth

We have studied demand trends in the industry for the past decade and project an acceleration in the next three to five years. This is seen in the increased public awareness and interest in financial planning and insurance industries, the emergence of self-regulatory plans, and the increased volume of new and creative investment and insurance products.

We anticipate market demand at all-time high levels. Furthermore, we believe that larger competitors are not well-equipped to respond to the demand we expect. Smaller competitors are not planning to take advantage of the rapid growth in market demand.

Risks

11

The Competition Will Take Our Market Share

We are actively involved in two segments of the financial services industry: insurance and investment. We are also involved with the savings industry and related legal, accounting, and tax experts.

Smaller competitors lack the financial means to compete on the level of expansion that we will undertake in the next 36 months. They also cannot offer the high compensation rates that we provide to our professional sales force or offer the range of products we currently sell. Perhaps the greatest deterrent to growth among smaller competitors is the inability to build an internal staff to support and service a growing force of branch offices.

Larger, institutional competitors have already demonstrated their inability to respond to the consumer. Due to the size, bureaucracy, and high internal cost level of the big national firm, the consumer has a sense of alienation when dealing with one. This is our greatest competitive strength. It is also an important threat to our standards for quality. As we grow, we face the risk of becoming like other large companies—unable to identify and respond to the requirements of its customers. We will avoid this threat by identifying maximum supportable levels of growth and not exceeding those levels until we have the internal staff needed.

In addition to these specific risks, we face broader risks common to all businesses. These risks are in the areas of timing, competition, obsolescence, and economics.

Timing of an expansion plan can spell the difference between complete success and utter failure. We believe that the timing is right for the marketing plan identified by this plan.

Competition is a factor that must be kept in mind at all times. We have been a small company in a slow growth trend for many years and now face many smaller competitors. Our plans call for growth to a larger plateau. We intend to maintain the best attributes of small and large by being constantly aware of the need for quality and staff excellence and at the same time being able to offer an ever-growing range of products and services through our branch offices.

Obsolescence may occur in a number of ways. In the past, entire product lines became obsolete due to changes in the tax laws. Computerized systems may be made obsolete by cheaper, faster, more advanced systems. A management style may be rendered obsolete because in-

Risks

12

dividuals fail to change with the times. We have addressed each of these threats. We diversify our product lines and constantly look for new developments. Our network system will be updated and improved as new technology becomes available. We will remain highly flexible in our management style by encouraging staff members to participate in the direction we take and in decisions that affect our future.

Economics may directly affect our ability to execute our plan. In the past, recessionary trends and stock market sentiment have adversely affected our sales volume, and inflation, interest rates, and the money supply affect our customers' willingness and ability to invest money. We have minimized this risk by expanding our product lines and diversifying our company.

Financial Analysis

13

Financial Analysis

The following pages summarize our income forecast, cost and expense budget, and cash flow projections for the next three years. We have reported these estimates in quarterly breakdowns.

Income Forecast

Estimates of sales are based on a series of assumptions concerning the level of recruitment of new sales professionals. Through this method, we will be able to identify variances and take corrective action as needed.

Several factors will influence the accuracy of this forecast.

- Recruitment level. If the actual level of recruitment is slower than anticipated, we will not meet our sales forecast goals. Thus, great emphasis will be placed on maintaining the schedule we have developed.

- Attrition level. If the number of people who leave our company is greater than projected, we risk a slowdown in forecast sales volume. We have based our estimates on historical levels of attrition, which have been low. The estimate of future attrition is overly generous based on past levels.

- Average sales volume. We have observed that the average salesperson has generated $9,800 per quarter in concession income. Our future projections are based on a lower average of $9,400 per quarter. The average newly recruited salesperson has historically generated $7,000 during their first quarter. We have estimated sales volume for this group at $6,000.

Financial Analysis

14

1. Newly Recruited Salespeople

Quarter	Number	Less Attrition	Net	Dollar Average	Total Sales
1	10	–0	10	$6,000	$ 60,000
2	10	–0	10	6,000	60,000
3	10	–2	8	6,000	48,000
4	10	–2	8	6,000	48,000
5	12	–2	10	6,000	60,000
6	12	–2	10	6,000	60,000
7	12	–3	9	6,000	54,000
8	12	–3	9	6,000	54,000
9	14	–3	11	6,000	66,000
10	14	–3	11	6,000	66,000
11	14	–4	10	6,000	60,000
12	14	–4	10	6,000	60,000
				Total	$696,000

2. Existing Salespeople

Quarter	Number	Less Attrition	Plus New Recruits	Net	Dollar Average	Total Sales
1	98	3	0	95	$9,400	$ 893,000
2	95	3	10	102	9,400	958,800
3	102	3	10	109	9,400	1,024,600
4	109	3	8	114	9,400	1,071,600
5	114	3	8	119	9,400	1,118,600
6	119	3	10	126	9,400	1,184,400
7	126	3	10	133	9,400	1,250,200
8	133	3	9	139	9,400	1,306,600
9	139	3	9	145	9,400	1,363,000
10	145	3	11	153	9,400	1,438,200
11	153	3	11	161	9,400	1,513,400
12	161	3	10	168	9,400	1,579,200
					Total	$14,701,600
					Grand total	$15,397,600

Financial Analysis

15

Notes to the Sales Forecast Worksheet:

1. Newly recruited salespeople are estimated at per-quarter levels, with the assumption that attrition may occur at average delays of two months after start date.
2. After the initial quarter, newly recruited salespeople are expected to generate the same average as existing representatives. Thus, the totals carried from the first section to the second are delayed by one quarter and are reported on a net-of-attrition basis.

Summary of Sales Forecast:

	Total Volume		
Quarter	Newly Recruited	Existing	Total
1	$ 60,000	$ 893,000	$ 953,000
2	60,000	958,800	1,018,800
3	48,000	1,024,600	1,072,600
4	48,000	1,071,600	1,119,600
5	60,000	1,118,600	1,178,600
6	60,000	1,184,400	1,244,400
7	54,000	1,250,200	1,304,200
8	54,000	1,306,600	1,360,600
9	66,000	1,363,000	1,429,000
10	66,000	1,438,200	1,504,200
11	60,000	1,513,400	1,573,400
12	60,000	1,579,200	1,639,200
Total	$696,000	$14,701,600	$15,397,600

Financial Analysis

16

Expense Budget

Commission cost and general expense budgets are summarized by quarter for the next three years and shown in the format of a pro forma income statement.

	Quarter ($000)					
	1	**2**	**3**	**4**	**5**	**6**
Sales	953	1,019	1,073	1,120	1,179	1,244
Commissions	476	509	536	560	589	622
Gross income	477	510	537	560	590	622
Expenses						
Salaries	260	260	260	270	270	270
Payroll tax	29	29	29	30	30	30
Depreciation	1	1	1	1	1	1
Phone/utilities	2	2	2	3	3	3
Travel and entertainment	5	5	5	6	6	7
Advertising	98	98	100	100	105	105
Insurance	2	2	2	3	3	3
Office supplies	3	3	3	4	4	4
Auto expense	2	3	3	3	4	4
Licenses and fees	35	35	35	35	45	45
Legal and accounting	10	10	30	10	10	40
Meetings	5	5	15	5	60	5
Interest	6	5	5	4	8	7
Other expenses	3	4	5	6	3	4
Total expenses	461	462	495	480	552	528
Operating profit	16	48	42	80	38	94
Income taxes	2	7	6	12	6	14
Net income	14	41	36	68	32	80

Financial Analysis

17

Expense Budget (Continued)

	Quarter ($000)					
	7	**8**	**9**	**10**	**11**	**12**
Sales	1,304	1,361	1,429	1,504	1,573	1,639
Commissions	652	681	714	752	786	819
Gross income	652	680	715	752	787	820
Expenses						
Salaries	305	305	305	325	325	325
Payroll tax	34	34	34	36	36	36
Depreciation	1	1	1	1	1	1
Phone/utilities	3	3	4	4	4	4
Travel and entertainment	8	8	8	9	9	10
Advertising	110	115	115	120	125	125
Insurance	3	3	5	5	5	5
Office supplies	4	5	5	5	5	6
Auto expense	5	5	6	6	7	7
Licenses and fees	45	45	55	55	55	55
Legal and accounting	20	20	50	20	20	60
Meetings	5	75	10	10	75	10
Interest	6	5	8	6	4	2
Other expenses	6	7	5	7	10	12
Total expenses	555	631	611	609	681	658
Operating profit	97	49	104	143	106	162
Income taxes	15	7	16	21	16	24
Net income	82	42	88	122	90	138

Financial Analysis

18

Cash Flow Projection

Projections of cash flow are reported in quarterly summaries for the next 12 quarters. Each month's ending balance becomes the following month's beginning balance. Loan principal is reported separately from interest, which is accounted for as part of each quarter's net income.

	Quarter ($000)					
	1	**2**	**3**	**4**	**5**	**6**
Beginning cash	7	8	35	7	11	11
Plus						
Net income	14	41	36	68	32	80
Depreciation	1	1	1	1	1	1
Loan proceeds	200				150	
Subtotal	222	50	72	76	194	92
Less						
Loan principal	14	15	15	15	33	34
Fixed assets	200		50	50	150	50
Subtotal	214	15	65	65	183	84
Ending cash	8	35	7	11	11	8

	Quarter ($000)					
	7	**8**	**9**	**10**	**11**	**12**
Beginning cash	8	6	13	29	27	41
Plus						
Net income	82	42	88	122	90	138
Depreciation	1	1	1	1	1	1
Loan proceeds			150			
Subtotal	91	49	252	152	118	180
Less						
Loan principal	35	36	73	75	77	79
Fixed assets	50		150	50		100
Subtotal	85	36	223	125	77	179
Ending cash	6	13	29	27	41	1

Financial Analysis

19

Trend Analysis

We are keenly aware of the importance of maintaining a consistent and appropriate level in specific financial indicators. As part of our budgeting process, we have developed ratios for the future. The following summary shows turnover in working capital for the last eight quarters and projects that ratio for the coming 12 quarters.

Turnover in working capital:

Quarter	Sales	Current Assets	Current Liabilities	Turns
		Amount ($000)		
−8	972.1	325.0	186.0	7.0
−7	966.9	307.4	169.3	7.0
−6	1,001.4	339.9	196.8	7.0
−5	998.3	318.6	174.1	6.9
−4	1,026.4	342.0	191.8	6.8
−3	997.0	321.4	178.0	7.0
−2	1,047.2	366.9	212.1	6.8
−1	972.9	301.1	156.0	6.7
est 1	953.0	385.0	240.0	6.6
2	1,018.8	340.0	185.0	6.6
3	1,072.6	389.0	224.0	6.5
4	1,119.6	410.0	242.0	6.7
5	1,178.6	458.0	281.0	6.7
6	1,244.4	404.0	211.0	6.4
7	1,304.2	455.0	255.0	6.5
8	1,360.6	500.0	289.0	6.4
9	1,429.0	460.0	233.0	6.3
10	1,504.2	420.0	185.0	6.4
11	1,573.4	480.0	237.0	6.5
12	1,639.2	430.0	175.0	6.4

Turnover in working capital is computed by dividing total sales by the difference between current assets and current liabilities. The analysis reported on the previous page is summarized in visual form in Figure A-1. The moving average was computed using nine quarters. Thus, the first month in the study represents the average of the month plus historical information for the last eight quarters.

Financial Analysis

20

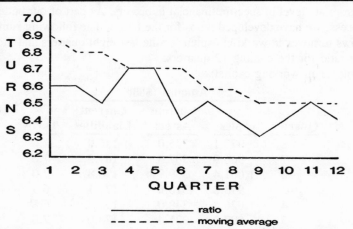

FIGURE A–1
Analysis: Turnover in Working Capital

Debt/Equity Ratio

A second critical ratio is the relationship between debt and equity. We have tracked this carefully throughout the company's history.

Our decision to seek financing for our three-year expansion plan will change this ratio from historical levels. However, we believe our plan is realistic and will be achieved; that with rapid loan repayments, the ratio will return to today's level by the end of the 36-month period; and that the temporary change in the debt/equity ratio will be justified by higher future profits.

The following summary shows the debt/equity ratio for the last eight quarters and the next 12 projected quarters.

Financial Analysis

21

Quarter	Amount ($000) Total Liabilities	Tangible Net Worth	Ratio
-8	186.0	410.9	45.3%
-7	169.3	398.1	42.5
-6	196.8	421.0	46.7
-5	174.1	400.6	43.5
-4	191.8	416.2	46.1
-3	178.0	403.0	44.2
-2	212.1	499.1	42.5
-1	156.0	426.2	36.6
est 1	640.0	907.0	70.6
2	655.0	976.0	67.1
3	660.0	1,033.0	63.9
4	630.0	1,058.0	59.5
5	625.0	1,114.0	56.1
6	615.0	1,158.0	53.1
7	610.0	1,225.0	49.8
8	600.0	1,277.0	47.0
9	600.0	1,342.0	44.7
10	625.0	1,419.0	44.0
11	650.0	1,496.0	43.4
12	670.0	1,556.0	43.1

The debt/equity ratio is computed by dividing total liabilities by tangible net worth. The trend is summarized visually in Figure A-2 using a moving average to show the estimated change over the 36-month (12-quarter) period. The moving average was based on a total of nine quarters. Thus, the first month includes that month's debt/equity ratio, plus the previous eight debt/equity ratios by quarter.

Financial Analysis

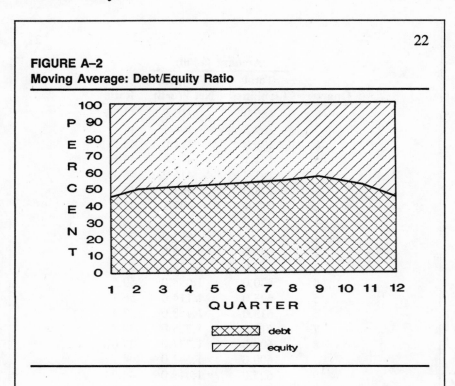

22

FIGURE A–2
Moving Average: Debt/Equity Ratio

Loan Repayment Plan

We have developed a tentative schedule for repayment of the line of credit within 36 months. Amortization has been computed so that payments are increased to meet that deadline. We are assuming 11.5 percent interest.

Financial Analysis

23

Repayment Schedule:

Month	Amount Drawn	Monthly Payment	Interest	Principal	Balance
1	200,000	6,595.22	1,916.67	4,678.55	195,321.45
2		6,595.22	1,871.83	4,723.39	190,598.06
3		6,595.22	1,826.56	4,768.66	185,829.40
4		6,595.22	1,780.86	4,814.36	181,015.04
5		6,595.22	1,734.73	4,860.49	176,154.55
6		6,595.22	1,688.15	4,907.07	171,247.48
7		6,595.22	1,641.12	4,954.10	166,293.38
8		6,595.22	1,593.64	5,001.58	161,291.80
9		6,595.22	1,545.71	5,049.51	156,242.29
10		6,595.22	1,497.32	5,097.90	151,144.39
11		6,595.22	1,448.47	5,146.75	145,997.64
12		6,595.22	1,399.14	5,196.08	140,801.56
13	150,000	13,621.26	2,786.85	10,834.41	279,967.15
14		13,621.26	2,683.02	10,938.24	269,028.91
15		13,621.26	2,578.19	11,043.07	257,985.84
16		13,621.26	2,472.36	11,148.90	246,836.94
17		13,621.26	2,365.52	11,255.74	235,581.20
18		13,621.26	2,257.65	11,363.61	224,217.59
19		13,621.26	2,148.75	11,472.51	212,745.08
20		13,621.26	2,038.81	11,582.45	201,162.63
21		13,621.26	1,927.81	11,693.45	189,469.18
22		13,621.26	1,815.75	11,805.51	177,663.67
23		13,621.26	1,702.61	11,918.65	165,745.02
24		13,621.26	1,588.39	12,032.87	153,712.15
25	150,000	26,913.47	2,910.57	24,002.90	279,709.25
26		26,913.47	2,680.55	24,232.92	255,476.33
27		26,913.47	2,448.31	24,465.16	231,011.17
28		26,913.47	2,213.86	24,699.61	206,311.56
29		26,913.47	1,977.15	24,936.32	181,375.24
30		26,913.47	1,738.18	25,175.29	156,199.95
31		26,913.47	1,496.92	25,416.55	130,783.40
32		26,913.47	1,253.34	25,660.13	105,123.27
33		26,913.47	1,007.43	25,906.04	79,217.23
34		26,913.47	759.17	26,154.30	53,062.93
35		26,913.47	508.52	26,404.95	26,657.98
36		26,913.45	255.47	26,657.98	-0-

Financial Analysis

24

Total Payments by Quarter:

Quarter	Interest	Principal	Total
1	5,615.06	14,170.60	19,785.66
2	5,203.74	14,581.92	19,785.66
3	4,780.47	15,005.19	19,785.66
4	4,344.93	15,440.73	19,785.66
5	8,048.06	32,815.72	40,863.78
6	7,095.53	33,768.25	40,863.78
7	6,115.37	34,748.41	40,863.78
8	5,106.75	35,757.03	40,863.78
9	8,039.43	72,700.98	80,740.41
10	5,929.19	74,811.22	80,740.41
11	3,757.69	76,982.72	80,740.41
12	1,523.16	79,217.23	80,740.39
Total	65,559.38	500,000.00	565,559.38

Financial Analysis

25

FINANCIAL CONSULTING GROUP
BALANCE SHEET
December 31, 19___

	Current Year	Previous Year
Current Assets		
Cash in Bank	7,400	8,100
Accounts Receivable	263,700	190,500
Marketable Securities	30,000	120,000
Total	301,100	318,600
Long-Term Assets		
Furniture and Equipment	34,044	4,984
Office Building	201,500	201,500
Land	85,000	85,000
	320,544	291,484
Accumulated Depreciation	39,444	35,384
Net	281,100	256,100
Total Assets	582,200	574,700
Current Liabilities		
Accounts Payable	29,300	16,200
Notes Payable	0	13,600
Taxes Payable	700	1,800
Commissions Payable	126,000	142,500
Total	156,000	174,100
Long-Term Liabilities	0	0
Total Liabilities	156,000	174,100
Net Worth		
Capital Stock	200,000	200,000
Retained Earnings	226,200	200,600
Total	426,200	400,600
Total Liabilities and Net Worth	582,200	574,700

Financial Analysis

26

FINANCIAL CONSULTING GROUP
INCOME STATEMENT
January 1, 19__ through December 31, 19__

	Current Year	Previous Year
Total Revenues	4,043,500	3,938,700
Commissions Paid	2,001,100	1,933,000
Gross Profit	2,042,400	2,005,700
General Expenses		
Salaries and Wages	1,042,100	1,018,900
Payroll Taxes	113,200	112,400
Depreciation	4,100	4,200
Telephone and Utilities	9,400	9,800
Travel and Entertainment	19,600	22,100
Advertising	384,000	441,800
Insurance	8,600	7,400
Office Supplies	10,900	14,700
Automotive Expenses	9,300	10,100
Licenses and Fees	186,300	107,000
Legal and Accounting	107,200	94,100
Meetings and Conventions	101,600	103,200
Other Expenses	16,000	37,400
Total Expenses	2,012,300	1,983,100
Operating Profit	30,100	22,600
Provision for Income Taxes	4,500	3,400
Net Profit	25,600	19,200

Financial Analysis

27

FINANCIAL CONSULTING GROUP
STATEMENT OF CASH FLOWS
January 1, 19__ through December 31, 19__

	Current Year	Previous Year
Net Income	$25,600	$19,200
Plus Non-Cash Expenses: Depreciation	4,100	4,200
Funds Provided by Operations	$29,700	$23,400
Increases in Fixed Assets	29,100	$ 0
Net Increase in Working Capital	$ 600	$23,400

Auditor's Opinion

We have examined the balance sheet of Financial Consulting Group as of December 31, 19_ and the related statements of income and of cash flows for the year ended December 31, 19__. Our examination was made in accordance with Generally Accepted Auditing Standards and included such tests of the accounting records and other such auditing procedures as we considered necessary.

In our opinion, the financial statements present fairly the financial position of Financial Consulting Group as of December 31, 19__, and the results of their operations and the changes in their financial position for the year ended December 31, 19__, in conformity with Generally Accepted Accounting Principles applied on a consistent basis.

(Signature)

APPENDIX B

BUSINESS PLAN

A sample business plan designed for submission to a venture capital company is shown on the following pages. The fictitious company is called Casper, Inc., a mail-order and retail clothing company.

The exact format of a business plan for a venture capital company should be varied based on the requirements that company imposes. Thus, it must be assumed that before preparing the plan the owner contacted the company and determined

- The format and sequence of the plan.
- Whether the company participated in equity ventures with this type of business and at the amount desired.
- Whether the dividend and liquidation plans were in line with the venture capital company's policies.

**CASPER, INC.
BUSINESS PLAN**

(Date)

Contents

CASPER, INC.

Contents

Introduction

1

Introduction

This business plan proposes a marketing expansion plan for Casper, Inc. The plan will require an investment in the amount of $900,000 to be repaid after 60 months from investment date. The investor will gain a 45 percent share in corporate stock, with options to acquire additional shares in the event a dividend payment is missed. Based on the venture capital company's own schedule, the percentage may rise to 100 percent in the event that payments are not made according to schedule.

Casper, Inc. is a national mail-order clothing sales company. In addition, the corporation owns four retail stores in a two-city area. The lines of clothing sold appeal to men and women. We specialize in practical, simple designs at an affordable price and avoid high-fashion and overpriced items.

This plan shows how our retail division can be expanded to add an additional 10 stores during the next 10 months and how catalog sales can be increased dramatically. This is a rapid and aggressive expansion plan; however, we believe that our current management team is aware of the dangers and will succeed in the plan. We have identified the personnel and procedures for adding retail outlets without experiencing the problems that commonly occur when expansion is undertaken too quickly and without the necessary support and control.

The rapid pace of growth is justified by the market opportunity we face today. Response to our lines has grown steadily over the last three years, and we project a continuing rise in this demand trend. However, in order for the plan to succeed, we will need to raise equity capital in the amount of $900,000. This will be used for organizational expenses and the acquisition of capital assets over a 10-month period.

The $900,000 capital, plus interest earned on short-term marketable securities, will fund organizational costs for the expansion plan on the following schedule:

Automated system upgrades	$ 80,000
Four quarterly catalogs	120,000
Salaries and wages	320,000
New store costs	400,000
Total	$920,000

Introduction

2

This plan explains the use of funds and shows how increased future profits and net worth will minimize the risks. We intend to pay the venture capital investor a quarterly dividend of $22,500, an annual return of 10 percent. This will continue for six years, at which time a repayment will be made in the amount of $1.8 million, twice the amount invested. This represents an average annual return of 27.9 percent.

Company History

3

Company History

Casper, Inc. was founded nine years ago by Maria Casper, the sole stockholder. Ms. Casper spent several years as a clothing consultant and designer and designs the company's catalogs.

Brian Admundsen is marketing director and oversees retail store managers. He is also in charge of catalog promotions and has developed our internal tracking system. Mr. Admundsen has more than 20 years' experience in marketing and was previously a vice president of a national clothing manufacturing company.

Sharon Paulson is administrative vice president. She is responsible for the office staff and for supervising accounting, administrative, and customer service departments. Ms. Paulson is a certified public accountant with several years of experience in auditing and development of internal control systems.

An additional seven home office staff members perform customer service, computer operation, accounting, clerical, and marketing functions. Four stores managers and six salespeople are on the payroll as well.

Objective

4

Objective

Casper, Inc. markets men and women's clothing through direct-mail catalogs as well as retail outlets. We sell simple, practical clothing that is affordable, of the highest possible quality, and at a reasonable and competitive price. Our staff ensures prompt response to the customer as the highest ideal of the organization.

Purpose

5

Purpose

Casper, Inc. has prepared this business plan for the purpose of raising additional equity capital. The funds will be used to achieve a plan of expansion that will be initiated over a 10-month period. The results of this expansion will be a higher volume of sales with accompanying greater profit margins. This will be achieved through stabilized fixed expenses and careful controls over direct costs and cash flow.

Historical growth in volume and profits establish management's ability to control a growing company and to build in profits. During the last two years, fixed overhead levels have risen due to a rapidly changing structure. During this period, three of the four existing retail stores were opened and put into operation. We believe that upon completion of our 10-store expansion phase, overhead growth will level out.

Catalog sales have also been promising. We now generate a higher volume in orders from past customers than from first-time orders. The plan calls for increasing from a twice-annual publication to catalogs produced each quarter.

Our goals for the coming year are

1. Acquire additional equity capital in the amount of $900,000. This will be used to finance the expansion plan described in this plan.

2. Open one new store per month in high-volume suburban malls and prime downtown locations that management has already identified. Locations for the next three months have been committed with lease holding deposits. Four additional locations are under negotiation. Each store's opening expenses will require $40,000 for lease deposits, interior design and shelving, advertising, and purchase of initial inventory. Deadline: Open one store per month for the next 10 months.

3. Increase catalog mailings from the current level of one catalog every six months to one per quarter. As volume increases, so will the typical printing and mailing. We have estimated that the average cost for the next year will be $30,000 per catalog, including design, printing, and mailing costs. Deadline: Three months for production of our next catalog, followed by three-month intervals thereafter.

4. Increase the volume of sales for our private label clothing line.

Purpose

6

We have produced limited quantities of designs by the corporation's owner, due to higher than average costs for low volume. With substantial growth in overall retail and catalog volume, our own designs can be manufactured at a lower cost. We subcontract this process with another clothing company to avoid the high investment cost in facilities, equipment, and labor. Private label merchandise produced at adequate volume produces a gross profit of approximately 54 percent, compared to averages of 41 percent on retail sales of other manufacturers' lines. Retail store and catalog responses have been promising, and our own line has established its popularity with our markets. Deadline: Six months to the first large-volume order.

5. Produce profits and cash flow to pay quarterly dividends to our equity partner equal to 10 percent per year, or $90,000 paid in quarterly installments. With the planned repayment in six years at twice the amount invested, the total return to the equity partner will average 27.9 percent per year. Deadline: Payments to begin six months after investment date.

Assumptions

7

Assumptions

Our business and marketing plan is based on a series of assumptions, including

1. The trend of growing mail-order volume will continue as forecast, as long as we are able to continue providing high-quality and affordable merchandise.

2. Sales volume in retail outlets will be adequate to produce profits, and volume goals will be achieved on schedule.

3. The expense of upgrading our existing automated system is necessary to handle a higher volume of inventory and sales activity. We believe our cost estimates are realistic.

4. Our existing management is capable of creating the internal monitoring and control procedures to produce higher profits with more outlets and greater volume.

5. The potential for marketing our own private label line of clothing will produce evergrowing average gross margins in the future.

6. The mail-order side of the business is where future profits will grow most substantially over the long term. Within six years, major store chains will be interested in acquiring rights to our retail stores and will want to establish boutique-style departments with our name in their larger stores.

7. Payments for acquisition of rights to the retail side of our business will be adequate to liquidate the 45 percent stock position of our venture partner within six years.

8. Our 10-month expansion plan is a rapid one. However, with proper capitalization and internal controls, it will be profitable and will produce a positive cash flow.

In addition to these broad assumptions concerning our marketing plan, our sales forecast, cost and expense budget, and cash flow projections are based on a series of detailed assumptions. These will be made available upon request.

Marketing Strategy

8

Marketing Strategy

Our marketing plan calls for rapid growth on several levels, all within a 10-month period. In other circumstances, a more methodical approach might be justified. We believe the 10-month plan is appropriate in our case, because

- We believe the most significant growth in the future will occur in private label sales, where gross profit margin is the highest. In order to achieve that margin, however, we must first be able to justify a very large order size. With higher store and catalog volume, this will be possible.
- Market response to the merchandise we offer has been positive beyond our own estimates. We believe that momentum is critical, especially in catalog sales. We will take advantage of this trend by increasing the frequency of our catalog publication.
- Our internal management team is very aware of the dangers involved in expansion, most especially when it occurs within a short period of time. We plan to emphasize cost and expense controls and development of the plan according to a strict budget and timetable.

The elements of our marketing strategy must be orchestrated with great care. This plan will depend on several developments, each of which must take place in a timely manner. These elements will affect both retail sales volume and catalog activities. On the retail side, our greatest concerns will be in finding prime locations and excellent on-site management. On the catalog side, we will emphasize creative catalog design and expansion of our list, as well as tracking of buying trends.

The elements of our plan include

1. Development of private label designs in consideration of our marketing deadline and production requirements.
2. Expansion of our mail list and response system to ensure maintenance of our effective customer service program.
3. Carefully controlled retail store procedures, based on recruitment of professional managers and leasing of prime locations.
4. Inventory control for catalog and retail sales, including a plan for a centralized inventory and delivery system for stores, reduction of backorder volume, and expansion of sizes and colors in many lines.

Marketing Strategy

9

5. Consistent and timely production of a quarterly catalog available to an expanded mail list of customers.
6. Development of internal support systems that will be effective but not overly complex. This will require staff training and an upgraded automated tracking and reporting system.

We have defined our expansion plan in terms of capital requirements over the next 10 months. The four categories of our expansion plan will include

1. Automated system. Costs of developing and installing upgraded software, purchase of additional hardware, and training of personnel. The total is estimated at $80,000.
2. Catalog. The cost of design, printing, and mailing. Each catalog's cost is estimated at $30,000, or a total cost of $120,000 for the next year.
3. Salaries and wages. Salary plus payroll taxes and benefits for newly hired store managers. Total cost: $320,000.
4. Store organizational costs. Estimated at $40,000 per store and including leasehold improvements, initial inventory, and advertising.

We consider all of these costs and expenses as organizational costs to be capitalized and amortized over a 60-month period.

Spending schedule:

Month	Automated System	Catalogs	Salaries and Wages	Stores	Total
1	15,000	30,000	5,800	40,000	90,800
2			11,700	40,000	51,700
3	15,000		17,500	40,000	72,500
4		30,000	23,300	40,000	93,300
5	20,000		29,200	40,000	89,200
6	15,000		35,000	40,000	90,000
7		30,000	40,800	40,000	110,800
8			46,700	40,000	86,700
9	15,000		52,000	40,000	107,000
10		30,000	58,000	40,000	128,000
Total	80,000	120,000	320,000	400,000	920,000

Risks

10

Risks

We have identified risks in four classifications, as well as the means for reducing those risks as our expansion plan progresses.

1.Timing

The most apparent risk in our business and marketing plan involves the rapid sequence of deadlines and new openings. We believe, however, that this plan is realistic and can be managed by our existing staff plus the managers we will recruit in the next 10 months.

Because the retail side of our business is seasonal, a second form of timing risk must involve store openings. Some months are more advantageous than others when timed to maximize high-volume seasons. We believe, however, that a store opened in a relatively slow period can establish its position and visibility over a longer period, ultimately increasing high-season volume and profits.

A third risk is that desirable mall and downtown space will not be available at the time we want to open a new store. Finding the right location requires research and site inspection. We have the first three locations committed and are investigating additional promising sites. By staying ahead of critical deadlines, we do not anticipate a timing problem in this respect.

2. Competition

The second classification of risk deals with competitive factors. A large number of mail-order and retail clothing outlets are available to our market. We depend on original catalog design and excellent customer service combined with our standard to emphasize affordable and practical lines to offset competitive threats.

On the retail side, we believe that our pricing will enable us to achieve our volume goals, which were developed conservatively and based on historical sales growth.

Mail-order sales will continue to grow as an increasing number of buyers return with subsequent orders. By increasing the frequency of new catalog editions, we expect the rate of growth to increase significantly.

A competing clothing label is another competitive concern. The limited exposure of our own designs is promising with the market

Risks

11

responding very positively. We believe that increasing our private label design sales activity will improve our gross margin in the future.

3. Obsolescence

The third classification is the risk that our designs will become obsolete, based on what the public wants to buy, or that our investment in automated processing will be more expensive or less efficient than we expect.

We intend to introduce practical designs to the market. Our clothing appeals more to the middle-income buyer on a budget than to those seeking high fashion and status symbols. We do not believe this approach poses a serious risk of market obsolescence.

Our investment in upgrading our automated system is as important and as valuable as our mailing list. The existing system works, but it has limitations. As we grow, we will want to be able to access information and analyze sales trends with greater flexibility. We do not expect this system to become obsolete for many years.

4. Economics

Two economic factors could affect future profitability and cash flow: buying trends and our own costs. We do not expect our customer's buying habits to change. Rather, the risk is that our designers will lose touch with what the typical Casper-line customer wants and will pay for. We are aware of this danger in our business and intend to maintain our creative and practical outlook through constant awareness of what the customer wants.

If our suppliers and manufacturers raise their wholesale costs, we will have to make a decision: either pass on the price increases to the customer or reduce gross margins and maintain profits through higher margins. Every clothing business must contend with this problem constantly and cannot fully escape the risk. We plan to hold the balance between affordability and acceptable gross margins.

Projections

12

Projections

We have prepared a number of worksheets showing historical financial results and estimating future growth. The purpose is to demonstrate that our marketing plan is both realistic and achievable within the next 10 months.

The first estimate is a summary of interest income on the $900,000 equity investment. This amount will be spent over a 10-month period, with unused funds kept in short-term marketable securities. We anticipate earning 7 percent.

Month	Amount Spent	Ending Balance	7% Interest	Balance
Equity				900,000
1	90,800	809,200	4,720	813,920
2	51,700	762,220	4,450	766,670
3	72,500	694,170	4,050	698,220
4	93,300	604,920	3,530	608,450
5	89,200	519,250	3,030	522,280
6	90,000	432,280	2,520	434,800
7	110,800	324,000	1,890	325,890
8	86,700	239,190	1,400	240,590
9	107,000	133,590	780	134,370
10	128,000	6,370	35	6,405
11	0	6,405	35	6,440
12	0	6,440	40	6,480
Total	920,000		26,480	

Summary

Amount of equity investment	$900,000
Plus interest earned	26,480
Less transfers to operations	−920,000
Balance, end of year	$ 6,480

Projections

13

Our second financial analysis estimates the annual dividend payments and six-year repayment of the equity investment.

Initial investment	$ 900,000
Dividends	
Year 1	$ 67,500
Year 2	90,500
Year 3	90,500
Year 4	90,500
Year 5	90,500
Year 6	90,500
Liquidation payment	1,800,000
Total repayments	$2,407,500
Average annual return =	27.9%

The amounts transferred from short-term marketable securities and used to finance our expansion plan will be capitalized as organization expenses and amortized over 60 months. The schedule for the first year:

Month	Spending Balance	Monthly Amortization
1	$ 90,800	$ 1,513
2	142,500	2,375
3	215,000	3,583
4	308,300	5,138
5	397,500	6,625
6	487,500	8,125
7	598,300	9,972
8	685,000	11,417
9	792,000	13,200
10	920,000	15,333
11	920,000	15,333
12	920,000	15,333

We have summarized historical levels of gross sales, to establish the trend and to support our forecasts for sales during the coming year.

Projections

14

Gross Sales Volume, Two Years
A. Retail Stores

	Total Gross Sales ($000)				
Month	**Store 1**	**Store 2**	**Store 3**	**Store 4**	**Total**
−24	23.9	0	0	0	23.9
−23	22.4	0	0	0	22.4
−22	26.3	0	0	0	26.3
−21	28.0	13.3	0	0	41.3
−20	27.6	16.9	0	0	44.5
−19	32.4	16.2	0	0	48.6
−18	37.1	15.4	0	0	52.5
−17	38.3	18.3	0	0	56.6
−16	34.6	12.5	17.7	0	64.8
−15	41.3	20.0	22.3	0	83.6
−14	46.8	28.8	25.9	0	101.5
−13	54.4	32.6	29.6	0	116.6
−12	28.2	20.9	19.3	0	68.4
−11	26.0	21.3	19.1	0	66.4
−10	27.9	20.6	18.6	0	67.1
− 9	27.3	21.4	22.4	0	71.1
− 8	29.6	24.2	25.5	20.4	99.7
− 7	32.4	27.3	27.1	22.3	109.1
− 6	38.6	29.5	33.4	24.8	126.3
− 5	40.1	29.0	35.0	24.5	128.6
− 4	36.6	28.4	34.5	24.7	124.2
− 3	41.2	29.6	36.2	29.0	136.0
− 2	48.6	31.7	34.0	29.6	143.9
− 1	56.6	34.3	36.5	34.4	161.8
Total	846.2	492.2	437.1	209.7	1,985.2

Projections

15

B. Mail Order

Month	Total Sales ($000)		
	New Orders	**Repeat Orders**	**Total**
−24	11.1	6.4	17.5
−23	14.3	6.2	20.5
−22	9.4	5.8	15.2
−21	9.6	5.8	15.4
−20	8.2	7.2	15.4
−19	16.1	7.4	23.5
−18	14.2	8.1	22.3
−17	11.3	7.7	19.0
−16	8.5	7.2	15.7
−15	8.2	8.4	16.6
−14	8.7	8.5	17.2
−13	15.9	9.3	25.2
−12	15.7	11.9	27.6
−11	9.6	9.5	19.1
−10	9.9	10.2	20.1
− 9	10.1	12.4	22.5
− 8	8.5	11.5	20.0
− 7	15.6	14.8	30.4
− 6	15.9	17.4	33.3
− 5	13.2	14.7	27.9
− 4	9.5	11.1	20.6
− 3	10.6	16.3	26.9
− 2	10.1	14.3	24.4
− 1	8.9	18.5	27.4
Total	273.1	250.6	523.7

Projections

16

C. Summary, All Sales

Month	Amount	Month	Amount
−24	41.4	−12	96.0
−23	42.9	−11	85.5
−22	41.5	−10	87.2
−21	56.7	− 9	93.6
−20	59.9	− 8	119.7
−19	72.1	− 7	139.5
−18	74.8	− 6	159.6
−17	75.6	− 5	156.5
−16	80.5	− 4	144.8
−15	100.2	− 3	162.9
−14	118.7	− 2	168.3
−13	141.8	− 1	189.2
		Total	2,508.9

Notes Regarding Historical Sales:

We used historical sales trends as part of our forecast of future volume, for existing and new stores, as well as for mail order. We observed these trends:

- Seasonal variations are predictable.
- Average volume increases with the length of time a store has been open.
- Reorder mail-order volume now is higher than new-order volume.

Projections

17

Forecast of Gross Sales, One Year
A. Existing Retail Stores

	Gross Sales ($000)			
Month	Store 1	Store 2	Store 3	Store 4
1	30	22	20	18
2	28	22	20	18
3	30	22	20	18
4	30	22	22	19
5	32	25	24	20
6	35	25	24	21
7	38	27	26	24
8	42	30	28	27
9	38	30	30	30
10	42	30	34	32
11	50	35	34	30
12	55	38	36	35
Total	450	328	318	292

B. New Retail Stores

	Gross Sales ($000)				
Month	Store 5	Store 6	Store 7	Store 8	Store 9
1	5	0	0	0	0
2	5	5	0	0	0
3	5	5	5	0	0
4	7	5	5	5	0
5	7	7	5	5	5
6	8	8	6	5	5
7	11	9	7	6	5
8	12	10	8	7	6
9	12	10	8	8	7
10	14	12	10	9	8
11	18	14	12	10	10
12	20	18	15	12	12
Total	125	93	81	67	58

Projections

18

	Gross Sales ($000)				
Month	Store 10	Store 11	Store 12	Store 13	Store 14
1–5	0	0	0	0	0
6	5	0	0	0	0
7	5	5	0	0	0
8	5	5	5	0	0
9	6	5	5	5	0
10	8	6	5	5	5
11	10	8	7	5	5
12	12	10	9	8	7
Total	51	39	31	23	17

C. Mail-Order and Interest Income

	Gross Sales ($000)			
	Mail-Order Sales			Interest
Month	New	Repeat	Total	Income
1	17	20	37	5
2	17	20	37	4
3	11	22	33	4
4	11	22	33	3
5	12	22	34	3
6	10	22	32	3
7	18	24	42	2
8	18	24	42	1
9	14	24	38	1
10	11	24	35	0
11	13	26	39	0
12	13	26	39	0
Total	165	276	441	26

Projections

19

D. Sales, All Sources

	Gross Sales ($000)			
Month	Retail Sales	Mail Order	Interest Income	Total Sales
1	95	37	5	137
2	98	37	4	139
3	105	33	4	142
4	115	33	3	151
5	130	34	3	167
6	143	32	3	178
7	163	42	2	207
8	185	42	1	228
9	194	38	1	233
10	220	35	0	255
11	248	39	0	287
12	287	39	0	326
Total	1,983	441	26	2,450

Notes regarding the gross sales forecast:

We predict total gross sales of $2.45 million dollars during the next 12 months. This compares to last year's gross of $1.6 million, an increase of 53 percent. The previous year's volume grew over the year before by 77 percent.

Gross Profit Trends

We intend to track and stabilize the rate of change in gross profit margin, both during and after our planned expansion period. We have observed a gradual decline in profit margin over the past two years as sales volume increased; however, the current gross profit margin is acceptable in our opinion.

Projections

1. Retail sales, historical gross margin.

	($000)
Total sales, last 2 years	$1,985.2
Cost of goods sold	1,154.6
Gross profit	$ 830.6
Average margin	41.8%

2. Mail order, historical gross margin.

	($000)
Total sales, last 2 years	$ 523.7
Cost of goods sold	224.6
Gross profit	$ 299.1
Average margin	57.1%

Projections

21

Net Profit Trends

Our after-tax profit for the last 24 months totaled $66,394 ($47,388 this year and $19,006 the year before). We estimate that net profits during the coming 12 months will be $139,000. This increase in the rate of profits will result from stabilized cost and general expense levels.

Pro Forma Summary

Below is our estimate of next year's gross margin and net profits by month.

Month	Gross Profit	Expenses	Operating Profit	Income Taxes	Net Profit
1	64	60	4	1	3
2	64	60	4	1	3
3	64	60	4	1	3
4	66	61	5	1	4
5	73	65	6	1	7
6	77	67	10	2	8
7	88	74	14	2	12
8	95	78	17	3	14
9	96	79	17	3	14
10	101	82	19	3	16
11	114	86	28	4	24
12	128	91	37	6	31
Total	1,030	863	167	28	139

Projections

22

Pro Forma without Added Capital

We estimate that growth during the coming year will occur without an additional equity investment to the following levels:

	Amounts ($000)		
	Retail	Mail Order	Total
Gross sales	1,388	379	1,767
Cost of goods sold	833	168	1,001
Gross profit	555	211	766
Expenses			707
Operating profit			59
Income taxes			9
Net profit			50

Cash Flow Projection

	Month 1	Month 2	Month 3	Month 4	Month 5	Month 6
Balance	7	7	7	9	13	21
Plus						
Income	3	3	3	4	7	8
Depreciation	1	1	1	1	1	1
Amortization	2	2	4	5	7	8
Transfers	91	52	73	93	89	90
Total	104	65	88	112	117	128
Less						
Expansion	91	52	73	93	89	90
Loan	4	4	4	4	4	4
Increases in accounts receivable	2	2	2	2	3	3
Dividends	0	0	0	0	0	23
Total	97	58	79	99	96	120
Balance	7	7	9	13	21	8

Projections

23

	Month 7	Month 8	Month 9	Month 10	Month 11	Month 12
Balance	8	24	43	40	64	95
Plus						
Income	12	14	14	16	24	31
Depreciation	1	1	1	1	1	1
Amortization	10	11	13	15	15	15
Transfers	111	87	107	128	0	0
Total	142	137	178	200	104	142
Less						
Expansion	111	87	107	128	0	0
Loan	4	4	4	4	4	4
Increases in accounts receivable	3	3	4	4	5	5
Dividends			23			23
Total	118	94	138	136	9	32
Balance	24	43	40	64	95	110

Financial Statements

24

CASPER, INC.
BALANCE SHEET

December 31, 19___

	Current Year	Prior Year
Current Assets		
Cash in Bank	7,114	6,051
Accounts Receivable	47,830	50,304
Inventory	298,500	292,650
	353,444	349,005
Long-Term Assets		
Furniture and Equipment	406,000	370,400
Computer System	42,350	42,350
	448,350	412,750
Less Accumulated Depreciation	192,065	179,813
	256,285	232,937
Total Assets	609,729	581,942
Current Liabilities		
Accounts Payable	106,227	75,175
Taxes Payable	9,054	11,477
Notes Payable	47,820	47,820
	163,101	134,472
Long-Term Liabilities		
Notes Payable	131,505	179,735
Total Liabilities	294,606	314,207
Net Worth		
Capital Stock	150,000	150,000
Retained Earnings	165,123	117,735
	315,123	267,735
Total	609,729	581,942

Financial Statements

25

CASPER, INC.
INCOME STATEMENT

For the Year Ended December 31, 19___

	Current Year	Prior Year
Total Sales	1,602,814	906,084
Cost of Goods Sold		
Inventory, January 1	292,650	264,000
Merchandise Purchased	887,839	502,046
Other Direct Costs	13,251	10,582
	1,193,740	776,628
Less Inventory, December 31	298,500	292,650
Cost of Goods Sold	895,240	483,978
Gross Profit	707,574	422,106
General Expenses	651,949	399,730
Operating Profit	55,625	22,376
Provision for Income Taxes	8,237	3,370
Net Profit	47,388	19,006

Financial Statements

26

CASPER, INC.
STATEMENT OF CASH FLOWS
For the Year Ended December 31, 19___

	Current Year	Prior Year
Funds Provided by Operations		
Net Income	47,388	19,006
Plus Depreciation	12,252	11,260
Total	59,640	30,266
Less		
Increases in Long-Term Assets	35,600	27,902
Reductions in Long-Term Debt	48,230	0
Total	83,830	27,902
Net Increase (Decrease) in Working Capital	(24,190)	2,364

Auditor's Opinion

We have examined the consolidated balance sheets of Casper, Inc. as of December 31, 19___, and December 31, 19___, the income statements, and the statements of cash flows for the periods ended December 31, 19___, and December 31, 19 ___. Our examination was made in accordance with Generally Accepted Auditing Standards and included tests of the accounting records and other auditing procedures as we considered necessary.

In our opinion, the consolidated financial statements present fairly the financial position of Casper, Inc. as of December 31, 19___, and December 31, 19___, and the results of operations for the years ended December 31, 19___, and December 31, 19___, in accordance with Generally Accepted Accounting Principles applied on a consistent basis.

(Signature)

INDEX

risk, 26, 95, 208, 237–238, 267
  statements, 40
Office of Business Loans (SBA), 111
Office of Investment (SBA), 110
Office of Management and Budget,
  105–106
options, equity, 154
organizational capital, 21
outside services, 61–62
overhead
  expense control, 132–133
  test, 4, 5
Overseas Private Investment Corporation,
  113

P

Painewebber Venture Management Company, 182
partnership
  active, 153
  conflicts, 3
  general, 166–168
  judgment, 168–171
  limited, 165
  motives, 15–17
  units, 153
Piper Jaffray Ventures, Inc., 182
planning
  analysis, 141–143, 161–163, 211–212
  context, 17–19
  contingencies, 27
  delegation, 58–60
  document, 89
  factors, 4–6
  farsighted, 158
  merits, 43–44
  organization, 136–139, 205–208
  outline, 42
  presentation, 135–136, 202–204
  projections, 212–215
  proof, 37–42, 139–141, 209–211
  realistically, 85–86, 172–173
  reports, 193–195

risks, 9
sample, 44–48, 225–253, 254–282
simplified, 35–37
standards, 191–192
systems, 60
validity, 9
profit
  history, 93–94
  net cash, 122–125
  plan, 94, 140–141
  ratio, 200
  test, 4, 5, 6–7
profitable volume, 70–74
Prudential-Bache Capital Partners, 183
public offering, 165–166
purpose section of the plan, 36, 45–46,
  137, 206, 230–231, 261–262

R

ratio
  collection, 142, 200
  current, 200, 245
  debt/equity, 100, 147–149, 246–248
  profit, 200
  sales, 200
  turnover in working capital, 98, 144–145, 146–147, 245–246
realistic plan, 85–86
repayment schedule, 9
Republic Venture Group, Inc., 183
risk
  borrowing, 94–96
  elimination, 9
  entrepreneurial, 51
  in start-up companies, 23–28
  managerial, 51
  planning, 3, 7–8, 9
  profile, 81–82
  section of the plan, 37, 41, 138, 207–208, 236–238, 266–267
Robertson, Coleman & Stephens, 183
Rothschild Ventures Inc., 183